D0319979

KEIGHLEY CAMPUS LIBRARY
LEEDS CITY COLLEGE

KC08045

UNDERSTANDING
BEHAVIORISM

Behavior Analysis and Society Series

UNDERSTANDING BEHAVIORISM

Science, Behavior, and Culture

William M. Baum
University of New Hampshire

📖 HarperCollins*CollegePublishers*

Acquisitions Editor: Catherine Woods
Project Editor: Diane Williams
Cover Design/Design Supervisor: Mary Archondes
Production Administrator: Valerie Sawyer
Compositor: University Graphics, Inc.
Printer and Binder: R. R. Donnelley & Sons Company
Cover Printer: New England Book Components, Inc.

KEIGHLEY COLLEGE
LIBRARY
44139 94-95
27 OCT 1994

Understanding Behaviorism: Science, Behavior, and Culture

Copyright © 1994 by HarperCollins College Publishers

All rights reserved. Printed in the United States of America. No part of this book may
be used or reproduced in any manner whatsoever without written permission, except in
the case of brief quotations embodied in critical articles and reviews. For information
address HarperCollins College Publishers, 10 East 53rd Street, New York, NY 10022.

Library of Congress Cataloging-in-Publication Data

Baum, William M.
    Understanding behaviorism: science, behavior, and culture /
William M. Baum.
        p.   cm.
    Includes bibliographical references and index.
    ISBN 0-06-500286-5
    1. Behaviorism (Psychology) I. Title.
BF199.B33   1994
150.19'43—dc20   93-5799
                                                     CIP

93 94 95 96 9 8 7 6 5 4 3 2 1

To my father, Mark Baum

CONTENTS

SERIES FOREWORD
BEHAVIOR ANALYSIS AND SOCIETY

Psychology is conceptually and theoretically fragmented to an unusual extent for a maturing scientific discipline. The absence of a consistent perspective across areas of interest within psychology constrains the interactions between basic researchers and persons with applied interests, and limits psychology's prospects for interdisciplinary collaboration at a time when great advances are being made at the boundaries between traditional scientific disciplines.

It is against this backdrop that we find huge appeal in the natural-science approach of behavior analysis to the study of relationships between behavior and its controlling variables. Behavior analysis is deeply rooted in the philosophy of science known as radical behaviorism. Radical behaviorism has been much maligned and misunderstood, but remains vital in its capacity to focus interest on measurable variables in the empirical search for causes of behavior. Such a focus, at first glance seemingly trivial or restrictive, has proven to have great heuristic value, promoting both a watchmaker's attention to detail in experimental methods, and an approach to behavior theory in which the analysis of diverse problems (including inner experience) is guided by principles derived from direct observation of behavior in its environmental context.

Laboratory studies of nonhuman behavior provided the early empirical foundations of behavior analysis, identifying a broad range of variables influencing behavior which in modern laboratories also are commonly explored through studies of human behavior. Over time, a conceptual and empirical framework has emerged for applying behavioral principles derived from the laboratory to socially relevant and practical problems in human culture. In the past half-century, great progress has been made toward unifying philosophical and methodological issues into a coherent body of knowledge equally applicable to basic and applied problems. As a result, the past 20 years have witnessed the maturing of behavior analysis into a discipline whose methods and theory extend into diverse areas of human endeavor—a feat rivaled by few other psychological disciplines.

The goal of the *Behavior Analysis and Society* series is to provide students, teachers, researchers, and practitioners with an accessible but challenging introduction to behavior analysis and its applications. Two "foundations" books introduce the philosophical and empirical underpinnings of behavior analysis. The remaining volumes address areas of social importance in which behavior analysis has made substantial contributions or is fast demonstrating the potential to do so, such as clinical psychology, psychopharmacology, developmental disabilities, education, health psychology, and industrial-organizational psychology. These books emphasize the functional problem-solving approach of behavior analysis over a comprehensive literature review or a specific set of practitioner guidelines—both of which are available elsewhere, and neither of which is likely to promote conceptual and empirical integration across disciplines. By using a common format to examine several significant areas in behavior analysis, the series seeks not only to summarize research and knowledge within each area but also to stimulate further intellectual unity and growth in the field.

Bill Buskist and Tom Critchfield
Series Editors

PREFACE

This book describes contemporary behaviorism and its links to philosophy, cognition, social psychology, anthropology, and evolutionary biology. If you regard yourself as a critic of behaviorism, you may be surprised by what you find here; the ideas bear little resemblance to the caricature common to psychology textbooks. You may remain a critic, but, using this book, you will be fighting a real dragon, rather than a papier-mâché imitation.

If you are neutral or if you regard yourself as a behaviorist, this book may surprise you too, but also may suggest uses in teaching. It can supplement a variety of courses on human behavior, animal behavior, and culture. It serves as a textbook for a course I teach to sophomores, and even to some freshmen who have taken only introductory psychology.

The book begins with a definition: Behaviorism consists of the proposition that *there can be a science of behavior.* It discusses what meaning of "science" might suit a science of behavior. It examines what "behavior" might mean for science. It explores implications of a science of behavior for purpose, knowledge, freedom, social relationships, culture, cultural change, and public policy.

I have aimed at a wide audience: psychologists, biologists, other social scientists, philosophers, undergraduates, graduate students, and anyone who might be interested in human behavior. Although I introduce some concepts current in behavior analysis, the language is predominantly nontechnical. Whether the book challenges you or pleases you, I doubt it will bore you.

❖ ACKNOWLEDGMENTS

My greatest intellectual debt is to my teachers, Fred Skinner and Dick Herrnstein, without whom I neither could have nor would have written this book. Invaluable help came from my two friends, Howie Rachlin and Tony Nevin, whose conversations over the years have been both instructive and inspiring. Two colleagues, Becky Warner and Tom Mawhinney, advised me on Chapter 11—although any defects are mine. Arguments with two cognitive psychologists in my department, John Limber and Ed O'Brien, helped by pushing me to formulate answers. Many students helped by asking questions and pointing out weaknesses. I wish to thank particularly Sandy Webster and Keith Beauregard for sharing their notes of my lectures and Dorothy Barrett and Steve Clark for analyzing student commentary. I also want to thank the following reviewers: William Buskist, Auburn University; Carl Cheney, Utah State University; John Malone, University of Tennessee; Jack Marr, Georgia Institute of Technology; Jay Moore, University of Wisconsin at Milwaukee; Edward Morris, University of Kansas; and Howard Rachlin, SUNY at Stony Brook. The University of New Hampshire helped me out in a big way with an extra semester of sabbatical leave through a Faculty Scholar Award. My friend Gerry Duffy and my wife Elizabeth gave me support throughout the project.

William M. Baum

PART ONE

WHAT IS BEHAVIORISM?

Behaviorism has been a controversial topic. Some objections arise from correct understanding, but misconceptions about behaviorism abound. The three chapters in this part aim to clarify what might be called the "philosophical stance" of behaviorism.

All that is genuinely controversial about behaviorism stems from its primary idea, that a science of behavior is possible. At some point in its history, every science has had to exorcise imagined causes (hidden agents) that supposedly lie behind or under the surface of natural events. Chapter 1 explains how behaviorists' denial of hidden agents leads to a genuine controversy, the question of whether behavior is free or determined.

Chapter 2 aims to forestall misconceptions that may arise because behaviorism has changed over time. An earlier version, called *methodological* behaviorism, was based on *realism,* the view that all experience is caused by an objective, real world outside of and apart from a person's subjective, inner world. Realism may be contrasted with *pragmatism,* which is silent about the origin of experience, but points instead to the usefulness of trying to understand and make sense out of our experiences. A later version of behaviorism, called *radical* behaviorism, rests on pragmatism, rather than on realism. Anyone failing to understand this difference is likely to misunderstand the critical aspect of radical behaviorism, its rejection of mentalism.

The behaviorists' critique of mentalism, explained in Chapter 3, underlies the remainder of the book, because it requires behaviorists to suggest nonmentalistic explanations of behavior (Part Two) and nonmentalistic solutions to social problems (Part Three).

CHAPTER 1

BEHAVIORISM: DEFINITION AND HISTORY

The central idea of behaviorism can be stated simply: *There can be a science of behavior.* Behaviorists have diverse views about what this proposition means, and especially about what science is and what behavior is, but every behaviorist agrees that there can be a science of behavior.

Many behaviorists add that the science of behavior should be psychology. This causes contention because many psychologists reject the idea that psychology is a science at all, and others who regard it as a science consider its subject matter something other than behavior. For better or worse, the science of behavior has come to be called *behavior analysis.* The debate continues as to whether behavior analysis is a part of psychology, the same as psychology, or independent of psychology, but professional organizations, such as the Association for Behavior Analysis, and journals, such as *The Behavior Analyst, Journal of the Experimental Analysis of Behavior,* and *Journal of Applied Behavior Analysis,* give the field an identity.

Since behaviorism is a set of ideas about this science called behavior analysis, not the science itself, properly speaking behaviorism is not science, but philosophy of science. As philosophy about behavior, however, it touches topics near and dear to us: why we do what we do, and what we should and should not do. Behaviorism offers an alternative view that often runs counter to traditional thinking about action, because traditional views have been unscientific. We shall see in later chapters that it sometimes takes us in directions radically different from conventional thinking. This chapter covers some of the history of behaviorism and one of its most immediate implications: determinism.

❖ HISTORICAL BACKGROUND

■ From Philosophy to Science

All the sciences—astronomy, physics, chemistry, biology—had their origins in, and eventually broke free from, philosophy. Before astronomy existed as a science, for example, philosophers speculated about the arrangement of the natural universe by starting from assumptions about God or some other ideal standard and reasoning to conclusions about the way the universe must be. For example, if all important events seem to occur on the earth, then this must be the center of the universe. Since a circle is the most perfect shape, the sun must travel about the earth in a circular orbit. The moon must travel in another, closer circular orbit, and the stars are arranged in a sphere, the most perfect three-dimensional form, around the whole. (To this day, the sun, the moon, and the stars are called heavenly bodies, because they were supposed to be perfect.)

The sciences of astronomy and physics came into existence when individuals began trying to understand natural objects and phenomena by observing them. When Galileo (1564–1642) trained a telescope on the moon, he observed that its crater-scarred landscape was far from the perfect sphere the philosophers supposed it to be. As for physics, Galileo observed the motion of falling objects by rolling a ball down a chute. In describing his findings, he helped invent the modern notions of velocity and acceleration. Isaac Newton (1642–1727) added concepts like force and inertia to create a powerful descriptive scheme for understanding the motion of bodies on the earth and as well as heavenly bodies such as the moon.

In creating the science of physics, Galileo, Newton, and many other thinkers of the Renaissance broke with philosophy. Philosophy reasons from assumptions to conclusions. Its arguments take the form, "If this were so, then that would be so." Science proceeds in the opposite direction: "This is observed; what could be true that would lead to such an observation, and what other observations would it lead to?" Philosophical truth is absolute: as long as the assumptions are spelled out and the reasoning is sound, the conclusions must follow. Scientific truth is always relative and provisional: it is relative to observation and susceptible to disconfirmation by new observations. Philosophical assumptions concern abstractions beyond the natural universe: God, harmony, ideal shapes, and so on. Scientific assumptions used in theory-building concern only the natural universe and the way it might be organized. Though Newton was a theologian as well as a physicist, he separated the two endeavors. About physics he said *"Hypotheses non fingo"* ("I do not make hypotheses"), meaning that when studying physics he had no concern for any supernatural entities or principles—that is, for anything outside the natural universe itself.

As well as physics, the ancient Greeks speculated about chemistry. Philosophers such as Thales, Empedocles, and Aristotle speculated that matter varied in its properties because it was endowed with certain qualities, essences, or principles. Aristotle suggested four qualities: *hot, cold, wet,* and *dry.* If a substance was a liquid, it possessed more of the wet quality; if a solid, more of the dry. As centuries passed, the list of qualities lengthened. Things that grew hot were said to possess the inner essence *caloric.* Materials that burned were said to possess *phlogiston.* These essences were considered real substances hidden somewhere within the materials. When thinkers turned away from such speculation and began relying on observations of material change, the science of chemistry was born. Antoine Lavoisier (1743–1794), among others, developed the concept of oxygen from careful observation of weights. Lavoisier found that when a metal is burned and transformed into a powder (oxide) in a closed vessel, the powder weighs more than the original metal, and yet the entire vessel retains the same weight. Lavoisier reasoned that this could occur if the metal combined with some material in the air. Such reasoning concerned itself only with natural terms; it left out the qualities suggested by philosophy and established chemistry as a science.

Biology broke with philosophy and theology in the same way. Philosophers reasoned that if living and nonliving things differed, it was because God had given something to the living things He had not given to the nonliving. Some thinkers considered this inner thing to be a soul; others called it *vis viva* (life force). In the seventeenth century, early physiologists began looking inside animals to see how they worked. William Harvey (1578–1657) found what seemed more like the workings of a machine than some mysterious life force. It appeared that the heart functioned like a pump, circulating the blood through the arteries and tissues and back through the veins to the heart. Again, such reasoning left out the hypothetical assumptions of the philosophers and referred only to the observation of natural phenomena.

When Charles Darwin (1809–1882) published his theory of evolution by natural selection in 1859, it created a furor. Some people were offended because the theory went against the biblical account of God creating all the plants and animals in a few days. Even many geologists and biologists were shocked by Darwin. Familiar with the overwhelming fossil evidence of the rise and extinction of many species, these scientists were already convinced that evolution occurred. Yet although they no longer took the biblical Creation account literally, these scientists still regarded the creation of life (hence, evolution) as the work of God. They were no less offended by Darwin's theory of natural selection than were those who took the biblical account literally.

What impressed Darwin's contemporaries most, pro and con, about the theory was its account of the creation of life forms that left out God or any other nonnatural force. Natural selection is a purely mechanical process. If creatures vary, and the variation is inherited, then any reproductive advantage enjoyed by one type will cause that type to replace all competitors. Modern evolutionary theory arose in the first half of the twentieth century when the idea of natural selection was combined with the theory of genetic inheritance. This theory continues to arouse objections because of its godless naturalism.

As it was with astronomy, physics, chemistry, physiology, and evolutionary biology, so it has been with psychology. Psychology's break with philosophy was recent. Until the 1940s it was unusual for a university to have a department of psychology, and professors of psychology were usually found in the philosophy department. If evolutionary biology, with its roots in the mid-1800s, is still completing its break with theological and philosophical doctrine, it is no surprise that today psychologists still debate among themselves about the implications of calling psychology a true science, and laypeople are only beginning to learn what those implications might be.

In the last half of the nineteenth century, it became common to call psychology the "science of mind." The Greek word *psyche* means something more like "spirit," but *mind* seemed less speculative and more amenable to scientific study. How to study the mind? Psychologists proposed to adopt the method of the philosophers: introspection. If the mind were a sort of a stage or arena, then one could look inside it and see what was going on; that was the meaning of the word *introspect*. This is a difficult task, and particularly so if one is trying to gather reliable scientific facts. To nineteenth-century psychologists it seemed that this difficulty could be overcome with enough training and practice. But, two lines of thought combined to undermine this view: objective psychology and comparative psychology.

■ Objective Psychology

Some nineteenth-century psychologists were uneasy with introspection as a scientific method. It seemed too unreliable, too open to personal bias, too subjective. Other sciences used objective methods which produced measurements that could be checked and duplicated in laboratories around the world. If two trained introspectors disagreed over their findings, it would be hard to resolve the conflict; however, with objective methods researchers could note differences in procedure that might produce different results.

One of the pioneers of objective psychology was the Dutch psychologist F. C. Donders (1818–1889), who was inspired by an intriguing astronomy problem: how to arrive at the exact time when a star is in a certain position in the sky. When a star is viewed through a powerful telescope, it appears to travel at considerable speed. Astronomers trying to make accurate time measurements were having difficulty estimating to the fraction of a second. An astronomer would listen to a clock ticking the seconds while watching a star, and count ticks. As the star crossed a line marked in the telescope (the "moment of transit"), the astronomer would mentally note its position at the tick just before transit, mentally note its position at the tick just after transit, and then estimate the fraction of the distance between the two positions that lay between the position just before transit and the line. The problem was that different astronomers watching the same moment of transit obtained different time estimates. Astronomers tried to get around this variation by finding an equation, called the "personal equation," for each astronomer that would compute the correct time from the particular astronomer's time estimates.

Donders reasoned that the time estimates varied because no two astronomers took the same time to judge the exact moment of transit, and he believed they were actually making their judgments by different mental processes. It seemed to Donders that this "judgment time" might be a useful objective measure. He began doing experiments in which he measured people's *reaction times*—the times required to detect a light or sound and then press a button. He found that it took a certain reliable amount longer to press the correct one of two buttons when one or the other of two lights came on than to press a single button when a single light came on. By subtracting the longer choice reaction time from the shorter simple reaction time, Donders argued that he could objectively measure the mental process of choice. This seemed a great advance over introspection because it meant that psychologists could do laboratory experiments with the same objective methods as the other sciences.

Other psychologists developed other methods that seemed to measure mental processes objectively. Gustav Fechner (1801–1887) attempted to measure subjective intensity of sensation by developing a scale based on the *just-noticeable difference*—the physical difference between two lights or sounds that a person could just detect. Hermann Ebbinghaus (1850–1909) measured the time it took him to learn and later relearn lists of nonsense syllables—consonant-vowel-consonant combinations with no meaning—to produce objective measures of learning and memory. Others used the method developed by I. P. Pavlov (1849–1936) to study learning and association by measuring a simple reflex transferring to new signals arranged in the laboratory. These attempts held the common promise that by following objective methods psychology could become a true science.

■ Comparative Psychology

At the same time that psychologists were trying to make psychology an objective science, the theory of evolution was having a profound effect on the discipline. No longer were human beings seen as separate from other living things. It was becoming recognized that not only do we share anatomical traits with apes, monkeys, dogs, and even fish, but we share with them many behavioral traits.

Thus arose the notion of the *continuity of species*—the idea that even if species clearly differ from one another, to the extent that they share a common evolutionary history, they also resemble one another. Darwin's theory taught that new species came into existence only as modifications of existing species. If our species evolved like any other species, then it too must have arisen as a modification of some other species. It was easy to see that we and the apes shared common ancestors, that apes and monkeys shared common ancestors, that monkeys and tree shrews shared common ancestors, that tree shrews and reptiles shared common ancestors, and so on.

There seemed to be every reason to expect that, just as we could see the origins of our own anatomical traits in other species, so we could see the origins of our own mental traits. It was assumed, of course, that our mental traits would appear in other species in simpler or rudimentary form, but the notion of making comparisons among species in order to learn more about our own gave rise to comparative psychology.

Comparisons between our species and others became common. Darwin himself wrote a book called *The Expression of the Emotions in Men and Animals.* At first, evidence of seemingly human mentality in other animals consisted of casual observations of wild and domestic creatures, often just anecdotes about pets or farm animals. With a little imagination one could see a dog that learned to open the garden gate by lifting the latch as having observed and reasoned from its owner's example. One could imagine further that the dog's sensations, thoughts, feelings, and so on must resemble ours. George Romanes (1848–1894) took this line of reasoning to its logical conclusion, even claiming that our own consciousness must form the basis of our guesses at whatever dim consciousness occurs in ants.

This "humanizing the beast," or *anthropomorphism,* seemed too speculative to some psychologists. In the last part of the nineteenth and early part of the twentieth century, comparative psychologists began to replace the loose anecdotal evidence with rigorous observation by conducting experiments with animals. Much of this early research relied on mazes, because any creature that moves about, from human to rat to fish to ant, can be trained to solve a maze. The time the creature took to traverse the maze and the number of errors it made could be measured, as could the decline in these two as the maze was learned. Carrying on the attempt to humanize the beast, these early researchers frequently added speculations about the animals' mental states, thoughts, and emotions. Rats were said to show disgust on making an error, confusion, hesitation, confidence, and so on.

The problem with these claims about animal consciousness was that they depended too much on individual bias. If two people introspecting could disagree over whether they were feeling angry or sad, it was even more true that two people could disagree over whether a rat was feeling angry or sad. Owing to the subjective nature of the observations, the disagreement could not be resolved by further experimentation. It seemed to John B. Watson (1879–1958), the founder of behaviorism, that inferences about consciousness in animals was even less reliable than introspection as a scientific method, and that neither could serve as the method of a true science.

■ Early Behaviorism

In 1913, Watson published the article "Psychology as the Behaviorist Views It," soon considered the manifesto of early behaviorism. Taking his lead from objective psychology, he articulated the growing unease among psychologists over introspection and analogy as methods. He complained that introspection, unlike methods in physics or chemistry, depended too much on the individual:

> If you fail to reproduce my findings . . . it is due to the fact that your intro-spection is untrained. The attack is made upon the observer and not upon the experimental setting. In physics and in chemistry the attack is made upon the experimental conditions. The apparatus was not sensitive enough, impure chemicals were used, etc. In these sciences a better technique will give repro-ducible results. Psychology is otherwise. If you can't observe 3–9 states of clearness in attention, your introspection is poor. If, on the other hand, a feel-ing seems reasonably clear to you, your introspection is again faulty. You are seeing too much. Feelings are never clear (Watson, 1913, p. 163).

Analogies between animals and humans were also unreliable. Watson complained that the emphasis on consciousness forced him into

> the absurd position of attempting to *construct* the conscious content of the animal whose behavior we have been studying. On this view, after having determined our animal's ability to learn, the simplicity or complexity of its methods of learning, the effect of past habit upon present response, the range of stimuli to which it ordinarily responds, the widened range to which it can respond under experimental conditions,—in more general terms, its various problems and its various ways of solving them,—we should still feel that the task is unfinished and that the results are worthless, until we can interpret them by analogy in the light of consciousness . . . we feel forced to say some-thing about the possible mental processes of our animal. We say that, having no eyes, its stream of consciousness cannot contain brightness and color sen-sations as we know them,—having no taste buds this stream can contain no sensations of sweet, sour, salt and bitter. But on the other hand, since it does respond to thermal, tactual and organic stimuli, its conscious content must be made up largely of these sensations. . . . Surely this doctrine which calls for an analogical interpretation of all behavior data may be shown to be false . . . (Watson, 1913, pp. 159–160).

Psychologists trapped themselves into such fruitless efforts, Watson argued, because they defined psychology as the science of consciousness. This definition was to blame for the unreliable methods and baseless speculations. It was to blame for psychology's failure to become a true science.

Instead, Watson wrote, psychology should be defined as the science of behavior. He described his disappointment when, seeing *psychology* defined by Pillsbury at the beginning of a textbook as the science of behavior, he found that after a few pages the book ceased referring to behavior and reverted instead to the "conventional treatment" of consciousness. In reaction, Watson wrote, "I believe we can write a psychology, define it as Pillsbury, and never go back upon our definition: never use the terms consciousness, mental states, mind, content, introspectively verifiable, imagery, and the like" (Watson, 1913, p. 166).

Avoiding the terms relating to consciousness and mind would free psychologists to study both human and animal behavior. If continuity of species could lead to "humanizing the beast," it could equally well lead to the opposite (bestializing the human?); if ideas about humans could be applied to animals, principles developed by studying animals could be applied to humans. Watson argued against anthropocentrism. He pointed to the biologist studying evolution, who "gathers his data from the study of many species of plants and animals and tries to work out the laws of inheritance in the particular type upon which he is conducting experiments. . . . It is not fair to say that all of his work is directed toward human evolution or that it must be interpreted in terms of human evolution" (Watson, 1913, p. 162). To Watson, the way seemed clear to turn psychology into a general science of behavior that covered all species, with humans as just one of the species.

This science of behavior Watson envisioned would use none of the traditional terms referring to mind and consciousness, would avoid the subjectivity of introspection and animal–human analogies, and would study only objectively observable behavior. Yet even in Watson's own time, behaviorists debated over the correctness of this recipe. It was unclear what *objective* meant or exactly what constituted *behavior*. Since these terms were left open to interpretation, behaviorists' ideas about what constitutes science and how to define behavior have varied.

Of post-Watsonian behaviorists, the best known is B. F. Skinner (1904–1990). His ideas of how to achieve a science of behavior contrast sharply with those of most other behaviorists. Whereas the others focused on natural-science methods, Skinner focused on scientific explanation. He argued that the way to a science of behavior lay through development of terms and concepts that would allow truly scientific explanations. He labeled the opposing view *methodological behaviorism* and styled his own view *radical behaviorism.* We shall discuss these more in Chapters 2 and 3.

Whatever their disagreements, all behaviorists agree with Watson's basic premises that there can be a natural science of behavior and that psychology can be that science. This central idea raises controversy paralleling the reaction to Darwin's naturalistic account of evolution. Whereas Darwin offended by leaving out the hidden hand of God, behaviorists offend by leaving out another hidden force: the power of individuals to direct their own behavior. Just as Darwin's theory challenged the cherished idea of God the creator, so behaviorism challenges the cherished idea of free will. Because this challenge often arouses antagonism, we take it up now.

❖ FREE WILL VERSUS DETERMINISM

▧ Definitions

The idea that there can be a science of behavior implies that behavior, like any scientific subject matter, is orderly, can be explained, with the right knowledge can be predicted, and with the right means can be controlled. This is *determin-*

ism, the notion that behavior is determined solely by heredity and environment.

Many people find determinism objectionable. It appears to run counter to long-standing cultural traditions assigning the responsibility for action to the individual, rather than to heredity and environment. These traditions have changed to some extent: delinquency is blamed on bad environment; famous artists acknowledge debts to parents and teachers; and some behavioral traits, such as alcoholism, schizophrenia, handedness, and IQ, are acknowledged to have a genetic component. Yet there remains the tendency to assign credit and blame to individuals, to assert that there is something more than heredity and environment in behavior, that people have freedom to choose their actions.

The name for the ability to choose is *free will.* It implies a third element besides heredity and environment, something within the individual. It asserts that despite inheritance and despite all environmental impacts, a person who behaves one way could have chosen to behave another way. It asserts something beyond merely experiencing that one has choice—it could seem to me that I can eat the ice cream or not, and yet my eating the ice cream could be entirely determined by past events. Free will asserts that choice is no illusion, that individuals themselves cause behavior.

Philosophers have tried to reconcile determinism and free will. Positions have been put forward called "soft determinism" and "compatibilist" theories of free will. A soft determinism attributed to Donald Hebb (a behaviorist; see Sappington, 1990), for example, holds that free will consists of behavior depending on inheritance and environmental history, factors less visible than one's present environment. But since such a view still considers behavior to result solely from inheritance and environment, past and present, it implies that free will is only an experience, an illusion, and not a causal relation between person and action. A compatibilist theory of free will proposed by philosopher Daniel Dennett defines free will as deliberation before action (Dennett, 1984). As long as I deliberate over eating the ice cream (Will it make me fat? Could I offset its effects with exercise? Can I be happy if I am always dieting?), my eating the ice cream is freely chosen. This is compatible with determinism because deliberation itself is behavior that might be determined by heredity and past environment. If deliberation plays any role in the behavior that follows, it would act only as a link in a chain of causality extending back into earlier events. However, this definition deviates from what people conventionally mean by free will.

Philosophers call the conventional idea of free will—the idea that choice really can be free of past events—*libertarian free will.* Any other definition, like those of Hebb and Dennett, that is compatible with determinism presents no problem for behaviorism or a science of behavior. Only libertarian free will conflicts with behaviorism. The history of the concept in Jewish and Christian theology suggests that it exists precisely in order to deny the sort of determinism that behaviorism represents. Parting with the philosophers, therefore, we will refer to libertarian free will as "free will."

■ Arguments For and Against Free Will

Proving free will (in other words, disproving determinism) would require that an act go counter to prediction even though every possible contributing factor is known. Since such perfect knowledge is impossible in practice, the conflict between determinism and free will can never be resolved by evidence. If it seems that middle-class children from good homes who become drug addicts must have chosen freely to do so because there is nothing in their backgrounds that would account for the behavior, the determinist can insist that further investigation would reveal the genetic and environmental factors that lead to such addictions. If it seems that Mozart's musical career was entirely pre-dictable on the basis of his family background and the way society in Vienna worked in his day, the free will advocate can insist that little Wolfgang freely chose to please his parents with musical efforts rather than play with toys like the other children. If evidence cannot persuade, then whether a person accepts determinism or free will may depend on the consequences of such belief, and these can be social or aesthetic.

Social Arguments   Practically, it appears that denying free will could under-mine the whole moral fabric of our society. What will happen to our judicial system if people cannot be held responsible for their actions? We are already having trouble when criminals plead insanity and diminished competence. What will happen to our democratic institutions if people have no free choice? Why bother to have elections if choice among candidates is not free? Belief that people's behavior can be determined might encourage dictatorship. For these reasons, perhaps, it is good and useful to believe in free will, even if it cannot be proved.

Behaviorists must address these arguments; otherwise, behaviorism risks being labeled a pernicious doctrine. We shall address them in Part Three when we discuss freedom, social policy, and values. A brief survey now will give an idea of the general direction taken later.

The perceived threat to democracy derives from a false assumption. Although it is true that democracy depends on choice, it is false that choice becomes meaningless or impossible if there is no free will. The idea that choice would disappear arises from an oversimplified notion of the alternative to free will. If there are two ways that a person might vote in an election, which vote actually occurs depends not only on the person's long-term history (back-ground, upbringing, or values), but also on events right before the election. Campaigning goes on for precisely this reason. I can be swayed by a good speech, and without it I might have voted for the other candidate. People need not be free; it is only necessary that their behavior be open to influence and persuasion (shorter-term environmental determinants) for elections to be meaningful.

We favor democracy not because we have free will but because we find that, as a set of practices, it works. People in a democratic society are happier and more productive than under any known monarchy or dictatorship. Instead of worrying over the loss of free will, one can more profitably ask what it is about democracy that makes it better. If we can analyze our democratic institutions to discover what makes them work, we might be able to find ways to make them even more effective. Political freedom consists of something more practical than free will: it means having choices available and being able to affect the behavior of those who govern. A scientific understanding of behavior could be used to increase political freedom. In this way, the knowledge gained from a science of behavior could be put to good use; there is no necessity that it be abused. And after all, if we really do have free will, presumably no one need worry about the use of such knowledge anyway.

What about morals? Jewish and Christian theology incorporated free will as the means to salvation. Without such teaching, will people still be good? One way of answering this question is to point to that part of humanity, by far the majority, which lacks this commitment to the notion of free will. Do Buddhists and Hindus in China, Japan, and India behave less morally? In our own society, the rise of public education has increasingly moved moral training from church and home into the schools. As we lean more heavily on schools to produce good citizens, behavior analysis is already helping. There is no reason why the science of behavior cannot be used to educate children to be good, happy, effective citizens.

As for the justice system, it exists to deal with our failures, and there is no need to regard justice as a purely moral issue. We will always need to "hold people responsible for their behavior" in the practical sense that actions are assigned to individuals. Once it has been established that someone has transgressed, then practical issues arise as to how to protect society from this person and how to make it unlikely that the person will behave so in the future. Jailing criminals has proven to be of dubious worth. A science of behavior could help both to prevent crime and to treat it more effectively.

Aesthetic Arguments Critics of the notion of free will often point to its illogic. Even theologians who promoted the idea have puzzled over its paradoxical conflict with an omnipotent God. Saint Augustine put the matter clearly: If God does everything and knows everything before it happens, how is it possible for a person to do anything freely? Just as with natural determinism, if God determines all events (including our actions), then it is only our ignorance—here, of God's will—that allows the illusion of free will. The common theological solution is to call free will a mystery; somehow God gives us free will despite His omnipotence. This is unsatisfactory because it defies logic and leaves the paradox unresolved.

In its conflict with determinism, godly or natural, free will seems to depend on ignorance. Indeed, it can be argued that free will is simply a name for ignorance of the determinants of behavior. The more we know of the reasons behind a person's actions, the less we are likely to attribute them to free will. If a boy who steals cars comes from a poor environment, we are inclined to attribute the behavior to the environment, and the more we know about how he was abused and neglected by his family and society the less likely we are to say that he chose freely. When we know that a politician has accepted a bribe, we no longer consider that politician's positions to be taken freely. When we learn that an artist had supportive parents and a great teacher, we wonder less over his talent.

The other side of this argument is that no matter how much we know, we still cannot predict exactly what a person will do in a given situation. This unpredictability has sometimes been considered evidence of free will. However, the weather is also unpredictable, but we never regard it as the product of free will. Many natural systems exist, the momentary behavior of which we cannot predict but which we never consider free. Would we set a higher standard for a science of behavior than for the other natural sciences? In addition, the logical error involved is easy to spot. Free will does imply unpredictability, but this in no way requires the converse, that unpredictability implies free will.

In a way, it should even be false that free will implies unpredictability. My actions may be unpredictable by another person, but if my free will can cause my behavior, I should know perfectly well what I am going to do. This requires that I know my will, because it is difficult to see how a will that was unknown could be free. If I decide to go on a diet, and I know this is my will, then I ought to predict that I shall go on the diet. If I know my will, and my will causes my behavior, I should be able to predict my behavior perfectly.

The notion that free will causes behavior raises a thorny metaphysical problem as well. How can a nonnatural event like free will cause a natural event like eating ice cream? Natural events can lead to other natural events, because they can be related to one another in time and space. Sexual intercourse leads to a baby just about nine months later. The phrase *leads to* implies that the cause can be placed in time and space. By definition, however, nonnatural things and events cannot be placed in time and space. (If they could be placed in time and space, then they would be natural.) How, then, can a nonnatural event *lead to* a natural event? When and where does willing take place, that it can lead to my eating ice cream? (Another version of this problem, the mind–body problem, will occupy us in Chapter 3.) The murkiness of such hypothetical connections led to Newton's *Hypotheses non fingo.* Science admits unsolved puzzles, because puzzles may ultimately yield to further thought and experimentation, but the connection between free will and action cannot be so illuminated. It is a mystery. Science's aim of explaining the world excludes mysteries that cannot be explained.

The mysterious nature of free will, for example, runs counter to the theory of evolution. First, there is the problem of discontinuity. If animals lack free will, how did it suddenly arise in our species? It would have to have been presaged in our nonhuman ancestors. Second, even if animals could have free will, how could such a nonnatural thing evolve? Natural traits evolve by modification from other natural traits. One can imagine even the evolution of a natural mechanical system that could behave unpredictably from moment to moment. But there is no conceivable way that natural evolution could result in a nonnatural free will. This may be a powerful reason that some religious groups oppose the theory of evolution; conversely, it is an equally powerful reason to exclude free will from scientific accounts of behavior.

❖ SUMMARY

All behaviorists agree that there can be a science of behavior, which has come to be called behavior analysis. Behaviorism is properly viewed as philosophy about that science.

All the sciences originated in and broke away from philosophy. Astronomy and physics arose when scientists turned from philosophical speculation to observation. In so doing, they dropped any concern with supernatural things, observing the natural universe and explaining natural events by referring to other natural events. Similarly, chemistry broke with philosophy when it abandoned hidden inner essences as explanations of chemical events. As it became a science, physiology dropped the inner *vis viva* in favor of mechanistic explanations of the body's workings. Darwin's theory of evolution was widely perceived as an attack on religion because it proposed to explain the creation of life forms with natural events only, and without the supernatural hand of God. Scientific psychology, too, grew out of philosophy and may still be breaking away from it. Two movements, objective psychology and comparative psychology, promoted this break. Objective psychology emphasized observation and experimentation, the methods that distinguished other sciences. Comparative psychology emphasized the common origin of all species, including human beings, in natural selection, and helped promote purely natural accounts of human behavior.

John B. Watson, who founded behaviorism, took his lead from comparative psychology. He attacked the idea that psychology was the science of mind by pointing out that neither introspection nor analogies to animal consciousness produced the reliable results produced by the methods of other sciences. He argued that only by studying behavior could psychology achieve the reliability and generality it needed to become a natural science.

The idea that behavior can be treated scientifically remains controversial because it challenges the notion that behavior arises from an individual's free choice. It promotes determinism, the idea that all behavior originates from genetic inheritance and environmental effects. The term *free will* names the supposed ability of a person to choose behavior freely, without regard to inheritance or environment. Determinism asserts that free will is an illusion based on ignorance of the factors determining behavior. Since soft determinism and compatibilist theories of free will affirm the idea that free will is only an illusion, they present no challenge to a science of behavior. Only *libertarian free will*, the idea that people really have the ability to behave as they choose (espoused by Judaism and Christianity), conflicts with determinism. Since the argument between determinism and free will cannot be resolved by evidence, the debate about which view is right rests on arguments about the consequences—social and aesthetic—of adopting one view or the other.

Critics of determinism argue that belief in free will is necessary to preserve democracy and morality in our society. Behaviorists argue that probably the opposite is true—that a behavioral approach to social problems can enhance democracy and promote moral behavior. As for aesthetics, critics of free will note that free will is illogical when paired with the notion of an omnipotent

God (as it usually is). Whether actions are determined by natural events or by God's will, they still cannot logically be attributed to an individual's free will. Supporters of free will retort that since scientists can never predict an individual's actions in detail, free will remains possible, even if it is a mystery. Behaviorists respond that its mysterious nature is precisely what makes it unacceptable, because it raises the same problem that other sciences had to overcome: How can a nonnatural cause lead to natural events? Behaviorists give the same answer as was given in the other sciences: Natural events arise only from other natural events.

❖ FURTHER READING

Boakes, R. A. (1984). *From Darwin to behaviorism: Psychology and the minds of animals.* Cambridge: Cambridge University Press. This is an excellent historical account of the rise of early behaviorism.

Dennett, D. C. (1984). *Elbow room: The varieties of free will worth wanting.* Cambridge, MA: MIT Press. This includes a thorough discussion of free will and an example of a compatibilist theory.

Sappington, A. A. (1990). Recent psychological approaches to the free will versus determinism issue. *Psychological Bulletin, 108,* 19–29. This article contains a useful summary of various positions.

Watson, J. B. (1913). Psychology as the behaviorist views it. *Psychological Review, 20,* 158–177. Watson lays out his original views in this classic paper.

CHAPTER 2

BEHAVIORISM AS PHILOSOPHY OF SCIENCE

The idea that there can be a science of behavior is deceptively simple. It leads to two thorny questions. The first is, "What is science?" This might prompt an answer like, "Science is the study of the natural universe." But this raises further questions: What makes something "natural"? What does "study" entail? If we rephrase the question to be, "What makes science different from other types of human endeavor, such as poetry and religion?" an answer might be that science is objective. But what is it to be "objective"?

The second question is, "What does it take to make the study of behavior scientific?" How we answer this question depends on how we have answered the first question. Perhaps behavior is part of the natural universe. Perhaps there is something unique about the way we would talk about behavior from a scientific point of view.

This chapter will focus on the first question. The primary focus of Chapter 3 will be the second question, although the full answer to the question of what it means to study behavior scientifically will be fleshed out by the rest of the book.

❖ REALISM VERSUS PRAGMATISM

Radical behaviorists' ideas about science differ from those voiced by both early behaviorists and many pre-twentieth-century thinkers. Radical behaviorism accords with the philosophical tradition known as *pragmatism,* whereas the earlier view derived from *realism.*

■ Realism

As a world view, realism is so pervasive in Western civilization that many people accept it without question. It is the idea that the trees, rocks, buildings, stars, and people I see really are there—that there is a real world out there that gives rise to our experiences of it. If I turn my back on a tree, I expect that when I turn around I shall see the tree again. It seems like common sense that the tree is part of a real world outside me, whereas my experience of the tree, my perceptions, thoughts, and feelings, are inside me. This seemingly straightforward notion entails two not-so-simple presumptions. First, this real world seems somehow to be *out there,* in contrast with our experience, which somehow seems to be *in here.* Second, our experiences are *of* this real world; they are separate from the world itself. As we shall see, both of these may be doubted, with remarkable results.

The Objective Universe   Several early Greek philosophers who lived in the sixth century B.C. are credited with originating scientific thinking. One of them, Thales, proposed a view of the universe that differed fundamentally from the widely accepted Babylonian view, which held that the god Marduk had created the world and continued to govern all happenings in it. Thales proposed that the sun, moon, and stars moved mechanically across the sky each day, and at night moved around the flat earth back to their places in the east to rise the next morning (Farrington, 1980). However far this may seem from our ideas today, Thales's version of the universe was useful. Farrington (1980, p. 37) comments, "It is an admirable beginning, the whole point of which is that it gathers together into a coherent picture a number of observed facts *without letting Marduk in.*" To put it positively, Thales proposed that the universe is a comprehensible mechanism.

In the context of realism, a comprehensible mechanism means a real mechanism that is "out there," and about which we learn as we study it. Its comprehensibility means that as we learn more about it, this mechanical universe seems less puzzling. Its being "out there" makes it objective—that is, regardless of how our conceptions about it may change, the universe remains just what it is.

Discovery and Truth   If there is an objective universe that we can learn about, then it is proper to say that when we study the universe scientifically, we discover things about it. If we can discover something about the way the universe works, it is proper to say that we discover the truth about it. In such a view, bit by bit, discovery upon discovery, we approach the whole truth about the way the universe works.

Sense Data and Subjectivity   To the realist, our approach to the truth is slow and uncertain because we cannot study the objective world directly. We have direct contact only with what our senses tell us. As George Berkeley (1685–1753) wrote in an essay called "Principles of Human Knowledge":

> It is indeed an opinion strangely prevailing amongst men, that houses, mountains, rivers, and in a word all sensible objects, have an existence, natural or real, distinct from their being perceived by the understanding . . . yet whoever shall find in his heart to call it in question may, if I mistake not, perceive it to involve a manifest contradiction. For what are the forementioned objects but the things we perceive by sense? and what do we perceive *besides our own ideas or sensations?*

In other words, since we have no direct contact with the real world, but only with our perceptions of it, we have no logical reason to believe that the world is actually there.

Although some philosophers after Berkeley joined his skepticism about realism and accepted the idea that the objects of the world are only inferences, philosophers of science tended to stick to realism and deal with Berkeley's point differently. Bertrand Russell (1872–1970), for example, writing in the early part of this century, substituted the concept of *sense data* for Berkeley's "ideas" and "sensations." He proposed that the scientist studies sense data to try to learn about the real world. The sense data, being "in here," are subjective, but are the means to understand the objective real world "out there."

Explanation   In the framework of realism, explanation consists in the discovery of the way things really are. Once we know the orbit the earth takes around the sun, then we have explained why we have seasons and why the position of the sun in the sky shifts as it does. It is like having the workings of an automobile engine explained: The crankshaft turns because the pistons push it around as they go up and down.

To the realist, explanations differ from mere descriptions, which only detail how our sense data go together. Descriptions of the shifts of the sun's position in the sky existed long before it was generally accepted that the earth moves around the sun in an elliptical orbit. Description only tells how things appear on the surface—once the underlying truth about the way things work is discovered, then the events we perceive are explained.

■ Pragmatism

Realism can be contrasted with pragmatism, a view that was developed by philosophers in the United States, particularly Charles Peirce (1839–1914) and

William James (1842–1910), during the last half of the nineteenth century and early part of the twentieth century. The fundamental notion of pragmatism is that the power of scientific inquiry lies not so much in our discovering the truth of the way the objective universe works, but in what it allows us to *do*. (Hence the name *pragmatism*, from the same root as *practical*.) In particular, the great thing that science permits us to do is to make sense out of our experience. It makes our experience seem comprehensible; for example, that rain falls not because of some mysterious god but because of water vapor and weather conditions in the upper atmosphere. Sometimes science even allows us to predict and control, if we have the means, what will happen. We listen to weather forecasts because they are helpful. We take antibiotics because we know they combat infection.

James (1907) presented pragmatism as a method for settling disputes and as a theory of truth. He pointed out that some questions lead only to endless arguments with no satisfactory resolution:

> Is the world one or many?—fated or free?—material or spiritual?—here are notions either of which may or may not hold good of the world; and disputes over such notions are unending. The pragmatic method in such cases is to try to interpret each notion by tracing its respective practical consequences. What difference would it practically make to any one if this notion rather than that notion were true? If no practical difference whatever can be traced, then the alternatives mean practically the same thing, and all dispute is idle. Whenever a dispute is serious, we ought to be able to show some practical difference that must follow from one side or the other's being right (pp. 42–43.)

In other words, if the answer to a question would not change the way science would proceed, then the question itself is at fault and merits no attention.

James and Peirce considered the question of whether there is a real, unchanging, objective world out there as one of those questions about which dispute is idle. James wrote that our conception of an object consists of nothing beyond its practical effects: "what sensations we are to expect from it, and what reactions we must prepare" (1907, p. 43). What matters about a bicycle is that I see it, call it by its name, may lend it to a friend, may ride it myself. Pragmatism remains agnostic about whether there is a real bicycle behind these effects.

With such an attitude toward questions, pragmatism must imply a special attitude toward the truth of answers. As a theory of truth, pragmatism roughly equates truth with explanatory power. If the question of whether there is a real universe out there is idle, then so too is the question of whether there is some final, absolute truth. Instead of ideas being simply true or false, James proposed that ideas can be more and less true. One idea is more true than another if it allows us to explain and understand more of our experience. James put it this way: "Any idea upon which we can ride, so to speak; any idea that will carry us prosperously from any one part of our experience to any other part, linking things satisfactorily, working securely, simplifying, saving labor; is true

KEIGHLEY COLLEGE LIBRARY

for just so much, true in so far forth, true *instrumentally*" (1907, p. 49). The idea that the sun and stars move around the earth explained only why they move across the sky; thus, it is less true than the idea that the earth orbits the sun while rotating on its axis, which also explains why we have seasons. According to pragmatism, however, we will never know whether the earth *really* revolves around the sun; another, truer, theory could conceivably come along.

In support of his view, James pointed out that in practice all scientific theories are approximations. Rarely, if ever, does one theory explain all the facts of experience. Instead, one theory often does well with one set of phenomena while another does well with another set. James wrote,

> and so many rival formulations are proposed in all the branches of science that investigators have become accustomed to the notion that no theory is absolutely a transcript of reality, but that any one of them may from some point of view be useful. Their great use is to summarize old facts and to lead to new ones. They are only a man-made language, a conceptual shorthand, . . . in which we write our reports of nature . . . (1907, pp. 48–49).

James's modern counterpart is Thomas Kuhn (1970), who wrote *The Structure of Scientific Revolutions.* In this book, he argued that science cannot be characterized as unending progress toward some ultimate truth. The apparently progressive quality of scientific thinking is, according to Kuhn, largely illusory. Most of the time, during periods of "normal science," some puzzles yield to research and inquiry while new puzzles crop up. When too many puzzles remain unsolved, a totally different view of the domain of the science may begin to gain acceptance and eventually overthrow the old view. A revolution in thinking occurs, and the new view (called a *paradigm*) usually explains more than the old view did. However, it doesn't explain all that the old view did, and it presents its own puzzles, too. This conception of science might be seen not as a march toward ultimate truth but as a busy dance hall, in which each dancer tries out different steps and figures, and in which every so often the band begins to play an entirely different tune.

Science and Experience   Pragmatism influenced modern behaviorism indirectly as a result of a friendship between William James and the physicist Ernst Mach (1838–1916). James's influence appears in Mach's book *The Science of Mechanics,* a history that applied pragmatism to that branch of physics. Since this book greatly influenced Skinner, and Skinner greatly influenced modern behaviorism, in a roundabout way modern behaviorism owes a great debt to James.

Following James, Mach argued that science has to do with experience and particularly making sense of our experience. He considered science to originate in the need for people to communicate efficiently, economically, with one another. This is essential to human culture because it permits understanding about the world to be passed easily from one generation to the next. Economy requires the invention of concepts that organize our experiences into types or categories, allowing us to use one term instead of many words. Mach compared science to the body of knowledge possessed by artisans, who he characterized as a social class that practices a certain craft:

> A class of this sort occupies itself with particular kinds of natural processes. The individuals of the class change; old members drop out, and new ones come in. Thus arises a need of imparting to those who are newly come in, the stock of experience and knowledge already possessed; a need of acquainting them with the conditions of the attainment of a definite end so that the result may be determined beforehand (1960, p. 5).

A potter's apprentice, for example, learns about different kinds of clay, working the clay, glazes, firing, kilns, and so on. Without such instruction, the apprentice could not be sure what procedures to follow to get a good finished product. Without the concepts that allow such instruction, each new generation of potters would have to experiment and discover the techniques all over again. This would not only be inefficient; it would prevent accumulation of knowledge over many generations. Imagine the state of house-building today if carpenters had no way to benefit from the experiences of carpenters a hundred years ago!

Conceptual Economy   As it is for any skilled performance, so it is for science. If I am teaching you to drive a car, I would be foolish indeed to put you behind the wheel and say, "OK, go ahead and experiment." Instead, I will explain to you concepts like starting, steering, braking, accelerating, shifting gears, and so on. Then you will know what to do if I say, "When you are entering a curve, let up on the accelerator, and then if the steering is easy, you can accelerate again." You might discover such rules on your own by experimenting, but it is a lot easier to be told. Just as the concepts of shifting and accelerating allow us to pass on an understanding of driving, so do scientific concepts allow us to pass on an understanding of experiences with other aspects of the natural world. As Mach wrote:

> To find, then, what remains unaltered in the phenomena of nature, to discover the elements thereof and the mode of their interconnection and interdependence—this is the business of physical science. It endeavors, by comprehensive and thorough description, to make the waiting for new experiences unnecessary; it seeks to save us the trouble of experimentation, by making use, for example, of the known interdependence of phenomena, according to which, if one kind of event occurs, we may be sure beforehand that a certain other event will occur (1960, pp. 7–8).

In other words, science creates concepts that allow one person to tell another what goes with what in the world and what to expect if such-and-such happens—to predict on the basis of past experience with such events. When scientists make up terms like *oxygen, satellite,* and *gene,* each word contains a whole story of expectations and predictions. These concepts allow us to talk about such expectations and predictions economically, without having to continually make long explanations.

As an example of the way science invents economical summarizing terms, Mach recounted how the concept of "air" developed. He began in the time of Galileo (1564–1642):

> In Galileo's time philosophers explained the phenomenon of suction, the action of syringes and pumps by the so-called *horror vacui*—nature's abhorrence of a vacuum. Nature was thought to possess the power of preventing the formation of a vacuum by laying hold of the first adjacent thing, whatsoever it was, and immediately filling up with it any empty space that arose. Apart from the ungrounded speculative element which this view contains, it must be conceded, that to a certain extent it really represents the phenomenon (1960, p. 136).

If you've ever put a drinking glass over your mouth and sucked the air out of it so that it would stick to your face, you felt the vacuum in the glass "pulling" your cheeks into the glass. Nowadays we would describe this as the action of air pressure. One crucial step in this change of view was the observation that air had weight:

> Galileo had endeavored . . . to determine the weight of the air, by first weighing a glass bottle containing nothing but air and then again weighing the bottle after the air had been partly expelled by heat. It was known, accordingly, that the air was heavy. But to the majority of men the *horror vacui* and the weight of the air were very distantly connected notions (1960, p. 137).

It was Torricelli (1608–1647) who first saw the connection between suction and the weight of air. He saw that a tube closed at one end, filled with mercury, and inverted with the open end in a bowl full of mercury, would contain a vacuum at the top and a column of mercury of a certain height below it. Mach commented:

> It is possible that in Torricelli's case the two ideas came into sufficient proximity to lead him to the conviction that all phenomena ascribed to the *horror vacui* were explicable in a simple and logical manner by the pressure exerted by the weight of a fluid column—a column of air. Torricelli discovered, therefore, the pressure of the atmosphere; he also first observed by means of his column of mercury the variations of the pressure of the atmosphere (1960, p. 137).

Invention of the vacuum pump made possible many further observations about what happens when air is exhausted from a vessel. Many of these observations were made by Guericke (1602–1686), who had one of the first efficient vacuum pumps. Mach wrote:

> The phenomena which Guericke observed with this apparatus are manifold and various. The noise which water in a vacuum makes on striking the sides of

the glass receiver, the violent rush of air and water into exhausted vessels suddenly opened, the escape on exhaustion of gases absorbed in liquids . . . were
immediately remarked. A lighted candle is extinguished on exhaustion,
because, as Guericke conjectures, it derives its nourishment from the air. . . .
A bell does not ring in a vacuum. Birds die in it. Many fishes swell up, and
finally burst. A grape is kept fresh in vacuo for over half a year (1960, p. 145).

In Mach's view, the concept of air allowed all these observations (i.e.,
experiences) to be seen as connected, instead of discrete and disorganized. The
word *air* allows them to be spoken of as related to one another, easily, and
with relatively few words. The concept provides our discussion with economy.

Explanation and Description   In some of the preceding quotes, Mach suggests that the aim of science is description. For realism, we noted that the aim
of science was not "mere" description, but explanation based on discovery of
the reality beyond our experience. In such a view, description only summarizes appearances, whereas explanation speaks of what is really true. To pragmatists like James and Mach, however, there is no such distinction because,
practically speaking, all that science has to go on is appearances—that is,
observations or experiences. For pragmatism, explanation and description are
one and the same.

What matters to the pragmatist is that in describing our observations we
use terms that relate one phenomenon to another. When we can see relations,
see how one observation is connected to others, then our experiences seem
orderly and comprehensible, instead of chaotic and mysterious. Mach argued
that the job of science begins when some events seem out of the ordinary, puzzling. Science then seeks out commonalities in natural phenomena, elements
that are the same despite all apparent variation. You puzzle over a statue of
Mickey Mouse on your boss's desk until you learn it is a telephone. As a child
I was accustomed to the idea that things fall when you let them go because
they have weight; therefore, I was surprised when a helium balloon flew into
the sky when I let go of it. Later in life, I learned about the concepts of density
and floating (common elements) and understood that a helium balloon floats
in air much as a boat floats in water.

Mach argued that this process of describing a phenomenon in common,
familiar terms is exactly what we mean by explanation:

> When once we have reached the point where we are everywhere able to detect
> the *same* few simple elements, combining in the ordinary manner, then they
> appear to us as things that are familiar; we are no longer surprised, there is
> nothing new or strange to us in the phenomena, we feel at home with them,
> they no longer perplex us, they are *explained* (1960, p. 7).

Scientific explanation consists only in describing events in terms that are
familiar. It has nothing to do with revealing some hidden reality beyond our
experience.

You might be surprised at the subjective tone of this: Events are explained
when we "feel at home" with them. In realism, what makes an event "familiar"

is nothing about the event itself—nothing objective—but something about our experience with this or similar events—something subjective. When a helium balloon rises, whether that event seems mysterious or familiar depends, to the realist, on nothing about the objective event, but rather on our subjective appreciation of the event.

In pragmatism, however, if there were to be a distinction between subjectivity and objectivity, it would differ altogether from that made in realism. It would be fair to say that the conflict between subjectivity and objectivity is for the pragmatist resolved in favor of subjectivity. Since there need not be an objective real world, objectivity, if it has any meaning at all, at most could be a quality of scientific inquiry. It would be consistent with pragmatism simply to drop the two terms altogether.

It might seem peculiar that in some of the quotes from Mach he uses the word *discover* in speaking of scientists' activities. Discovery seems to imply getting beyond appearances to the way things really are, an idea consistent with realism. To Mach, "discovering" the common elements in phenomena is the same as inventing concepts. Each common element corresponds to a category or type, and its label is the concept or term. Take the type of event we call "floating"—boats float in water and helium balloons float in air. The behavior of the helium balloon becomes comprehensible once we have invented (or discovered) the concept of floating. Just as the distinction between subjectivity and objectivity disappears for pragmatism, so does the distinction between discovery and invention. Commenting on the concept of air, Mach wrote, "What indeed could be more wonderful than the sudden *discovery* [italics added] that a thing which we do not see, hardly feel, and take scarcely any notice of, constantly envelopes us on all sides, penetrates all things; that it is the most important condition of life, of combustion, and of gigantic mechanical phenomena" (p. 135). Yet he could just as well have said that air, the concept, was a wonderful invention.

In the same way, Lavoisier, who "discovered" oxygen, discovered a new way of talking about combustion. We could just as well say that he invented a new term, *oxygen*. (The interested reader should refer to Kuhn's *The Structure of Scientific Revolutions* for a more recent discussion of the identity of discovery and invention.)

Later in the book (particularly Chapter 7), we shall discuss scientific terms again, because in the behavioral view neither word—*invention* or *discovery*—describes science so well as the idea that scientific talk is, after all, behavior. We shall see that a scientist is someone who engages in certain types of behavior, including certain types of verbal behavior. Right now, however, we continue at a more general level.

❖ RADICAL BEHAVIORISM AND PRAGMATISM

Modern, radical behaviorism is based on pragmatism. To the question, "What is science?" it gives the answer of James and Mach: Science is the pursuit of economical and comprehensible descriptions of human natural experience (i.e., our experience of the "natural world"). The goal of a science of behavior is to describe behavior in terms that render it familiar and hence "explained." Its methods aim to enlarge our natural experience of behavior through precise observation.

Old, methodological behaviorism was based on realism. In the context of studying behavior, realism would hold that there is some real behavior that goes on in the real world, and that our senses, whether used with instruments or in direct observation, provide us only with sense data about that real behavior, which we never know directly. If we make the observation that a man is moving his feet one in front of the other rapidly in the street, someone might object that this fails to capture the sense of the description that the man is running along the street. But someone else might object that this still falls short, because the man might be exercising, running from the police, or running a race. Even if we determine that the man is running a race, he still might be described as training for the Olympics or impressing his family and friends.

To the realist (methodological behaviorist), the best way to deal with diverse possible descriptions is to stick close to the first, to describe running in the street in as mechanical terms as possible, perhaps even going into the muscle groups involved, because those mechanical movements would supposedly bring us as close as we can get to the real behavior. The man's reasons for engaging in this behavior would be dealt with separately.

The pragmatist (radical behaviorist), having no commitment to any idea of real behavior, asks only which way of describing the man's behavior is most useful, or in Mach's terms, most economical—that is, which gives us the best understanding or the most coherent description. That is why radical behaviorists tend to favor the types of description that include the man's reasons for running. A useful description might be, "The man is running in a race along this street as part of an attempt to enter the Olympics." As we shall see in later chapters, we might refine this further, by incorporating the reasons behind the attempt to enter the Olympics and in other ways.

Being realists, methodological behaviorists distinguished between the objective world and the subjective world. Since science seemed to them to concern only the objective world, they considered science to consist of methods for studying the world "out there." Since realism assumes that the same objective world is out there for everyone, whereas each person's subjective world is different and inaccessible to anyone else, methodological behaviorists thought that the only route to a science of behavior would be through methods that were objective, that gathered sense data about the world out there, the world that everyone shares and could potentially agree about. That is why it is true to say of old behaviorism that it was the "psychology of the other one," that it proposed for study only the public behavior of a person that could be observed by someone else, and that it ignored consciousness.

Radical behaviorism, in contrast, makes no such distinction between the subjective and the objective worlds. Instead of focusing on methods, it focuses on concepts and terms. Just as physics advanced with the invention of the term *air*, so a science of behavior advances with the invention of its terms. Historically, behavior analysts have used concepts such as *response, stimulus,* and *reinforcement.* The uses of these concepts have changed as the science has progressed. In the future, their use may continue to change, or they may be replaced by more useful terms. In the chapters that follow, we shall take up many terms, old and new, and evaluate them for their usefulness. We will ask again and again which terms make for economical, comprehensible descriptions.

How does radical behaviorism answer the question, "What is behavior?" The answer is pragmatic. The terms we use to talk about behavior not only allow us to make sense of it, but also define it. Behavior includes whatever events we can talk about with our invented terms. Radical behaviorism inquires after the best, the most useful ways to talk about it. If, for example, it is useful to say that a person is running a race in order to qualify for the Olympics, then running a race in order to qualify for the Olympics constitutes a behavioral event. In Chapter 4, when we take up some of the concepts used by behavior analysts today, we shall also be able to define behavior more specifically.

This pragmatic emphasis on talk, terms, and descriptions—as opposed to methods of observation—leads to one of the striking contrasts between methodological and radical behaviorism. Conscious phenomena, being among those things we can talk about, are included in the study of behavior for the radical behaviorist. We shall discuss how this is done in the next chapter.

❖ SUMMARY

The idea that there can be a science of behavior raises two questions: (1) What is science? (2) What view of science applies to behavior? Radical behaviorists view science within the philosophical tradition of pragmatism. Pragmatism contrasts with realism, the view adopted by many pre-twentieth-century scientists and by early twentieth-century behaviorists. Realism holds that there is a real world outside of us and that that outer real world gives rise in each of us to internal experiences. The outer world is considered objective, whereas the world of inner experience is considered subjective. In realism, science consists in discovering the truth about the objective universe. Since, however, we have no direct knowledge of the outer world, but only of our inner experience, which comes to us through our senses, philosophers like Bertrand Russell argued that science must proceed by reasoning from sense data about what the objective universe must be like. Our experiences of the real world are explained when our reasoning leads us to the ultimate truth about it. Pragmatism, in contrast, makes no assumption of an indirectly known real world outside. It focuses instead on the task of making sense of our experiences. Questions and answers that help us to understand what happens around us are useful. Questions that can make no difference to our understanding, such as whether there is a real universe outside us, merit no attention. There is no absolute ultimate truth; rather the truth of a concept lies in how much of our experience it allows us to link together, organize, or comprehend. For pragmatists like William James and Ernst Mach, this process of linking together various parts of our experience is what constitutes explanation. In Mach's view, speaking effectively about our experiences—that is, communication—was one and the same as explanation. He argued that insofar as we can talk about an event in familiar terms, the event is explained. To the extent that talking about events in familiar terms is called description, explanation and description are the same. Science discovers only concepts that render our experience more comprehensible.

Whereas radical behaviorism is based on pragmatism, methodological behaviorism was based on realism. To the realist, real behavior occurs in the real world, and this real behavior is accessible only indirectly through our senses. Accordingly, the methodological behaviorist tries to describe behavioral events in terms as mechanical as possible, as close to physiology as possible. The radical behaviorist looks instead for descriptive terms that are useful for understanding behavior and economical for discussing behavior. Pragmatic descriptions of behavior include its ends and the context within which it occurs. To the radical behaviorist, descriptive terms both explain behavior and define what behavior is.

❖ FURTHER READING

Berkeley, G. (1939). Principles of human knowledge. In E. A Burtt (Ed.), *The English philosophers from Bacon to Mill* (pp. 509–579). (Originally published in 1710.) New York: Random House. This classic essay includes Berkeley's criticism of realism.

Day, W. (1980). The historical antecedents of contemporary behaviorism. In R. W. Rieber & K. Salzinger (Eds.), *Psychology: Theoretical-historical perspectives* (pp. 203–262). New York: Academic Press. In this article, Day discusses the relationship between pragmatism and radical behaviorism.

Farrington, B. (1980). *Greek science*. Nottingham: Russell Press. An excellent book on early Greek science.

James, W. (1974). *Pragmatism and four essays from The meaning of truth.* New York: New American Library. (Originally published in 1907 and 1909.) James's ideas about pragmatism may be found in this book.

Kuhn, T. S. (1970). *The structure of scientific revolutions* (2nd ed.). Chicago: University of Chicago Press. Kuhn's extension of pragmatic thinking is summarized in this book.

Mach, E. (1960). *The science of mechanics: A critical and historical account of its development.* (Originally published in 1933.) La Salle, IL: Open Court Publishing. Mach's application of pragmatism to physical science.

Russell, B. (1965). *On the philosophy of science.* New York: Bobbs-Merrill. Russell's views on science may be found in this collection of essays.

CHAPTER 3

PUBLIC, PRIVATE, NATURAL, AND FICTIONAL

We saw in Chapter 2 that radical behaviorism makes no distinction between subjective and objective phenomena in the traditional sense. We shall see in this chapter that, although it makes little of the distinction between public and private events, which roughly correspond to the objective and subjective worlds, it does draw some other distinctions. The most important is between natural events and fictional events.

❖ MENTALISM

The term *mentalism* was adopted by B. F. Skinner to refer to a type of "explanation" that really explains nothing. Suppose you ask a friend why he or she bought a pair of shoes, and the friend replies, "I just wanted them" or "I did it on impulse." Even though these statements sound like explanations, you are really no further ahead than before you asked. Such nonexplanations are examples of mentalism.

In defining a science of behavior, radical behaviorists often focus on distinguishing valid explanations from phony explanations. For the pragmatists James and Mach (see Chapter 2), a valid explanation was a description in comprehensible terms. In the same vein, radical behaviorism seeks a set of terms that render an event like buying a pair of shoes comprehensible. In developing such a set of terms, it will be helpful also to see why terms like *wanted* and *impulse* fall short.

■ Public and Private Events

Public events are events that can be reported on by more than one person. A thunderstorm is a public event, because you and I talk about it together. Of course, many public events go unreported. We may both hear a bird singing, but we don't necessarily talk about it. Even if I hear the bird when I am alone, it is still public, because you and I could talk about it if you happened to be near.

Private events are events that can never be reported on by more than one person, no matter how many other people may be present. Aaron cannot tell what Shona is thinking at this moment because Shona's thoughts are private events. Only Shona can report on her thoughts.

Two points are important about this public–private distinction. First, to the radical behaviorist the distinction is of little significance. The only difference between public and private events is the number of people who can report on them. Otherwise, they are the same sort of events, having all the same properties. Skinner (1969) expressed this by writing, "The skin is not all that important as a boundary." To give the distinction some other importance would reinstate the old objective–subjective distinction in a different form.

Second, public and private events are both *natural* events. If I think, *It is a beautiful day,* that is a natural event. If I say, *It is a beautiful day,* that is a natural event. If I go to the beach, that too is a natural event. They are all of the same type.

■ Natural Events

Every science deals with natural events, whether moving objects, chemical reactions, tissue growth, exploding stars, natural selection, or bodily action. Behavioral analysis is no different.

The particular natural events that make up the subject matter of behavior analysis are those assigned to whole living organisms. The behavior of stones and stars is outside of the subject matter because these objects are not living. The behavior of a cell, liver, or leg is outside because these are not whole organisms. However, when my dog barks, that event (my dog's bark) is assigned to the whole organism (my dog). If I say, *The sky is blue,* that utterance (event) is assigned to me; it is, so to speak, my saying of *The sky is blue.* The same is true of private events. If I think, *The car is making a new noise,* that event is assigned to me as a whole organism; it is my thinking. These are the sorts of events that in this book we will simply refer to as *behavior,* with the additional phrase "of the whole organism" being understood.

Private events can be included in behavior analysis because science requires only that events be natural; there is no requirement that they be observable. In Chapter 2, we saw that one of Mach's points about air was that, although we observe many phenomena that we attribute to air, we cannot observe air itself.

■ Natural, Mental, and Fictional

In everyday talk, all sorts of things are considered *mental*—thoughts, feelings, sensations, emotions, hallucinations, and so on. *Mental* is the adjective form of *mind*. What do all the things called *mental* have to do with the mind?

Most English-speaking people will assert that they have minds; many would be insulted to be told they have none. Mindlessness is bad. It seems that English has this theory built into it: To have a mind means to have thoughts, feelings, emotions, and so on, and since we have those, we are inclined to conclude that each of us has a mind. The reasoning, however, is circular. The only reason we suppose that each of us has a mind is that we all know we have thoughts—that is, we all know that we think.

If we examine English constructions with *mind* in them, it seems there are two main uses of the word. Sometimes it is a place or space, a sort of arena or theater, as when we say, "I have something in mind" or "I must be out of my mind." Sometimes it seems to be an actor or agent, acting in its own right, as when we say, "My mind is made up" or "I had a mind to tell him just what I thought" or "I can see it in my mind's eye." But where is this space or object? What is it made of?

The notion of mind is troublesome for a science of behavior because the mind is not a part of nature. We expect that if a surgeon opens up your skull, inside will be sitting a brain. The brain could be taken out, held in the hands, weighed, have its volume measured; we could even play catch with it. Nothing of the sort could be said of your mind. It has none of these properties of a natural object.

The most revealing English phrases with *mind* in them are those in which the word appears as a verb or in an adverb, as when we say, "Mind how you go!" or "I was minding my own business" or "I was mindful of the danger." These all suggest that mind or mindfulness is a quality of certain types of behavior—deliberate, thoughtful, conscious behavior. Some behavior is called careful, some is called intelligent, some is called purposive, and some is private. Whenever behavior appears purposive, intelligent, or private, one is tempted to take the further step of supposing that it involves the mind. But one need not, and the radical behaviorist maintains that in a science of behavior one must not. As we shall see in later chapters, however, it remains interesting to ask why certain behavior is called conscious, purposive, or intelligent.

I cannot know that I have a mind the way that I know that I think, sense, and dream. Thoughts, sensations, and dreams are private events, natural and often observable by the one to whom they belong. In contrast, the mind and all its parts and processes are *fictional*.

Everyday talk about mental things and events includes both private events and fictional things and events. Thinking and seeing are private and natural, whereas mind, will, psyche, personality, and ego are all fictional. When methodological behaviorists allowed public things and events and ruled out mental (in the everyday sense) things and events, they ruled out private events along with fictional things and events. In contrast, radical behaviorists allow all natural events, including both the public and the private, and rule out only the fictional. The distinction between natural and fictional, moreover, has nothing to do with how these are studied (i.e., methodology).

To say the mind is fictional is to say that it is made up, make believe. I no more have a mind than I have a fairy godmother. I can talk to you about my mind or about my fairy godmother; that cannot make either of them any less fictional. No one has ever seen either one. When I was giving a recent talk, a philosopher in the audience objected that he was seeing the working of my mind as I was talking. I was tempted to reply, "You are actually seeing the working of my fairy godmother; she is here at my elbow, whispering in my ear." It makes as much sense to regard speech or problem solving as the workings of mind as to regard love and marriage as the workings of a fairy godmother. One can do either, of course, for fun or in poetry, but such talk is no help in a science.

Fictional things and events are unobservable, even in principle. No one has observed a mind, urge, impulse, or personality; they are all inferred from behavior. A person who behaves aggressively, for example, is said to have an aggressive personality. No one will ever see the personality, though; one sees only the behavior.

Being unobservable, however, need not be a drawback. We have seen the example of air, and other acceptable unobservable concepts are easy to think of: atoms, molecules, radiation, electricity, genes. All of these could be called inventions as much as discoveries. So what is wrong with mental fictions?

■ Objections to Mentalism

Mentalism is the practice of invoking mental fictions to try to explain behavior. Mind, will, ego, and the like are often called *explanatory fictions,* not because they explain anything, but because they are supposed to explain. The key objection to them is that they fail to explain. There are two sorts of reason why they fail: *autonomy* and *superfluity.*

Autonomy: Mental Causes Obstruct Inquiry   Autonomy is the ability to behave. A thing is autonomous if we assign its behavior to it. A person, rat, or fish is autonomous in this sense, because we say that each behaves. There is no problem with assigning behavior to organisms; a problem arises when behavior is assigned to parts of organisms, particularly hidden parts.

In the realist's view of behavior, when the distinction is drawn between "in here" and "out there," it seems that there must be a real me—my self— somewhere inside who controls my external body. It is as if there were a little person inside—a homunculus—who receives the sense data from the sense organs and then controls bodily movements. This little person is often depicted in cartoons and animated films as occupying an inner control room with video screens, loudspeakers, levers, and knobs. It is easy to see that this is no explanation of behavior, but the realist's view, if less literal, falls prey to the same problems as the homunculus.

Problems arise because the little person or the self inside is autonomous. If it were true that my outward behavior is only a result of the behavior of this inner self, then a science of behavior would have to study the behavior of this inner self. It is impossible to study the inner self for the same reason that it is impossible to study the inner homunculus: Both are fictions that are made up to try to make sense of behavior in the light of the prior division between "in here" and "out there." A science of behavior based on such distinctions could never succeed, any more than could a science of mechanics based on the inner emotions of matter or a science of physiology based on an inner *vis viva.* Instead, the events of interest are assigned to the objects under study, the rock or ball in mechanics, the cell or tissue in physiology, and the whole organism in a science of behavior.

When events are assigned to some hidden inner entity, not only is scientific inquiry deflected toward the impossible task of understanding the hidden entity, but curiosity tends to rest. Further inquiry is impeded not only by the seeming difficulty of the task, but also by the semblance of an explanation being taken for the real thing. These effects occur all the time in normal social intercourse, when a person, asked "Why did you do that?," replies "I felt like it" or "I had an impulse" or "The devil made me do it." We are put off by such evasions; it would be discourteous to inquire further, and the offering of some sort of explanation keeps us from inquiring further. As scientists, however, we would sooner or later have to see the inadequacy of such nonexplanations and inquire further. This inadequacy brings us to the second great defect of mentalism.

Superfluity: Explanatory Fictions Are Uneconomical   Even if we overlook the way autonomous inner entities impede inquiry, they are unacceptable because by normal scientific standards they are not real explanations. All explanatory fictions, autonomous or not, fall short. Apart from impeding inquiry, "The devil made me do it" and "My inner self made me do it" both fail as explanations. Even if an inner impulse were not considered autonomous, "I did it on an impulse" fails as an explanation for the same reason: The devil, the inner self, and the impulse are all *superfluous.*

Mentalistic explanations proceed by inferring a fictional entity from behavior and then asserting that the inferred entity is the cause of the behavior. When a person is said to eat vegetables because of a desire for health or a belief in vegetarianism, such talk arises in the first place because of the act of eating vegetables; thus, the reason for saying there is a desire or belief is the action. This "explanation" is perfectly circular: The person has the desire because of the behavior and exhibits the behavior because of the desire. We are no further ahead than with the original observation, because to say that Naomi believes in vegetarianism is to say that she eats vegetables. It may say something more— that she reads vegetarian magazines, goes to meetings of a vegetarian society, and so on—but her belief is still inferred from her behavior.

The science of mechanics faced the same sort of problem when *horror vacui* was thought to explain the facts of suction, and physiology faced it when *vis viva* was thought to explain cell metabolism. *Horror vacui* was inferred from the facts of suction; *vis viva* was inferred from cell metabolism. These inferred causes cannot truly be said to explain at all because they offer no simpler view of suction or cell metabolism. Instead they sit, so to speak, behind the observed events, mysteriously producing them.

Horror vacui, vis viva, and mental fictions are all useless because they are uneconomical, to use Mach's term. Mental fictions are uneconomical because, instead of simplifying our perception of events by describing them with a few understood concepts, they make matters more complicated, in two ways. First, as we have already seen, they merely restate the original observation with some added superfluous concept. If we accept the idea that Naomi eats vegetables because of her belief in vegetarianism, now we have to explain both her eating habits and her belief, whereas before we had to explain only her eating habits.

Second, this added concept has no clear relationship to the observed events. If a teenager is said to steal cars because of low self-esteem, we now have to wonder how this low self-esteem could lead to stealing cars. In Chapter 1 we saw that one problem with the notion of free will is that the connection between free will, a nonnatural event, and eating ice cream, a natural event, remains forever a mystery. The same problem arises with any nonnatural event in the mind. In this context, the problem is called the *mind–body* problem and expressed: How can a nonnatural thing affect a natural thing? Mental causes all pose this mysterious-connection problem. Like the mind, all fictional mental causes, if they existed, would be nonnatural. They cannot be found in the body—no one has ever found a belief, attitude, personality, or ego in anyone's heart, liver, or brain. They are never measured, except by behavior, such as answers to a questionnaire. How can such things cause behavior?

The mind–body problem has never been and never will be solved because it is a *pseudo-question,* a question that itself makes no sense. How many angels can dance on the head of a pin? What happens when an irresistible force encounters an immovable object? Each of these questions implies a nonsensical premise—that an angel could dance on the head of a pin and that it is possible for an irresistible force to coexist with an immovable object. The nonsensical premise underlying the mind–body question is the idea that fictions like a mind, an attitude, or a belief could cause behavior at all.

In response to this argument, it is often suggested that attitudes, beliefs, wishes, and the like exist as things in the brain. Our present level of understanding of the brain, however, allows no such assertion. Perhaps someday the working of the brain will be well enough understood to shed light on the mechanisms underlying studying for an examination or robbing a store, but that day appears to lie far in the future, if it will ever arrive at all. Behavior analysis needs wait on discoveries about the nervous system no more than physiology needed to wait on discoveries about biochemistry. Nowadays cell function is often explained with biochemistry, but physiologists understood cell function with concepts like membrane, osmosis, metabolism, and mitosis before chemists were any help at all. Similarly, behavior analysis can understand behavior at the level of its interaction with the environment without any help from neurophysiologists. Indeed, when help from the neurophysiologists is forthcoming, behavior analysts will have described the phenomena that could be explained further by reference to bodily mechanisms.

The radical behaviorist's objection to mentalism is really an objection to *dualism,* the idea that two sorts of existence, material and nonmaterial, or two sorts of terms, referring to the material and the nonmaterial, are necessary to understand behavior fully. All the sciences, not just behavior analysis, reject dualism because it is confusing and uneconomical. When Newton said, *"Hypotheses non fingo"*—"I do not make hypotheses"—by *hypotheses* he meant nonmaterial, supernatural causes somehow underlying natural events.

The writings of René Descartes (1596–1650) were influential in establishing dualism in psychology. Although Descartes made many wonderful contributions to mathematics and philosophy, his view of behavior has not been helpful. He proposed that the bodies of animals and humans were complicated machines, working according to simple natural mechanisms. He thought the brain and nerves were filled with a thin fluid—*animal spirits*—which flowed to the muscles to cause action. In accordance with Christian theology, he maintained that, whereas animals were merely machines, humans had in addition a soul. He thought the soul influenced behavior by moving a gland in the middle of the brain, the pineal gland, which affected the flow of the animal spirits. Although this particular idea never caught on, the notion that human behavior depends on the soul remained. Later, as psychology grew more scientific, psychologists distanced themselves from Christian theology by replacing the soul with the mind. Neither the pineal gland nor the mind solved the problem raised by Descartes's dualism: the mystery of the ghost in the machine. Even if the movements of the pineal gland did affect behavior, the mystery remains: how does the soul move the pineal gland? Even if the mind is not transcendental, it is still nonmaterial (nonnatural) and, in relation to behavior, just as ghostly as the soul. There is no room for such mysteries in a science.

❖ CATEGORY MISTAKES

The philosopher Gilbert Ryle (1900–1976) also attacked mentalism, but took a different approach from Skinner's. Whereas Skinner proposed to exclude terms like *mind, intelligence, reason,* and *belief* from a behavior analysis, Ryle thought that the terms might be useful if we could avoid using them illogically. The trouble with a term like *intelligence* is only that people will say that Tom displays intelligent behavior *and* intelligence. Whereas Skinner would regard intelligence as a mental fiction inferred from the intelligent behavior, Ryle argued that intelligence *is* intelligent behavior, and to consider the one to be the cause of the other or even to consider the two to be conjoined in any way involves a logical error, a *category mistake.*

If we are naming examples of fruit (a category), and I offer a carrot as an instance, that is a category mistake because a carrot is not a fruit. There are various types of category mistakes, various ways in which a supposed instance can fail to belong to a category to which it is mistakenly assigned. Ryle was concerned with a particular type of category mistake.

Suppose we are naming fruits again, and someone suggests *vegetables*. That is an error in a different way than *carrot*. *Vegetables* does not merely belong in another, similar category; it is itself the label of another category like fruits. It would seem even more strange in our fruit-naming game if someone were to suggest *fruits*. Not only is *fruits* a category label rather than a possible instance, but it is the label of the very category of which we are naming instances. This error of treating *fruits* as if it were an instance of fruits is exactly the sort of error that Ryle considers to occur in mentalism.

Suppose our game switches to naming intelligent behaviors. Players suggest long division, playing chess, designing a house, choreography, and so on. Then someone suggests *intelligence*. This would seem mistaken, according to Ryle's view, for the same reason as responding *fruits* in our fruit-naming game. *Intelligence* is the label of the category to which such behaviors as long division, chess-playing, house design, and choreography belong. Those behaviors are all instances of intelligence. The error is treating the category label as if it were an instance of the category.

The likely objection to this argument would go, "No, what I mean by intelligence is not all those behaviors, but something underlying those behaviors, that makes them possible, that causes them." But where is this intelligence? What is it made of? How could it cause behavior? Its ghostly nature derives from its being the label, rather than an instance, of the category. The reason the logical error occurs so readily is that the objection exemplifies a common theory about behavior which Ryle called the *para-mechanical hypothesis*.

■ Ryle and the Para-Mechanical Hypothesis

The para-mechanical hypothesis is the idea that terms which are logically category labels refer to ghostly things in some ghostly space (the mind), and that these ghostly things somehow mechanically cause behavior. This is exactly the same idea that Skinner called mentalism. Whereas Skinner emphasized the practical problems with mentalism—that it is distracting and useless—Ryle emphasized the logical problems with it.

To illustrate, Ryle pointed to the concept of team spirit. When we watch a football game and see the players shout encouragement to one another, pat one another on the back when they make mistakes, and hug one another when they succeed, we say they are showing team spirit. We do not mean that some ghostly spirit is running up and down the field with them, hovering around their heads. If a foreigner were to ask, "I see them shouting, patting, and hugging, but where is that famous team spirit?" we would think the question odd and that the questioner failed to understand the concept. We might explain that the shouting, patting, and hugging *are* the team spirit. We would mean that those actions are instances of the category of actions which we label *team spirit*. They are not the only instances; we could expand the list greatly.

The foreigner's error arose because of the way we talk about team spirit: We say the team *shows* it. That is why the foreigner thought it correct to conjoin shouting, patting, hugging, and showing team spirit. It is the same error as conjoining long division, chess-playing, choreography, and showing intelligence. Just as *showing team spirit* is a label for a category of behavior, so *showing intelligence* is a label for a category of behavior. Long division and chess are instances of showing intelligence. There is no ghostly intelligence, no thing, intelligence, to be shown.

Ryle applied his argument to all sorts of mental capacities and states that are said to be shown in behavior or to cause behavior: knowledge, purpose, emotion, and others. For instance, why do we say, "John is in love with Sally"? He buys her flowers, writes poetry to her, stammers and blushes in her presence, declares his love to her, and so on. John does not do those things *and* love Sally or *because* he loves Sally; John's doing those things *is* his being in love with Sally.

We shall see how Ryle's argument applies to other terms in some of the following chapters. Although he attacked mentalism primarily on logical grounds, his arguments and Skinner's differ mainly in emphasis: the germs of Skinner's pragmatic objections can be found in Ryle's writings, and the basics of Ryle's logical objections can be found in Skinner's writings. The main disagreement between them seems to be that, whereas Skinner wished to exclude mentalistic terms from technical discussions of behavior, Ryle implied that they could be used if only we remember that love, belief, expectation, attitude, and the like are really only labels of categories of behavior.

■ Rachlin's Molar Behaviorism

Howard Rachlin, a contemporary behaviorist, took Ryle's argument a step further. Since at least the 1930s, some behaviorists have suggested that behavior cannot be understood by focusing on events of the moment. In the nineteenth century and first half of the twentieth century, atomistic views of mind and behavior abounded. Since the only well-understood unit of behavior was the reflex, talk about behavior tended to be couched in terms of *stimulus* and *response,* events that occur in a moment; and the most important relation between events was considered to be their momentary closeness in time, or *contiguity.*

Critics of theories emphasizing momentary events and contiguity called such views *molecular* and proposed instead analyses that they called *molar.* Molar theorists argue that molecular views of behavior must fail, for two reasons. First, present behavior depends not only on present events, but on many past events. These past events affect behavior as an aggregate, not as momentary happenings. The reason I avoid eating rich food today is that I ate rich food many times in the past and gained weight; none of this happened at any particular moment in time. Second, behavior cannot occur in a moment; no matter how brief, it always takes some time. Brushing my teeth may be a single event, but it takes me a while. If I put together all the activities of my day, they must add up to 24 hours.

Rachlin saw in Ryle's ideas a justification and an extension of this second tenet of molarism, that the units of behavior (e.g., activities) extend through time. John's loving Sally occurs at no particular time because it is a whole category of actions that occur at different times. It would seem absurd to say that John does not love Sally at this moment because he is working instead of giving her flowers, paying her compliments, or any of the other actions in the category. It seems perfectly reasonable to say that John loves Sally now and has done so for years, even though he has been spending most of that time working and sleeping. The common "solution" to this problem of John loving Sally all the time and yet not showing love for Sally all the time is the para-mechanical hypothesis; invent a ghostly love-thing, a mental fiction, that is there all the time to cause John's loving behavior when it occurs and bridge the time gaps in between. However attractive this idea might seem, we have seen that it is no real solution, because it is confusing and uneconomical (Skinner) and it fails logically (Ryle).

According to Rachlin's view, what matters about John's love is how often his loving actions occur. John's loving Sally and John's showing love for Sally are really just two labels for the same behavior category. It makes sense to say that John has loved Sally for years because over those years the love-category actions have occurred with relatively high frequency. John has shown not some ghostly inner mental love, but a high rate of loving actions. These actions need not be the only things he does; they just need to occur often enough. Indeed, their rate is crucial. If John telephoned Sally just once a month and brought her flowers only once a year, she might well doubt his sincerity, particularly if he is calling Dolores every day and giving her flowers twice a week. If John declares that he loves Sally now and forever, he is predicting that his love-category actions will go on occurring at a high frequency.

Rachlin's argument applies to all terms that seem to refer to inner causes of behavior, whether states of mind like love and anger or behavioral dispositions like intentions and beliefs. He illustrated this with a discussion of what it means to be in pain (Rachlin, 1985). As with love, being in pain is the same as showing pain and engaging in actions that fall in the category of pain-behavior—grimacing, groaning, clutching oneself, screaming, rolling around, limping, and so on. Whether or not someone is said to be in pain depends only on how often such actions occur and in what contexts they occur. If a person groans only once a week or only when his mother is in the room, then we are inclined to conclude that he is faking. An actor may completely convince us that she is in pain on the stage, but when we see her after the play laughing and chatting, we say she was only acting. We assert confidently that someone is in pain only if pain-behavior occurs at a consistent, high rate. If being in pain is just showing pain-behavior often and in all circumstances, just as with being in love, then there is no ghostly inner mental pain, just as there was no ghostly inner mental love.

An objection arises. Perhaps there is no ghostly inner mental love, but pain in no way seems ghostly. Rather, it seems to be a sensation, a real private event.

Rachlin's response to this is best understood from his answer to the objection, "But I can feel pain and not show it." He argues that it is impossible to feel pain and not show it because to feel pain *is* to show it. One philosopher tried to refute Rachlin's whole argument by relating that for years he had severe headaches without ever letting on to anyone about them. Rachlin's reply was, "If so . . . his parents, his doctor, his closest friends, and his spouse and children (if any) must, to this day, still not know about those headaches. Does anyone want to bet?" Although this might seem facetious, the serious point is that one cannot be in pain without showing it, either to others or to oneself. Rachlin's argument only seems counter to experience as long as one insists that it is possible to be in pain and show it to no one. Alone in my room, I may be in pain and get over it before anyone sees me. Was I not in pain? I was, if I showed it, but the whole episode was private only in the sense that no other person happened to be present; had another person been there, that person would also have said that I was in pain. My way of knowing that I have a headache is the same as your way of knowing that I have a headache: I frown, groan, shut my eyes, complain, and take aspirin. If I did none of those things, I would be no more inclined to say I had a headache than you would be.

Paradoxical though it might seem, Rachlin's idea that pain consists of public behavior rather than private experience has plenty of evidence to back it up. In particular, reports of pain and other pain-behavior depend greatly on circumstances. Many of us have had injuries that should have been painful but were not because we were distracted. Having twisted an ankle, an athlete may go on running and report that the ankle began to hurt after the race. The same injury under nonrace circumstances would have resulted in immediately "feeling pain." Research on pain has produced many examples like this. Although childbirth is considered painful in our culture, anthropologists have described cultures in which women show no signs of pain, give birth while working in the fields, and go on working as soon as the baby is born, while the father lies at home in bed and groans and shows every sign of being in intense pain. A particularly striking example was reported by Henry K. Beecher, an anesthesiologist who compared the behavior of wounded soldiers in a World War II combat hospital to the behavior of civilians who were undergoing surgery that involved wounds similar to the soldiers' wounds. He found that whereas only about one-third of the soldiers complained of pain enough to receive morphine, four out of five of the civilian patients did so. Although the soldiers reported feeling little or no pain whereas the civilians reported severe pain, Beecher observed that the difference was not that the soldiers were insensitive to painful stimuli, because they complained as much as anyone when a vein puncture was botched. Beecher concluded:

There is no simple direct relationship between the wound per se and the pain experienced. The pain is in very large part determined by other factors, and of great importance here is the significance of the wound. . . . In the wounded soldier [the response to injury] was relief, thankfulness at his escape alive from the battlefield, even euphoria; to the civilian, his major surgery was a depressing, calamitous event (quoted by Melzack, 1961, pp. 42–43).

These observations support Rachlin's view, because instead of the same trauma producing the same pain, as the para-mechanical hypothesis would require, the whole category of pain-behavior, including the report of feeling pain, depends on circumstances. Even though our apparent inner experience of pain seems compelling, clinical and experimental evidence support the idea that being in pain, like being in love, or any other mental state, consists primarily of public behavior.

With such a view, Rachlin lays much less emphasis on private events than Skinner. It becomes a matter of little importance for Rachlin whether private events really occur or not, because his view deemphasizes momentary events and isolated actions in general, whether public or private. John's being in love with Sally might include his thinking about her, but if none of the public actions in the category occur, both Sally and John should doubt John's sincerity. For Rachlin, neither love nor pain need exist as a private thing, because in practice what people say about themselves or others always relies most heavily on public behavior. In this molar perspective, it can truly be said that the way I know myself is the same way that others know me.

Although Rachlin's denial of private events might seem like a return to methodological behaviorism, it is not. Both methodological behaviorists and Rachlin advocate the study of public events, but for different reasons. Methodological behaviorists regard public events as objective, and rule out of bounds mental things and events because they are subjective. Approaching behavior with a molecular view, they hoped to predict momentary actions. Rachlin never raises the objective–subjective distinction and never rules out mental things and events. Instead, he asserts that one can study mental things and events because the terms (*pain, love, self-esteem,* and so on) that supposedly refer to them are really labels for molar activities and action categories. Therefore, we study them by studying the public events that these activities and categories embrace. Rachlin parts with methodological behaviorism and aligns himself with radical behaviorism on two grounds: anti-dualism and pragmatism. Like any radical behaviorist, he denies the existence of mental fictions, and especially mental causes of behavior. Since he never raises the subjective–objective distinction, instead measuring the truth of his view by its explanatory power (usefulness), his ideas belong in the tradition of pragmatism rather than realism. He need neither deny nor affirm the existence of private events because the categories of behavior that people talk about always include many public actions. Indeed, people would not talk about them if they did not—but that is a topic for a discussion of verbal behavior. (See Chapter 7.)

❖ PRIVATE EVENTS

For Skinner, private events are natural and in all important respects like public events. Even if thoughts are natural events and may be said sometimes to affect behavior, still they never cause behavior in the sense of originating it. Although the origins of behavior lie in the present and past environment, private events figure importantly in Skinner's analysis of certain types of behavior, particularly self-reports, which we shall consider now and in Chapter 6, and problem solving, which we shall take up in Chapter 8.

■ Private Behavior

Since private events are assigned to the person, rather than to the environment, they are best understood as behavioral events. Broadly speaking, there are two kinds: thinking events and sensing events.

Thinking, for the present discussion, is speaking privately. This may seem too narrow, because *thinking* is used in many other ways in everyday talk. "I am thinking of going to a movie" means I am inclined, or likely, to go to a movie. "I am thinking of a painting I once saw" means I am imagining the painting, and is best understood as a sensing event.

Thinking is usefully set apart from sensing events, because thoughts have a relationship to public speech that sensing events do not. A thought may be stated publicly or privately. (Skinner uses the words *overt* and *covert*.) I may say aloud to myself, *I wonder what will happen if I push this button,* or I may whisper it to myself, or I may think it privately. These events are all much the same; the first two might be overheard, whereas the third cannot be. Sensing events, however, have no public counterparts. Seeing a tree, hearing an orchestra, feeling an itch, smelling a skunk—all these are private events only.

Sensing events are best understood in contrast with the usual view of sensation and perception, which Skinner calls "copy theory." Some ancient Greek philosophers, puzzling as to how it was possible to see objects at a distance, thought that the objects must send copies of themselves to our eyes. If I see a tree across the road from me, it must be because the tree sends little copies of itself to my eyes. The modern view is similar, except we now say that the tree reflects light which passes through the pupils of my eyes to form images on the membranes at the rear of my eyeballs. These images substitute for the Greek copies.

This notion may be useful in understanding some things about the eyes, but it in no way explains seeing. The problem of how the tree is seen is now replaced by the problem of how the copy of the tree is seen. Copy theory has all the defects of mentalism. The appearance of an explanation—you see the tree because there is a copy of it in your eye or in your brain—distracts us from our attempt to understand what seeing is. The copy is superfluous, because the question remains the same whether we ask about seeing the tree or seeing the copy: What is it to see something? In particular, the theory fails to explain why seeing is selective. Not all objects that reflect light to our eyes are seen. Why do I see the tree and not the road? How is it possible for one person to point something out to another, to "get" you to see something? How is it possible for someone to look right at a sign and yet not see it?

To the radical behaviorist, sensing and perceiving are behavioral events, actions. The thing that is seen, heard, smelled, felt, or tasted is a quality of the event—that is, part of the definition of the event. Seeing a wolf is qualitatively different from seeing a bear. The two events have much in common—they are both acts of seeing, rather than hearing or walking—but they are also different. They are different acts, just as walking to the store differs from walking to the bank. If I say, *It's a nice day* on one occasion and, *There's a tiger behind you* on another, both are instances of speech, but the two acts differ in the same way as the two acts of walking; the nice day and the tiger are part of the definition of the act. Just as it is impossible to walk without walking somewhere and talk without saying something, it is impossible to see without seeing something. The somewhere and the somethings differentiate among different acts of walking, talking, and seeing, but not as attachments to them. They are different acts, not the same action applied to different things.

That the goal or object of a sensing event is a quality of the event can be seen more clearly when we talk about other senses than vision. In such talk we rarely fall prey to copy theory. If I hear a violin playing, it would be unusual for someone to assert that my action of hearing somehow fastens onto the sound of the violin. The sound is part of the act or perhaps the result of the act. Hearing a violin and hearing an oboe are different acts of hearing, not the same action applied to different sounds. An ancient Japanese puzzle goes, "If a tree falls in the forest, and no one is there to hear it, does it make a sound?" The behaviorist's answer is "no," because a sound exists only as part of an act of hearing. In the same way that hearing a violin differs from hearing an oboe, so seeing a bear differs from seeing a wolf.

The relationship between seeing and the thing seen becomes clearer still when we examine instances of what Skinner calls "seeing without a thing seen." If I dream of a wolf, is a wolf present? If I imagine my childhood home, is my home there? It almost seems as if copy theory were invented to try to explain such instances. If I am seeing, there must be a something there to see; since there is neither a wolf nor a house, there must be a copy, held up somehow to my vision (not to my eyes!). Copy theory used this way is a form of mentalism; the apparent explanation is no explanation at all. Where is the ghostly mental copy, what is it made of, and how can it be seen? Where before we had an act of seeing to explain, now we have the same act plus a mysterious copy with a mysterious relationship to the act. The alternative is to consider seeing a wolf with eyes closed to resemble seeing a wolf with eyes open. The two acts differ—we can usually tell them apart—but they have much in common. This leaves unanswered such questions as, "How do I dream and imagine things I have never actually seen?" and "Is it possible to practice imagination?" Viewing dreaming and imagining as acts, however, allows these questions to be framed for scientific study more effectively than by copy theory.

Copy theory attempts to explain dreaming and imagining by the idea that copies are stored in and retrieved from memory. Questions about recollection become questions about ghostly mental processes of encoding, storage, and retrieval. If when I imagine my childhood home I see my father there, that is supposedly because the two memories are somehow linked together. If when someone says, "Think of birds," I think of sparrows, finches, and ostriches, that is supposedly because the memories of those things are linked in some way.

In contrast, the behavioral view points to facts of life. When I was a child, seeing my childhood home, I saw my father, too. When I heard about birds, I often heard about sparrows, finches, and ostriches. If these things are linked, it is not in memory, but in time and place. Recollection is repetition. When I recall a visit to the ocean, I resee the sky, water, and sand, rehear the waves, and resmell the sea air. Those acts of imagining differ from the original acts of seeing, hearing, and smelling, but they are similar also. Much of our behavior is repeated every day. I comb my hair every morning. Does it help to understand how or why I do that to say that there must be somewhere inside me a memory of hair-combing? Someday, neurophysiologists may have something to say about the brain mechanisms by which these things occur. In the meantime, there is much to be understood about seeing and reseeing as acts.

Sensory acts are modified by experience; they are subject to learning. First-year medical students see a brain differently from their instructors. Once upon a time, the instructors saw as little as their students; someday the students will see as much as their instructors. We learn to pick things out of a landscape or a symphony. If I say to you, "See that barn across the fields" or "Listen to the oboe," you see or hear something that you didn't a moment ago. Figure 3.1 shows two droodles. If you have never seen them before, they look like collections of lines. (If you have seen them before, then remember the first time you saw them.) Now I tell you that the top one shows a bear climbing a tree (it's on the other side), and the bottom one shows a soldier and his dog going behind a fence. You see them differently. Your behavior has changed as a result of reading these words. After we take up discrimination and stimulus control in Chapters 6 and 7, it will be easier to understand how this behavioral change could be called *discriminated seeing*.

■ Self-Knowledge and Consciousness

The word *conscious* is used in a variety of ways. "Having consciousness" appears to be the same as "being conscious," because consciousness is not a thing but a property. A person may be said to have consciousness or to have lost it, to be conscious or unconscious; both contrasts refer to the same possibilities. Whether we call a person conscious or unconscious depends on what the person does, particularly in response to environmental events like questions and pinpricks. From time to time someone asks whether nonhuman animals are conscious or not. The answer to the question depends on what the

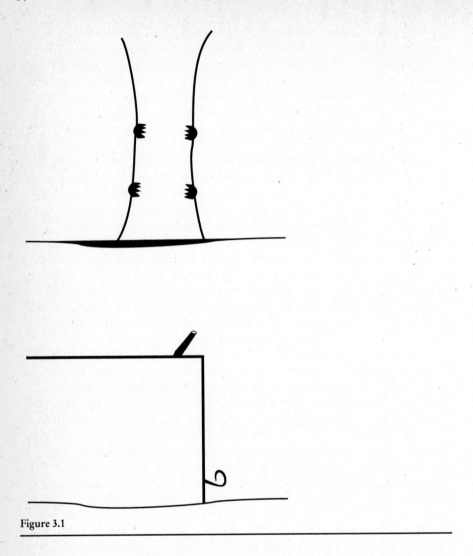

Figure 3.1

animal does and what we will accept as evidence of consciousness. Some acts are said to be conscious, others not. Jurors frequently have to judge whether a person decided to commit a crime consciously or not.

Many different criteria for making judgments about consciousness have been proposed, but there has been no consensus about what it means for a person or an act to be conscious. Debate continues about whether dogs and bats are conscious. When debate is endless, the scientist begins to suspect that the fault lies less with the answers than with the question itself.

To the behaviorist, it may be interesting to try to understand when people are inclined to use the word *conscious,* but the notion is of no use for the scientific understanding of behavior. The vagueness and uselessness of the idea of consciousness derives from its ties to Skinner's homunculus and Ryle's para-mechanical hypothesis. Consciousness belongs to the little person or autonomous self inside, who looks out at the external world through the senses or looks within the inner world of the mind and is thus conscious of both worlds. Call into question this view of inner world, outer world, inner self, and mind, and you call into question the notion of consciousness, because the notion of consciousness hardly has meaning apart from this view.

Inquiring what makes people use phrases such as "losing consciousness" and "being conscious" of something, the behaviorist asks how people learn such talk or what events occasion such talk. Although there is considerable variation from one social group to another, everyone seems to agree on one type of evidence: If people can talk about their behavior, then they are considered to be conscious and conscious of their behavior. I cannot usually tell you about all the acts involved in my driving to work—they are unconscious—but if you specifically asked me to notice, then I could tell you in some detail. I can do it to some extent even if you never prompted me. To the extent that I can talk about them, people will say my acts are conscious. My acts of driving or walking may be conscious or unconscious, depending on whether I can tell someone else about them. Even acts of speaking may be designated conscious or unconscious, depending on whether the speaker can repeat what he or she said. How often people say things and a minute later deny having said them! We say, "It was said unconsciously."

Like other acts, seeing and other sensing acts may be conscious or unconscious, depending on whether the person talks about them. If a police officer stops my car and asks me, "Didn't you see that stop sign?" I could honestly answer "no" because, even if I had looked in its direction, I might have failed to see the sign, just as when you first looked at the droodles in Figure 3.1 and failed to see the bear and the soldier. If the officer asks me, "Do you see the sign now?" I will look and say "yes." Both answers are reports on behavior: the first a report on the absence of an event, and the second a report on the occurrence of an event. Although the event being reported on is private, in Skinner's view reporting on one's private acts is the same as reporting on one's public acts. We learn to talk about what we see, hear, smell, and think in the same way as we learn to talk about what we eat, where we go, and what we say. Self-knowledge consists of such talk. In Chapter 7, we shall see that this talk is verbal behavior, a social product, under control of stimuli that are both public and private.

Ryle and Rachlin share with Skinner the general view that self-knowledge can be understood as a type of behavior, but because they regard acts as instances of larger categories of behavior, they assign private acts a much lesser role in self-knowledge. To Ryle, seeing a robin is a category of behavior, just as walking to the store might be. Just as walking to the store includes such behavior as walking in a certain direction, talking about walking to the store, and afterward bringing home a purchase, so seeing a robin includes such behavior as looking in its direction, pointing at it, talking about it, and remarking when it is gone. Some of the behavior included in seeing a robin might be saying, "Look, there's a robin" or "I see a robin," or responding "yes" when someone else asks whether I see the robin. These are not reports on private events; they are simply instances of the category of seeing a robin.

In discussing pain, Rachlin was discussing a phenomenon that most people would consider a private sensing event. His view of feeling pain resembles Ryle's view of seeing a robin. Feeling pain in the leg includes such behavior as pointing to it, clutching it, limping, and talking about it. Saying "My leg hurts" is not reporting on a private event; it is simply an instance of the category pain in the leg. As far as Rachlin is concerned, the private event of pain remains outside the discussion. It is not only irrelevant but might not even exist. If a person complains of pain in the leg, and does so convincingly, we behave the same way whether the pain exists or not. Only later might we learn that the person was faking; perhaps the pain vanishes too suddenly or the person limps on the wrong leg. The same would be true of seeing or hearing. In the movie *The Heart Is a Lonely Hunter,* a deaf man pretends to be enjoying music by moving his body as if he were conducting an orchestra. His performance is convincing, but when the record stops and he continues, his companion realizes he was faking. Had he stopped when the record stopped, she would presumably have continued to regard him as having heard the music. Sooner or later, he was bound to slip up, but if a deaf person could fake perfectly, to all intents and purposes that person could hear, because faking perfectly would mean that no one knows the difference.

Someone might object that even if a deaf person fooled everyone around him, he would himself know he was faking. However, if he succeeded in all instances, how could he know? For all he knows, this behavior *is* hearing. Only if his own behavior differed from other people's behavior could he himself know he was faking. Suppose a hearing person listening to music fakes enjoyment. If she does all the right things, why should she not believe that she really enjoys it? The only clue to her or to others would be a difference between her behavior and the behavior of those who are said to really enjoy music. They smile, relax, resist being interrupted, and talk about the music afterward. Do I enjoy the music less because I do not talk about it afterward? Perhaps. Just as no private enjoyment need enter the discussion, so, for Rachlin, no private hearing need enter the discussion.

❖ SUMMARY

Although radical behaviorists hold a variety of views on many topics, they agree on the following basic points.

First, the mentalistic explanations of behavior that occur in everyday talk have no place in a science. Mental causes of behavior are fictional. The origins of behavior lie in heredity and in the environment, present and past. Because mental fictions give the appearance of explanations, they tend to impede inquiry into environmental origins, which would lead to a satisfactory scientific explanation. Mentalism is unsatisfactory because it is uneconomical (Skinner) and logically fallacious (Ryle).

Second, in a science of behavior, everyday mentalistic terms like *believe, expect,* and *intend* must either be avoided or carefully redefined. The extent to which behavior analysts should do one or the other remains to be seen. We shall see in subsequent chapters that some terms can be redefined fairly well, whereas others seem too foreign to be worth redefining. Some new terms, invented for behavior analysis, seem especially helpful.

Third, private events, if they need to be spoken of at all, are natural and share all the properties of public behavior. Even if they are to be spoken of, their origins lie in the environment, just like other behavior; behavior never originates in private events. Whereas Skinner gives them a role in situations involving talking about private behavior (self-knowledge; Chapters 6 and 7), molar behaviorists like Rachlin circumvent the need to give private events any explanatory role at all by conceiving of behavior as organized into categories that occur over extended periods of time.

❖ FURTHER READING

Melzack, R. (1961). The perception of pain. *Scientific American, 204* (2), 41–49. An excellent early paper summarizing the physiological and situational aspects of pain.

Rachlin, H. (1985). Pain and behavior. *The Behavioral and Brain Sciences, 8,* 43–83. This article describes Rachlin's ideas about pain and arguments and evidence in support of them. The journal's treatment includes commentary by several critics and Rachlin's replies to these critics.

Rachlin, H. (1989). *Judgment, decision, and choice.* New York: Freeman. A relatively advanced book describing theory and research on the topics listed in the title in a behavioral perspective. Rachlin reconciles the mentalistic approach with the behavioral approach by showing how mentalistic terms can be interpreted behaviorally.

Rachlin, H. (1990). *Introduction to modern behaviorism* (3rd ed.). New York: Freeman. An excellent introduction to behavior analysis in the molar perspective.

Ryle, G. (1984). *The concept of mind.* Chicago: University of Chicago Press. (Reprint of the 1949 edition.) Chapter 1 explains the para-mechanical hypothesis, the "ghost in the machine," and category errors. Subsequent chapters take up more specific topics, like knowledge, will, and emotion.

Skinner, B. F. (1969). Behaviorism at fifty. In *Contingencies of reinforcement* (pp. 221–268). New York: Appleton-Century-Crofts. Skinner's most famous discussion of private events in contrast with mental events.

Skinner, B. F. (1974). *About behaviorism.* New York: Knopf. Chapter 1 contains a comparison of methodological behaviorism with radical behaviorism. Chapter 2 discusses mental causes in contrast with private events. Chapter 5 discusses copy theory and seeing in the absence of the thing seen.

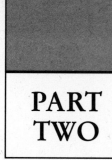

PART TWO

A SCIENTIFIC MODEL OF BEHAVIOR

To be clear and convincing about one's criticism of someone else's view, one must offer an alternative view that would be acceptable. To help see what is wrong with conventional mentalistic views of behavior, we need to consider explanations that might be scientifically acceptable. In Chapters 4–8 we will take up some basic concepts in behavior analysis and use them to suggest alternatives to unscientific mentalistic notions.

A warning is in order, however. Like all scientific explanations, the ones that we shall take up are considered by scientists to be tentative, open to dispute and to change. Any of these explanations may be considered incorrect in the future or may be disbelieved by some behavior analysts even today.

For our purposes, the possibility that a particular scientific explanation may eventually be discarded is unimportant. We need only to see that scientific explanations of behavior are possible. As behavior analysis moves ahead, the explanations accepted will change as new ones are devised. We need only to see, as an alternative to mentalism, what sort of explanation is scientifically acceptable.

EVOLUTIONARY THEORY AND REINFORCEMENT

Modern evolutionary theory provides a powerful framework within which to talk about behavior. Indeed, it no longer seems possible to discuss behavior outside such a context because biologists since Darwin have increasingly claimed behavior as part of their subject matter. In keeping with the assumption of continuity of species (Chapter 1), their attention has turned more and more to human behavior as well. Even more than in Watson's time, psychologists who ignore evolutionary theory today risk isolation from the mainstream of scientific development.

Our concerns with evolutionary theory in this chapter are twofold. First, the evolutionary history or *phylogeny* of any species—including our own—can help us understand the species's behavior. Most of the genes an individual inherits have been selected across many generations because they promote behavior that makes for successful interaction with the environment and reproduction. Second, evolutionary theory represents a type of explanation that is unusual among the sciences. Scientific explanations usually appeal to mechanism, or the way things are arranged at a certain time. The type exemplified by evolutionary theory, which we shall call *historical* explanation, is central to behavior analysis because the scientifically acceptable alternative to mentalism is historical explanation.

❖ EVOLUTIONARY HISTORY

When we talk about the phylogeny of a species, we are talking about no particular event, but a series or history of events over a long period. Physics offers a different sort of answer to the question, "Why does the sun rise in the morning?" than biology offers to, "Why do giraffes have long necks?" The explanation about the sun requires reference only to events occurring right at the moment—the rotation of the earth at the time of sunrise. The explanation about giraffes' necks requires reference to the births, lives, and deaths of countless giraffes and giraffe ancestors over many millions of years.

Darwin's great contribution was to see that a relatively simple mechanism could help explain why phylogeny followed the particular course it did. The history of giraffes' necks, Darwin saw, is more than a sequence of changes; it is a history of selection. What does the selecting? Not an omnipotent Creator, not Mother Nature, not the giraffes, but a natural, mechanical process: natural selection.

■ Natural Selection

Within any population of organisms, individuals vary. They vary partly because of environmental factors (e.g., nutrition), and also because of genetic inheritance. Among the giraffe ancestors that lived in what is now the Serengeti Plain, for instance, variation in genes meant that some had shorter necks and some had longer necks. As the climate gradually changed, however, new, taller types of vegetation became more frequent. The giraffe ancestors that had longer necks, being able to reach higher, got a little more to eat, on the average. As a result, they were a little healthier, resisted disease a little better, evaded predators a little better—on the average. Any one individual with a longer neck may have died without offspring, but on the average longer-necked individuals had more offspring, which tended on the average to survive a little better and produce more offspring. As longer necks became more frequent, new genetic combinations occurred, with the result that some offspring had still longer necks than those before, and they did still better. As the longer-necked giraffes continued to out-reproduce the shorter-necked ones, the average neck length of the whole population grew.

Figure 4.1 diagrams the process. The horizontal axis represents neck lengths, increasing from left to right. The upper vertical axis represents the relative frequency of various neck lengths in the population of giraffes or giraffe ancestors. Curve 1 shows the variation in short-necked giraffe ancestors. As selection proceeds, the distribution shifts to the right (Curve 2), indicating that neck length, while continuing to vary, got longer on the average. Curve 3 shows variation in present-day giraffes, a stable frequency distribution that no longer shifts toward longer necks.

For such a process of selection, three conditions must be met. First, whatever environmental factor makes having a longer neck advantageous (in our

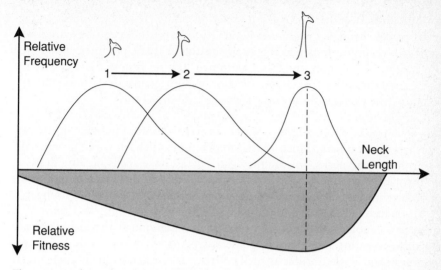

Figure 4.1 Evolution by natural selection.

example, the shift in vegetation) must remain present. Second, the variation in neck length must reflect, at least in part, genetic variation. Longer-necked individuals must tend to have more longer-necked offspring than shorter-necked. If, for example, all the variation in neck length were due to variation in diet, with no underlying variation in genes—the individuals that ate better had longer necks, instead of the other way around—selection would be impossible because generation after generation the same variation in diet and neck length would be repeated. Third, there must be competition. Since an area's resources can support only a certain size population of giraffes, overpopulation means that some offspring must die. The successful offspring will survive into the next generation to produce their own offspring.

These three factors are incorporated into the concept of *fitness.* The fitness of a genetic variant (a *genotype*) is its tendency to increase from one generation to the next relative to the other genotypes in the population. Any one genotype, even a shorter-necked one, could do well by itself, but in competition with others its fitness might be low. The greater the fitness of a genotype, the more that genotype will tend to predominate as generation succeeds generation. The vertical axis going downward in Figure 4.1 represents the fitness of the genotypes underlying the various neck lengths. The shaded curve shows how fitness varies with neck length. This remains the same throughout the selection process, because it represents the constant factors in the environment (the vegetation) that link neck length to reproductive success. Its maximum is at the vertical broken line, the same line that indicates the average neck length of today's giraffes. Once the average genotype in a population reaches the maximum fitness, the distribution of genotypes in the population stabilizes.

Once the population stabilizes, only the directional shift ceases; selection continues, selection that keeps the population stable. The fitness curve in Figure 4.1 passes through a maximum because too long a neck can be a disadvantage. Birth complications and the strain on the heart of pumping blood to a great height, for example, might set an upper limit on fitness. Since the fitness curve passes through a maximum, selection will go against deviations from the maximum (the average of the population) in both directions.

Darwin himself, and many biologists since, have recognized that behavior plays a central role in evolution. Selection occurs because individuals interact with their environment. Much of that interaction is behavior. In our example, giraffes have long necks because they eat. Turtles have shells because drawing into them affords protection. Reproduction, the key to the whole process, cannot occur without behavior such as courting, mating, and caring for young.

Those individuals that behave more effectively enjoy a higher fitness. The fitness of a genotype depends on its producing individuals that behave better than others—eating more, running faster, feeding offspring more, building a better nest, and so on. Insofar as such behavior is affected by genotype, natural selection may have acted to change it and to stabilize it.

■ Reflexes and Fixed Action Patterns

Reflexes Some behavioral traits are as much characteristics of a species as are anatomical traits. The simplest of these are called *reflexes,* because the earliest theory about them was that the bodily effect produced by a *stimulus*—an environmental event stimulating sense organs—was reflected by the nervous system into a *response*—an action. If your nose is tickled, you sneeze. If you are poked in the eye, you blink. If you are cold, you shiver. The tickle, poke, and cold are stimuli; the sneezing, blinking, and shivering are responses.

Reflexes are a product of natural selection. They invariably seem to involve maintaining health, promoting survival, or furthering reproduction. Sneezing, blinking, shivering, release of adrenalin in danger, and sexual arousal are examples. Individuals in which these reflexes were strong tended to survive and reproduce better than individuals in which they were weak or nonexistent. In Figure 4.1, if we substituted force of sneeze reflex or readiness of penile erection for neck length, we can imagine a similar history of selection. The fitness curve would pass through a maximum, because too weak a sneeze is too little protection and too slow an erection means fewer offspring, but too strong a sneeze would be damaging and too swift an erection would be an obstruction (not to mention a social problem). Over many generations, genotypes promoting a stronger reflex would tend to reproduce more frequently on the average (frequency distributions 1 and 2), until the maximum fitness arrived (frequency distribution 3).

Fixed Action Patterns More complex patterns of behavior can also enter into fixed relations to environmental events and be characteristic of a species. When a parent herring gull arrives at the nest, the chicks peck at a spot on its beak and the parent responds by depositing food on the ground. In other bird species, the chicks open their mouths wide and gape, and the parent puts the food into their mouths. When a female stickleback (a small fish) with eggs enters a male's territory, the male begins a series of movements around her, and she responds by approaching the male's nest. Such complex behavioral reactions are known as *fixed action patterns.* The environmental events that trigger these patterns are known as *sign stimuli* or *releasers*—the parent bird arriving, the blows on the beak, the wide-open mouth, the female stickleback's egg-laden belly. As with reflexes, these behavioral reactions can be seen as important to fitness and, hence, as products of a history of natural selection. As with reflexes, those individuals in which fixed action patterns are too weak or too strong have less fit genotypes.

Although releasers and fixed action patterns may seem more complex than the stimuli and responses in reflexes, no clear dividing line separates these types of reaction. Both can be considered relationships between an environmental event (stimulus) and an action (response). Both are considered characteristic of a species because they are highly reliable traits, as reliable as a giraffe's neck or a leopard's spots. Being so reliable, they are considered built-in, the result of genotype, and not learned.

Reflexes and fixed action patterns are reactions that enhance fitness by being available immediately when needed. When the silhouette of a hawk passes overhead, a baby quail crouches and freezes. If this reaction depended on experience, few baby quails would survive to reproduce. The pattern may be subject to refinement—gull chicks eventually peck more accurately at the parent's beak, and the young vervet monkey's single alarm call eventually becomes different calls for an eagle or for a leopard—but its great initial reliability derives from a history of selection for such reliability. The fitness of genotypes requiring that such patterns be learned from scratch would be less than genotypes that built in the basic form.

As with neck length or coloration, reflexes and fixed action patterns were selected over a long period in which the environment remained stable enough to maintain an advantage for those individuals that possessed the right behavior. The reflexes and fixed action patterns we see today were selected by the past environment. Although they enhanced fitness in the past, nothing guarantees that they will continue to enhance fitness in the future; if the environment changes suddenly, selection will have had no chance to change the built-in behavior patterns.

Do human beings possess such unlearned patterns? Among all species, ours seems to be the most dependent on learning. It would be a mistake, however, to imagine that human behavior is entirely learned. We have many reflexes: coughing and sneezing, startle, blinking, pupillary dilation, salivation, glandular secretion, and so on. What about fixed action patterns? These are hard to recognize in humans because they are so modified by later learning. Some can be recognized because they occur universally. One fixed action pattern is the smile—even people blind since birth smile. Another is the eyebrow flash of greeting: when one person sincerely greets another, the eyebrows rise momentarily. Neither person is usually aware of the response, but it produces a feeling of welcome for the greeted person (Eibl-Eibesfeldt, 1975). It should come as no surprise that humans possess fixed action patterns, even though they are modified or suppressed by cultural training. Indeed, we could hardly learn all the complex patterns we do without an elaborate base of built-in tendencies.

Respondent Conditioning   One simple type of learning that occurs with reflexes and fixed action patterns is *classical* or *respondent conditioning*. It is called conditioning because its discoverer, I. P. Pavlov, used the term *conditional reflex* to describe the result of the learning; he thought a new reflex was learned that was conditional upon experience. Pavlov studied a variety of reflexes, but his best-known research focused on responses to food. He found that when a stimulus such as a tone or light regularly precedes feeding, behavior in the presence of the stimulus changes. A dog begins after a number of tone–food pairings to salivate and secrete digestive juices in the stomach in the presence of the tone by itself. If Tom begins to salivate when he sees the roast turkey brought in to dinner on Thanksgiving, it seems clear that he was not born with that reaction; he salivates because in the past such events preceded eating. If Tom had grown up in an orthodox Hindu home in India, vegetarian from birth, it is unlikely that the sight of a roasted turkey would make him salivate. If, having grown up in the United States, he were to visit an Indian home, he might fail to salivate at some of the food served for dinner there.

The same conditioning that governs simple reflex reactions also governs fixed action patterns. Researchers after Pavlov found that in any situation in which eating has occurred often in the past, all behavior related to food, not just salivation, becomes more likely. Dogs bark and wag their tails, behavior that accompanies group feeding in wild dogs. As the time of feeding draws near, pigeons become likely to peck at almost anything—a light, the floor, the air, or another pigeon—until there is food to peck at.

Behavior analysts debate the best way to talk about such phenomena. The older way, derived from Pavlov's idea of conditional reflexes, speaks of responses *elicited* by stimuli, suggesting a one-to-one causal relation. This may work for reflex reactions like salivation, but many researchers find it inadequate when applied to the variety of behavior that becomes likely around feeding. To talk about the whole cluster of food-related behavior, the term *induce* has been introduced (Segal, 1972). Repeated feeding following a tone induces food-related behavior in the presence of the tone. For a dog, this means that salivation, barking, and tail-wagging all become likely when the tone is on.

What is true of food is true of other phylogenically important events. Situations that precede mating induce sexual arousal, a whole cluster of reflexes and fixed action patterns that varies widely from species to species. For humans, it entails changes in heart rate, blood flow, and glandular secretion.

Situations that precede danger induce a variety of aggressive and defensive behavior. A rat that is given electric shocks in the presence of another rat attacks the other rat. Similarly, people in pain often become aggressive, and any situation in which pain has occurred in the past induces aggressive behavior. How many doctors, dentists, and nurses have had to wrestle with unwilling patients before any pain was ever actually inflicted! Such situations induce a host of reflex reactions and fixed action patterns varying from one species to another. Some of this behavior has more to do with escape than with aggression. Creatures may become very likely to run in situations that signal danger. Sometimes, when a situation includes pain that in the past has been inescapable, the signs of danger induce extreme passivity, a phenomenon known as *learned helplessness* and sometimes speculated to resemble clinical depression in humans.

The debate over what all this means and how best to talk about it continues, but it need not detain us here. For our purposes, it is enough to note that a history of natural selection can have at least two sorts of result. First, it can ensure that events important to fitness, such as food, a mate, or a predator, reliably produce behavioral reactions, both simple reflexes and fixed action patterns. Second, it can ensure the susceptibility of a species to respondent conditioning. Tom may not come into the world salivating at roast turkey, but he does come in so constructed that he may learn this reaction if he grows up in the United States. If individuals that could learn to react to a variety of possible signals were more fit, then individuals today will possess a genotype, typical of the species as the result of a history of natural selection, that enables this type of learning. In a sense the genotype makes for individuality, because the exact signals that will induce the behavior will depend on the individual's own special history of those particular signals preceding a particular phylogenically important event.

These events that we have been calling *phylogenically important* tend to be important (in the sense of inducing behavioral reactions) to all members of a species. This uniformity suggests an evolutionary history in which those individuals in the population for which these events were important (in the present sense) were more fit. Those genotypes that made for individuals in whom food and sex failed to induce appropriate behavior (were unimportant) are no longer with us.

A distinction must be made between what was important long ago, during phylogeny, and what we consider important in our society today. The evolutionary history that made food, sex, and other events phylogenically important extended over millions of years. The circumstances in the environment that linked the events with fitness a million years ago could be absent today because human culture can change enormously in only a few centuries, an amount of time that could never produce any significant evolutionary change in our species. For example, if a new generation begins every 20 years, 300 years represents only 15 generations, far too few for much change in genotypes. All the changes that have occurred as a result of the Industrial Revolution—the growth of cities and factories, cars and airplanes, nuclear weapons, the nuclear family—can have had no effect on the behavioral tendencies supported by our genotypes. Thus, our evolutionary history may have prepared us poorly for some of today's challenges. When the doctor approaches to give you a shot, your tendency may be to tense up, prepare for the danger, and be ready for flight or aggression, when the appropriate response is to relax. With nuclear weapons in our hands, how much more important it becomes to curb aggressive tendencies that evolved at a time when a stick would have been a powerful weapon!

■ Reinforcers and Punishers

Why do we submit meekly to injections? Behavior analysts explain our tendency to submit rather than resist by the consequences of these actions. Resistance might avoid some pain in the short run, but allowing the shot is linked to more important consequences, such as health and reproduction, in the long run. The tendency of consequences to shape behavior serves as the basis for a second type of learning, *operant conditioning* or *learning*.

Phylogenically important events, when they are the consequences of behavior, are called *reinforcers* and *punishers*. Those events that during phylogeny enhanced fitness by their presence are called reinforcers, because they tend to strengthen behavior that produces them. Examples are food, shelter, and sex. If food and shelter are obtained by working, then I work. If sex is obtained by performing courtship rituals special to my culture—dating—then I date. Those events that during phylogeny enhanced fitness by their absence are called punishers, because they tend to suppress (punish) behavior that produces them. Examples are pain, cold, and illness. If I pet a dog and it bites me, I will be less likely to pet it again. If eating nuts makes me sick, I will be less likely to eat nuts. Such changes in behavior because of its consequences are examples of operant learning.

Operant Learning   Whereas respondent conditioning occurs as a result of a relationship between two stimuli—a phylogenically important event and a signal—operant learning occurs as a result of a relationship between a stimulus and an action—a phylogenically important event and the behavior that affects its occurrence. Broadly speaking, there are two types of relationships between behavior and consequences: *positive* and *negative*. If you hunt or work for food, this behavior tends to produce food or make it more likely. This is a positive relationship between a consequence (food) and an action (hunting or working). If Naomi is allergic to nuts, she checks the ingredients of prepared foods before eating them to make sure there are no nuts or nut oils in them and to avoid getting sick. This relationship is a negative one; the action (checking) prevents the consequence (sickness) or makes it less likely.

With two types of action—consequence relationships (positive and negative) and two types of consequences (reinforcers and punishers), we have four types of relations that can engender operant learning (Figure 4.2). The dependence between work and food is an example of positive reinforcement: *reinforcement* because the relation tends to strengthen or maintain the action (working), and *positive* because the action makes the reinforcer (food) likely. The relation between tooth-brushing and tooth decay is an example of nega-

Consequence:

	Reinforcer	Punisher
Positive	Positive Reinforcement	Positive Punishment
Negative	Negative Punishment	Negative Reinforcement

(row labels under "Action-Consequence Relation:")

Figure 4.2 Four types of relations engendering operant learning.

tive reinforcement: *reinforcement* because the relation tends to maintain tooth-brushing (the action), and *negative* because brushing makes tooth decay (the punisher) less likely. The relation between walking on icy patches and falling is an example of positive punishment: *punishment* because the relation makes walking on ice (the action) less likely, and *positive* because the action makes the punisher (falling) more likely. The relation between making noise while hunting and catching prey is an example of negative punishment: *punishment* because the relation tends to suppress making noise, and *negative* because making noise (the action) makes catching prey (a reinforcer) less likely.

Phylogenically important events are not the only reinforcers and punishers. The signals of phylogenically important events that enter into respondent conditioning also function as reinforcers and punishers. A dog that has been trained to press a lever to produce food will press the lever also to produce a tone that is followed by food. As long as the tone continues to signal the food—the relation of respondent conditioning—the tone serves to reinforce the dog's lever pressing. This explains why people work for money as well as food itself; as in respondent conditioning, money is paired with food and other goods. When a reinforcer or punisher is the result of respondent conditioning like this, it is called *acquired* or *conditional*. The phylogenically important events that bear directly on fitness are called *unconditional* reinforcers and punishers. Money and a tone signaling food are conditional reinforcers. Painful events in a doctor's office may make the office itself a conditional punisher.

In human society, the events that become conditional reinforcers and punishers are many and varied. They differ from culture to culture, from person to person, and from time to time within one's lifetime. When I was in the first grade, I strove for gold stars; today I encourage my child to strive for happy-face stickers. In the United States, when we are ill we make appointments with physicians; in other cultures people make appointments with magicians and shamans. Naomi, who is allergic to nuts, finds the smell and sight of peanut butter disgusting and avoids the stuff. I, who eat it daily for lunch, buy it at the store all the time. My problem is with green peppers; when I am served salad in a restaurant, I pick them out.

Whether such a stimulus becomes or remains a conditional reinforcer or punisher depends on its signaling an unconditional reinforcer or punisher. Money remains a reinforcer only as long as it signals the availability of food and other unconditional reinforcers. In the early years of the United States, the government issued currency called "continentals" that became worthless because it was backed by too little gold—that is, there was too little possibility of redeeming the paper for reliable money. People refused to accept the paper money as payment, and it ceased to function as a reinforcer. My friend Mark, who is a skydiver, was terrified the first time he jumped from an airplane, and hesitated for a long while before he finally jumped. However, after many jumps with no mishap, he now jumps without hesitation; jumping ceased to be a punisher. I, who have never jumped out of an airplane, can only marvel at the power of the conditional reinforcers that would maintain this behavior.

This last example illustrates an important point to remember when we are discussing reinforcement and punishment: behavior often has mixed consequences. Slogans like "No pain, no gain" and "Thank God it's Friday" point to this fact of life. Life is full of choices between alternatives that offer different mixes of reinforcement and punishment. Going to work entails both getting paid (positive reinforcement) and suffering hassles (positive punishment), whereas calling in sick may forfeit some pay (negative punishment), avoid the hassles (negative reinforcement), allow a vacation (positive reinforcement), and incur some workplace disapproval (positive punishment). Which set of relations wins out depends on which relations are strong enough to dominate, and that depends on both the present circumstances and the person's history of reinforcement and punishment.

■ Biological Factors

Reinforcement and punishment need to be understood in light of the circumstances in which our species evolved. Since sensitivity to reinforcement and punishment enhances fitness only under some circumstances, and some such sensitivities enhance fitness more than others, phylogeny has provided us with physiology that both helps and hinders the action of reinforcement and punishment in various ways. Behavior analysis considers three sorts of physiological influence.

First, no reinforcer functions as a reinforcer all the time. If you have just eaten three slices of apple pie and your gracious host offers yet a fourth, you are likely now to refuse. No matter how powerful the reinforcer, it is possible to have enough. If you have gone for a while without the reinforcer, it is likely to be powerful; this is *deprivation*. If you have had a lot of the reinforcer lately, it is likely to be weak; that is *satiation*. It is even possible for a reinforcer to become a punisher, as anyone knows who has ever overeaten. If you have already satiated on apple pie, having to eat another slice would actually be too much of a good thing, a punisher. Medieval water torture exploited the punishing effects of forcing a person to drink water beyond capacity. It seems likely that these tendencies for reinforcers to wax and wane and even turn to punishers evolved because individuals that possessed them survived and reproduced better than those that lacked them.

Second, we may come into the world physiologically prepared for certain kinds of respondent conditioning. Some conditional reinforcers and punishers seem to be more easily acquired than others. Some require a lot of experience and some very little. Even some seemingly unconditional reinforcers and punishers appear to depend a bit on experience. When I was a child, I hated mushrooms, but today I put them raw in my salad. Likewise, the reinforcing power of sex seems to grow with experience. On the other hand, some seemingly conditional reinforcers and punishers are easily acquired, so easily that they hardly seem conditional. To children and some adults, candy is a powerful reinforcer. Our ancestors, who ate a lot of fruit, benefited from a predilection for sweet-tasting food, because ripe (sweet) fruit is more nutritious than unripe fruit. As a result, most humans seem to come into the world prepared to develop a sweet tooth—unfortunately for some of us now that rapid cultural change has made sweets readily available.

Another example of such prepared learning is fear of snakes. Many children will handle snakes readily and show no fear of them, but show a special sensitivity to any suggestion that snakes are objects to be feared. The same child that a week ago handled a snake may today scream and hide at the sight of the same snake. To our ancestors snakes probably were a real hazard, and selection would have favored those individuals disposed to be fearful. Indeed, a sure way to create pandemonium in a cage of monkeys is to introduce a snake in their midst.

Humans seem to be especially sensitive also to signs of approval and disapproval from others. Some of these signs, such as the smile and the frown, are universal; others vary from culture to culture. Approval and disapproval may be expressed by sounds, gestures, and even bodily postures too subtle for an outsider to notice, but apparent to all who grow up in that culture. In a social species like ours, the fitness of each individual depends on good relations with other members of the community. It seems likely that our history of selection favored both a sensitivity to unconditional cues like smiles and frowns and an ability to learn any conditional cues especially easily.

Instead of trying to divide reinforcers and punishers into two categories, conditional and unconditional, it might be wiser to speak of a continuum of conditionality, from highly conditional to minimally conditional. Sweets and snakes might be minimally conditional, whereas money and failing an exam would be more conditional. Smiles and frowns might be minimally conditional, whereas subtle slights and boosts might be highly conditional. Whichever view we adopt, two points seem clear: (1) There is an extremely wide range of events that can be reinforcers and punishers, and (2) directly or indirectly, all reinforcers and punishers ultimately derive their power from their effects on fitness—that is, from a history of evolution by natural selection.

The third physiological influence is to prepare the way for certain types of operant learning. The structure of my body makes some learning unlikely. No matter how much I try to spread my wings, I never seem to learn to fly. An eagle, on the other hand, is exceedingly likely to spread its wings and learn to fly. Of course, it learns partly because it has wings, but also because it is predisposed to use them. Our species, too, is predisposed to behave in certain ways and learn certain skills. Children come into the world especially sensitive to speech sounds and begin to babble at an early age. Virtually all children, without special instruction, come to speak the language spoken around them by the age of two. Speaking is learned because of its consequences, by the effects it has on other people, who provide reinforcement and punishment. Children learn to request cookies because that is how they get someone to give them cookies. But this learning is highly prepared. For a human, speaking is so crucial to fitness that genes favoring learning to speak would be strongly selected. As a result, the physiology of our bodies makes it virtually a certainty that we will learn this skill.

As a result of our physiology, some skills will be especially easy to learn, whereas others, no matter how important in life today, will be less helped. Compare learning to speak with learning to read and write. The first requires no instruction; the other demands schools and teachers. Learning calculus can be helpful, but it remains a challenge to most people, whereas it seems almost anyone can learn to drive a car. The sort of coordination of eyes, hands, and feet required for driving, also important to hunting prey and evading predators, comes easily to us, whereas abstract thinking takes more effort. Hunting and being hunted went on for millions of years, whereas calculus was invented less than 400 years ago. This means that all skills are not equally easy to acquire, and that operant learning may work much better with some skills (speaking and driving) than with others (reading and calculus).

■ **Overview of Phylogenic Influences**

There seem to be five ways that a history of natural selection affects behavior.

1. It provides reliable patterns of behavior—reflexes and fixed action patterns—that aid survival and reproduction.

2. It can favor genotypes that provide the capacity for respondent conditioning, in which a variety of neutral stimuli can become promises and threats of up-coming situations (releasers) requiring fixed action patterns. If that capacity to learn enhanced fitness, then the physiological equipment necessary for it would have been selected.

3. It can favor genotypes that provide the capacity for operant conditioning, in which consequences (reinforcers and punishers) shape the behavior on which they depend. If operant learning enhanced fitness during phylogeny, then natural selection would have provided the

physiological equipment necessary for this type of flexibility. Those fixed action patterns that serve as a base for respondent conditioning (unconditional stimuli and responses, according to Pavlov) serve also as a base for operant learning, as unconditional reinforcers and punishers. The signals or conditional stimuli of respondent conditioning function as conditional reinforcers and punishers in operant learning.

4. It has provided physiological mechanisms of deprivation and satiation, by which reinforcers and punishers wax and wane in their power to affect behavior.

5. It selects biases that favor conditioning of certain signals in respondent conditioning and strengthening of certain actions in operant learning. If such signals and actions are especially important to fitness, but some flexibility is also good for fitness, then physiological mechanisms would have been selected that make such learning especially easy.

❖ HISTORY OF REINFORCEMENT

The term "history of reinforcement" in behavior analysis is really shorthand for "history of reinforcement and punishment," an individual's history of operant learning from birth. In this section we shall see that it is a history of selection by consequences analogous to phylogeny. Reinforcement and punishment shape behavior as it develops during an individual's lifetime (during the *ontogeny* of behavior) in the same way that reproductive success shapes the traits of a species during phylogeny.

■ Selection by Consequences

In Figure 4.1, individual giraffe ancestors that had shorter necks tended to produce fewer surviving offspring on the average than did those with longer necks. The lesser and greater fitnesses (reproductive successes) were consequences of the shorter and longer necks. As long as those differential consequences remained (Curves 1 and 2 in Figure 4.1), average neck length in the population continued to grow. When the process reached its limit (Curve 3), there were still differential consequences of neck length, except now either too short or too long a neck results in lower average reproductive success, because the variation in neck length spans the point of maximum fitness (the broken line in Figure 4.1). Now the differential consequences of neck length act to stabilize the population.

The general rule of thumb in phylogeny is that within a population of individuals that vary in genotype, those types that are more successful tend to become or remain the most frequent. An analogous rule holds for ontogeny by reinforcement and punishment; it is known as the *law of effect*.

The Law of Effect   Successful and unsuccessful behavior are defined by their effects. In everyday terms, successful behavior produces good effects, and unsuccessful behavior produces less good or bad effects. In operant learning, success and failure correspond to reinforcement and punishment. A successful action is one that is reinforced; an unsuccessful action is one that is less reinforced or punished.

The law of effect is the principle that underlies operant learning. It states that the more reinforced an action is, the more it tends to occur, and the more punished an action is, the less it tends to occur. The results of the law of effect are often spoken of as "shaping," because as more successful types of behavior wax and less successful types wane, it is like a sculptor molding a lump of clay, building up here, pressing down there, until the lump takes desired shape. When you were first learning to write, even the crudest approximations of letters like *o* and *c* were met with high praise. Some of these efforts were better than others, and the better ones were usually more praised. Really poor performance might even have produced disapproval. Gradually, your letters became better shaped. (Standards shifted, too; shapes that were praised at an early stage merited disapproval at a later stage.)

Shaping and Natural Selection   Behavior analysts think of the shaping of behavior as working in just the same way as the evolution of species. Just as differences in reproductive success (fitness) shape the composition of a population of genotypes, so reinforcement and punishment shape the composition of an individual's behavior. To clarify the parallel, think of the collection of all behavior of a certain sort—say, driving a car to work—that a person engages in over a certain period—say, a month—as being like a population of giraffes. Driving to work is a species of behavior, just as giraffes are a species of animal, and all the driving I do in a month is a population of driving actions, just as all the giraffes in the Serengeti Plain are a population of giraffes. Just as some giraffes are more successful at producing offspring, so some of my driving actions are more successful in getting me to work. Some maneuvers gain time; these are reinforced. Others lose time or prove dangerous; these are punished. The successful maneuvers tend to become more frequent or at least are maintained from month to month, and the unsuccessful maneuvers tend to become less frequent or at least remain rare from month to month, just as the more successful types of giraffes tend to remain more common and the less successful types of giraffes tend to remain rare. Just as more successful types of giraffes are selected by their success, so more successful types of driving are selected by their success. Over time, selection results in either evolution or stabilization of driving.

Suppose we take Figure 4.1 and substitute driving speed relative to the speed limit for neck length and efficiency (making good time without excessive danger) for fitness. The result is Figure 4.3. The three frequency curves might refer to different stages in my learning to drive. At first, I tended to drive at low speed (Curve 1). As I gained competence, I drove faster (Curve 2). Since those speeds tended to be less efficient (less reinforced), gradually my driving

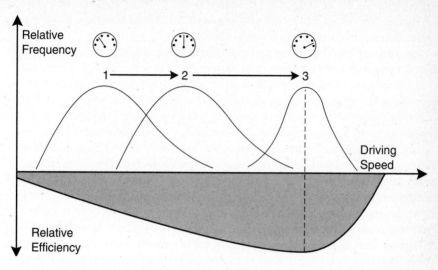

Figure 4.3 Shaping by reinforcement and punishment.

shifted to where it is today (Curve 3), coinciding on the average with the most efficient speed, represented by the broken line (about 5 miles per hour above the speed limit).

Just as with evolution, behavior shaping operates on the population and on the average. When my driving to work was being shaped (say, Curve 2 in Figure 4.3), greater speed meant greater efficiency only on the average. Sometimes greater speed was less efficient; perhaps I got stopped by a police officer or had an accident. Sometimes greater speed was no more efficient; maybe I went fast only to be trapped behind a school bus or at a railroad crossing in the final stretch. Not every action of a type need be reinforced or punished for the type to be strengthened or suppressed; the type only need be reinforced or punished more *on the average* over time.

For evolution or stabilization of a population by natural selection, three ingredients are necessary: variation, reproduction, and differential success. (1) For there to be selection among possibilities, there must be more than one possibility—that is, the individuals in the population must vary in the trait (neck length in Figure 4.1, speed in Figure 4.3, or coloration or a host of other traits). (2) The different variants must tend to reproduce themselves—that is, offspring should resemble their parents from generation to generation. For natural selection, this resemblance results from genetic inheritance. Long- and short-necked giraffes inherit their long and short necks from their parents. (3) Among the variants, some must be more successful than others (i.e., there must be competition). If all variants were equally fit—if instead of the fitness curve shown in Figure 4.1 fitness were represented by a flat line—then the trait (neck length) would neither shift in a particular direction nor remain stable, but drift unpredictably from time to time. Since too short a neck lowers fitness, the population moves steadily toward longer necks; when too long a neck also lowers fitness, the population remains stable.

Shaping by reinforcement and punishment requires the same three ingredients: variation, reproduction, and differential success. (1) For shaping, the variation occurs within the population of actions that serve a similar purpose (driving, in our example, which serves to get us places). You hardly ever do the same thing exactly the same way twice. Sometimes you brush your teeth hard, sometimes easy. Sometimes you speak in a high pitch, sometimes low. Sometimes I drive above the speed limit, sometimes below it. The population of harder and softer tooth brushings, higher- and lower-pitched utterances, or faster and slower driving varies just the same way as the population of shorter- and longer-necked giraffes. (2) For shaping to occur, actions must tend to repeat (reproduce) from time to time. If I go rock-climbing only once in my life, there is no chance for my rock-climbing to be shaped. Since I brush my teeth every day, there is plenty of chance for my tooth-brushing to be shaped. (3) For shaping, differential success means differential reinforcement and punishment. I speak loudly to my deaf grandmother; otherwise she cannot hear me and provide reinforcement for my speaking to her. If I speak too loudly, she reprimands me with, "Don't you shout at me, young man." Most of the time I find a loudness at which she and I can carry on a nice conversation; so, some loudnesses are more successful than others, just as in Figure 4.3 some speeds are more successful than others. As in natural selection, there is a limit to population size—you brush your teeth only two or three times a day, and I do only so much driving in a month. Since the more successful variants tend to reproduce more often from day to day or month to month, the less successful variants tend to become less frequent. As long as some variants are reinforced or punished more than others, the action population will either shift or remain stable, as in Figure 4.3.

When one person dispenses reinforcement and punishment purposefully to change the behavior of another person, it is called training, teaching, or therapy. Whether we are talking about an athletic coach training a team, an animal trainer training a bear to dance, a teacher teaching a child to read, or a therapist helping a client to be more assertive with superiors, the same principles of reinforcement and punishment apply. The only difference is that these instances of shaping constitute relationships—that is, two people are involved, both of whose behavior is being shaped. (More about this in Chapters 7, 9, and 11.)

Training, teaching, and therapy resemble selective breeding, the process in which reproductive success (which individuals get to breed) is determined by a person, rather than by the natural environment. When farmers breed only the cows that produce the most milk, they are capitalizing on the inheritance of milk production, just as natural selection capitalizes on the inheritance of advantageous traits in the natural environment. Darwin got the idea of natural selection in part from observing selective breeding. He saw that the same principles could apply on the farm and in nature. Similarly, the same principles of reinforcement and punishment apply in our "natural," unstructured environment and in situations structured especially for behavior change.

■ Historical Explanations

The parallel between natural selection and shaping is no accident, as both ideas exist to solve similar problems. In Chapter 1, we saw how Darwin's theory of natural selection provided the first scientific account of evolution. Prior to that, even if one rejected the exact account in the Bible, it was common to regard evolution as the result of God's design, intelligence, or purpose. From a scientific point of view, such an "explanation" is unacceptable, because it fails to advance understanding and impedes efforts to make true advances. Just as natural selection replaced divine purpose, selection by reinforcement and punishment replaces mentalistic "explanations" of behavior that refer to design, intelligence, or purpose inside the person or animal behaving.

Figure 4.4 shows a summary of the parallel between natural selection and shaping. Both ideas rely on the notion of gradual change through time—a history. In evolution by natural selection, the history is phylogeny, the gradual shift of genetically based traits. In behavior shaping, the history is the gradual shift of an individual's behavior due to interaction with the reinforcement and punishment relations in his or her environment (Figure 4.2). Your personal history of reinforcement and punishment includes all those times when your behavior produced food, money, approval, pain, or disapproval—all those consequences that shaped your behavior into what it is today. It is part of the ontogeny of your behavior.

Both ideas refer to a population within which variation occurs. In evolution, variation occurs within a population of individuals, the key variation being in the individuals' genotypes. In shaping, variation occurs within a population of action-types, all the different ways that an individual performs a certain task or action, such as tooth-brushing or going to the store.

Both ideas require reproduction of types. In natural selection, genotypes are passed from generation to generation by genetic inheritance. In shaping, actions repeat because the occasions for them repeat. I brush my teeth every morning and every night because I get up every morning and go to sleep every night. People often call such repetition "habit." The exact mechanism underly-

	History	Population (Variation)	Reproduction	Selection	"Explanation" Replaced
Natural Selection	Phylogeny	Genotypes	Genetic inheritance	Differential fitness	God the Creator
Shaping	History of reinforcement and punishment (ontogeny)	Action-types (behavior)	Repetition or "Habit"	Differential reinforcement and punishment	Purpose, will, intelligence (mentalism)

Fig. 4.4 Parallel between natural selection and shaping.

ing habit must lie in the nervous system, but much less is known about that than about the genetic transfer of characteristics from parents to offspring.

Both ideas attribute change to selection by differential success. In natural selection, change in the genotypes composing a population is due to differential fitness or reproductive success. In shaping, change in the ways an action is performed (the action-types) is due to differential reinforcement and punishment, the differences in effectiveness of the different action-types.

Finally, each idea replaces an earlier unscientific account. Natural selection replaces God the Creator, the hidden force guiding evolution, with an explanation in purely natural terms. The apparent intelligence and purposefulness of life forms are seen as the outcome of selection acting on variation. It is a good thing for giraffes that they have long necks, but neither they nor the Creator need be given credit for this, because the environment made long necks good and selected them as well. Shaping by reinforcement and punishment also replaces hidden forces, the mentalistic causes of behavior, with explanations in purely natural terms. The intelligence and purposefulness of actions are seen as the outcome of selection (reinforcement and punishment) acting on variation. It is a good thing for me that I drive as well as I do, but neither I nor any inner purpose or intelligence need be given any credit for this, because the environment made skillful driving good and selected it as well.

Historical explanations like natural selection and reinforcement differ from scientific explanations that rely on immediate causes. The sun's rising is explained by an immediate cause, the earth's rotation. In historical explanation, the "cause" of the event is nowhere present, but is a whole history of past events. The long neck of the giraffe cannot be explained by any event at its birth or even at its conception, but is explained by the long history of selection that produced it over millions of years. Similarly, my driving speed cannot be explained by any event while I am driving or even when I get into the car, but is explained by the history of shaping that produced it over many months or years.

Evolutionary biologists distinguish between *proximate* explanations and *ultimate* explanations (Alcock, 1989). The proximate explanation of a behavioral pattern points to the physiological mechanisms that determine the pattern's development from conception. An individual's genetic endowment explains, in a proximate way, why the individual sneezes, smiles, and is able to learn. But the larger question of why the individual has that genetic endowment in the first place cannot be explained by the moment of conception or any other moment. The ultimate explanation points to the individual's membership in a population or species and, strictly speaking, applies to the population and not to the individual at all. Human beings sneeze and learn because that reflex and that capacity enhanced fitness among humans and their ancestors over many millions of years; that is the ultimate explanation.

Ultimate explanations are historical explanations; proximate explanations are explanations in terms of immediate causes. If enough were known about the physiology of the nervous system, it might be possible to explain why I drove 55 miles per hour at 8:55 on the morning of June 10. That would be a proximate explanation of that particular instance of my behavior, just as molecular genetics and embryology might provide a proximate explanation of why I have two hands and feet. But why the population of my driving speeds is what it is month after month cannot be explained by the physiology of my nervous system, just as why human beings have two hands and feet cannot be explained by any one person's genetics or embryological development. The population requires an ultimate or historical explanation. On a particular occasion, I may hand over my wallet to a man with a gun; the historical explanation points to this event's membership in a population (or category, in Ryle's terms), called, say, "compliance with a threat," and the long history of reinforcement for compliance with threats, from the playground to the classroom to the streets of New York City.

People seem to prefer proximate explanations, probably because it is simpler to think of events like billiard balls knocking into one another. When an act appears to have no immediate cause, instead of pointing to the history of reinforcement that produced the action-category to which the act belongs, we may be tempted to provide an immediate cause by making one up. If the history of reinforcement responsible for Zack's going to a movie when he should have been studying is obscure, we may be tempted to say his will power collapsed. That, of course, is mentalism.

Chapter 3 criticized mentalism at length, but never offered any alternative; now we are in a position to suggest a scientifically acceptable account of purpose and intention. As we noted at the beginning of this part of the book, particulars of the account shall change as time goes on. We need only establish that a truly scientific account is possible. That is the subject of the next chapter.

❖ SUMMARY

The theory of evolution is important to behavior analysis in two ways.

First, much behavior originates in genetic inheritance derived from the species's evolutionary history (phylogeny). Natural selection provides reflexes and fixed action patterns, the capacity for respondent conditioning, the capacity for operant learning, reinforcers and punishers that change in power with time and context, and biases that favor certain types of respondent and operant conditioning.

Second, the theory of evolution provides a model of historical explanation, the type of explanation that applies to operant behavior. A history of reinforcement and punishment parallels a history of natural selection, except that the first operates on a type of behavior (population of actions) within the lifetime of an individual, whereas the second operates on a species (population of organisms) over many generations. Both concepts replace nonscientific accounts that refer to a hidden intelligent agent directing evolutionary or behavioral change.

Although explanations in physics and chemistry rely on immediate causes, historical explanations refer to the cumulative effects of many events over a long period of time. Changes produced in a population as a result of selection by consequences cannot be pinpointed at a particular moment. Like phylogeny, a history of reinforcement refers to many events of the past, all of which together produced present behavior.

❖ FURTHER READING

Several books are available at various levels that treat the topics of this chapter in greater depth.

Alcock, J. (1989). *Animal behavior: An evolutionary approach* (4th ed.). Sunderland, MA: Sinauer Associates. An excellent introductory textbook covering evolutionary theory and sociobiology.

Barash, D. (1982). *Sociobiology and behavior* (2nd ed.). New York: Elsevier. An excellent treatment, more advanced than Alcock's.

Eibl-Eibesfeldt, I. (1975). *Ethology: The biology of behavior* (2nd ed.). New York: Holt, Rinehart and Winston. This book has an excellent treatment of fixed action patterns, particularly in human beings.

Gould, J. L. (1982). *Ethology: The mechanisms and evolution of behavior.* New York: Norton. A more up-to-date, though not necessarily better, book than Eibl-Eibesfeldt.

Mazur, J. E. (1990). *Learning and behavior* (2nd ed.). Englewood Cliffs, NJ: Prentice-Hall. An advanced textbook on behavior analysis that provides a good overview of the field.

Rachlin, H. (1990). *Introduction to modern behaviorism* (3rd ed.). New York: Freeman. Although misnamed, this is an excellent introduction to the basics of modern behavior analysis.

Segal, E. F. (1972). Induction and the provenance of operants. In R. M. Gilbert & J. R. Millenson (Eds.), *Reinforcement: Behavioral analyses* (pp. 1–34). New York: Academic Press. An excellent technical review of induction, its interaction with reinforcement, and its effects on operant behavior.

Skinner, B. F. (1953). *Science and human behavior.* New York: Macmillan. The first textbook in behavior analysis, now of mostly historical interest, but containing many illuminating arguments and examples.

CHAPTER 5

PURPOSE AND REINFORCEMENT

S ay that someone told you that you should read *Moby Dick,* so you hunt for a copy in the local bookstores. The first store doesn't have any, so you go to another store. Such activity is often called *purposive* because it is supposedly driven by an inner purpose (obtaining and reading *Moby Dick*). Behavior analysts reject the notion that an inner purpose guides the action. What scientifically acceptable alternative can they offer?

Chapter 4 examined the close parallels between evolutionary theory in biology and reinforcement theory in behavior analysis. We saw that they both rely on historical explanations to replace unscientific notions about a hidden agent (Creator, intelligence, or will) behind the scenes. In this chapter, we shall see exactly how the idea of a history of reinforcement and punishment substitutes for traditional notions about purpose.

❖ HISTORY AND FUNCTION

We saw in Chapter 4 that historical explanations are ultimate explanations, and that ultimate explanations account for the existence of populations of organisms or actions and have little to say about the peculiarities of individual organisms or actions. Point to a zebra and ask an evolutionary biologist about its stripes; you will get an explanation about why zebras as a group have stripes. If you really want to know why that particular zebra has a pattern of stripes that make it different from other zebras, you will have to go to an embryologist or developmentalist. Point to a child and ask a behavior analyst why she is hitting a companion with a toy truck, and you will get an explanation about why that child exhibits the group of actions that we call aggressive behavior. If you want to know why the aggression involves that particular toy and those particular arm muscles, you will have to go to a physiologist. When evolutionary biologists or behavior analysts get more specific about a population, they do so by defining subpopulations or subcategories. White-crowned sparrows may sing a bit differently from one region to another, and I may drive faster when I am late than under other circumstances, but sparrows in a particular region and drives when I am late are still populations and are still explained historically.

Historical explanation and population-thinking, which go hand-in-hand, both take some getting used to. This is true for historical explanation used in behavior analysis because people are so prejudiced toward seeking explanations in causes present at the moment of action. As for population-thinking, people are unaccustomed to grouping actions along the lines of function—that is, along the lines of what they accomplish, rather than how they look. We turn now to a closer look at how historical explanations and functional definitions work.

■ Using Historical Explanations

At least since Freud's invention of psychoanalysis, psychologists and laypeople alike have grown accustomed to the idea that events in our childhood affect our behavior as adults. If I was abused as a child, I may tend to abuse my own children when I am an adult. If my family always sat down to supper together, this may seem essential to me when I am a parent. Such observations form the basis for historical explanations. I behave so as an adult *because of* the events of my childhood.

History Versus Immediate Cause   There seems to be an enormous temptation to represent somehow the events of childhood in the present. If no obvious cause can be found in the present, the temptation is to make one up. If I was traumatized as a child, then it is said that I have "anxiety" or a "complex" that causes maladaptive behavior today. If a teenager grew up in a dysfunctional family, then he misbehaves today because he has "low self-esteem."

Such notions are examples of mentalism, the practice of putting forward imaginary causes to try to explain behavior. Talking about anxiety, complexes, or self-esteem adds nothing to what is already known—the connection between past events and present behavior. Attributing delinquency to low self-esteem in no way explains the delinquency. Where did the low self-esteem come from? How can it cause delinquency? Is there any evidence of low self-esteem other than the behavior it is supposed to explain? Is low self-esteem anything other than the label for the category of behavior that it is supposed to explain?

The way to escape this trap is to accept that events long ago can affect present behavior directly. If a boy was beaten and neglected as a child, that can contribute to his stealing cars as a teenager, even across the gap of time.

Gaps of Time That an observed relation between environment and behavior spans a gap of time has no bearing on its scientific or practical importance. If people who were abused as children tend to be abusive as adults, the gap between childhood and adulthood does not change the usefulness of this fact, which may lead to therapy and a fuller understanding of the effects of early experience. Even though we have no idea of what bodily mechanisms allow such relations over time, we need neither to resort to mentalism nor to hesitate to make use of the observations.

The situation with gaps of time in behavior analysis resembles that in physics with action at a distance. The concept of gravity was slow to be accepted because it seemed strange that a body could exert an influence on another body even though it was far away. Gravity was finally accepted because it proved useful in explaining phenomena as diverse as falling bodies and the effect of the moon on tides. Ideas about its mechanism came much later.

With gaps of time, we unquestioningly tolerate relationships over small gaps. If I stub my toe and am still in pain a minute later, no one would quarrel with the idea that my behavior now is the result of the stubbing a minute ago. If a teacher tells a child, "Raise your hand if you are having trouble," and the child raises her hand after five minutes, we have no difficulty attributing this action to the combination of the teacher's instruction and the child's having trouble, even if five minutes elapsed between them.

Longer gaps, however—years or even hours—seem to give rise to a temptation to mentalism. In their effects on present behavior, there is no difference in principle between my stubbing my toe a minute ago and my having been traumatized 30 years ago. One occurred a lot longer ago than the other, but there is no need to invent a complex to explain the one any more than the other. Likewise, there is no difference in principle between combining the teacher's instruction with the child's having trouble and combining a promise made on Monday with a meeting on Friday. For each, the combination of the earlier event with the later event makes certain behavior likely at the later time. The gap of four days no more requires invention of "memory" to bridge it than does the gap of five minutes.

Responses to instructions and promises that involve gaps of five minutes or four days imply other, longer, gaps. Just as present responses to childhood trauma arise across a gap of many years, so do present responses to instructions and promises arise from long-ago events. Without a history of taking instructions and making promises, neither the child nor the teacher could behave appropriately. For the child to obey the teacher, there must have been many occasions when the child was told to do something, did it, and the behavior was reinforced. For you to go hunting for *Moby Dick* because a friend told you to read it requires past occasions when you followed such advice and the results were reinforcing. Likewise, the making and keeping of promises must have been reinforced many times in the past for someone now to make and keep a promise.

The particular instruction followed may never have been heard before, and the particular promise made may never have been spoken before, but each history comprises many instances similar to the present one. No one ever told you to read *Moby Dick* before, but people told you to do other things, some of which you did. The history need include neither the particular instruction nor the particular promise because "instruction-taking" and "promise-keeping" are categories based not on structure or appearance, but on *function*.

■ Functional Units

A functional class or category is defined by what the members do—how they act or function—rather than how they are composed or how they appear. A structural class might be "four-legged furniture," because a thing need only be put together in a certain way to belong, whereas "table" might be a functional class, because a thing need only exist for the purpose of having objects put on it to belong. A table may have three, four, six, or eight legs; it makes no difference how it is constructed.

A class or category is called a "unit" when it is treated as a single whole. If I say I am going to buy a table, the particular object that I will bring home remains unknown, but there is no doubt to what unit I am referring. Similarly, if I say I am going to Africa to look at giraffes, the particular individuals I will look at remain unknown, but there is no doubt about the unit "giraffes." If I say I will give you directions to my house, the particular instructions remain unknown, but there is no doubt about the unit "instructions."

Species as Functional Units   Before the advent of modern evolutionary theory, it was common to classify creatures according to how they looked, or according to their structure. This worked fairly well except that disputes arose when two species looked so much alike that it was practically impossible to tell them apart. Variation in coloration and skeletal structure within a species of lizard might make it impossible to say just by looking whether a particular specimen was a member of that species or another similarly varying species.

Nowadays, evolutionary biologists no longer define species according to their structure; instead, they define them according to how they reproduce. A species is a population, the members of which breed with one another, but not with members of other such populations. Each species is a reproducing unit, distinct from other such reproducing units because mating occurs within a species but not between species. There are two species of frog that are indistinguishable by appearance and anatomy, and yet one breeds at sunrise and the other at sunset. They are two distinct species, because members of the two never interbreed. Even if two frogs from different species can be made to inter-breed in the laboratory, if they never interbreed in the natural habitat they still belong to two distinct species. Hyenas look different from jackals, but what makes them different species is that hyenas and jackals do not breed with one another. What matters is what the species do—how they function reproductively—not how they look or sound or are constructed.

Operants as Functional Units   Skinner invented the noun *operant* to have a name for a functional category of behavior. It has usually been used to mean a category of acts that are *discrete*—that is, each instance begins at a certain point in time, ends at another point, and occupies all the time between those two points without interruption. For example, when someone opens a door, the act has a certain beginning (approaching the door) and end (letting go once it is open) and nothing else happens in between. Molar action categories like those discussed by Ryle and Rachlin (Chapter 3) are also functional, but their members may include actions that extend through time (e.g., John's loving Sally includes his writing about her in his diary) and may be interrupted by members of other categories (e.g., working). This difference only raises some practical considerations about how to measure different types of behavior. It is of no importance to our discussion of functional units. Everything we may say about operants applies equally well to molar categories.

An operant is a class of acts all of which have the same environmental effect. In the laboratory, commonly studied operants are the lever-press and the key-peck. The lever-press, for example, includes within it all the acts that have the effect of depressing the lever. It makes no difference whether the rat presses the lever with its left paw, right paw, nose, or mouth; all of these are instances of lever-press. In the world at large, we recognize operants when we speak of "opening the front door" or "walking downtown" as units. As with the lever-press, opening the front door comprises all acts that have the effect of getting the door open. It makes no difference whether I open it with my left hand or right hand; both are instances of opening the front door.

Speaking of behavior in terms of classes or categories is not really a choice, but a necessity. One has only to watch a rat to see that it actually does press the lever in a variety of ways. This variability might be reduced by specifying, for example, that only right-paw presses can be reinforced, but then the rat would press the lever with its right paw in a variety of ways. Careful observation would always reveal some variation, because the rat cannot press the lever exactly the same way twice. Each individual act is unique.

If this uniqueness of acts seems like a fatal blow to a science of behavior, it is well to remember that every science faces the same problem. To the astronomer, each star is unique; that is why they are given proper names. To understand stars, the astronomer groups them into categories: white giants, red dwarfs, and so on. Although every creature is unique, the biologist understands living things by grouping them into species. In a sense, it is the very business of science to group things and events into categories. Recognizing sameness is the beginning of explanation.

The units of behavior must be categories, but why functional categories? Why not group acts, for instance, according to which limbs or muscles are involved? The answer is that structurally defined categories cannot work for behavior any more than they can work for species. As with a species, you can tell an act is a member of the operant "lever-press" pretty well by looking, but any ambiguity will be resolved not by how the act looks but by what it does—whether the lever actually gets depressed. However much I may go through the motions of opening the front door, the act is not an instance unless the door opens.

An excellent illustration of the impossibility of defining an operant by its structure is the following excerpt from an announcement, written by Douglas Hintzman at the University of Oregon, of an upcoming lecture to be given by a scholar whom we shall call "Dr. X":

> I asked Dr. X to explain "reading." He replied that it is a method that millions have used to gain enlightenment. Practitioners of this art ("readers," as Dr. X calls them) adopt a sitting position and remain virtually motionless for long periods of time. They hold before their faces white sheets of paper covered with thousands of tiny figures and waggle their eyes rapidly back and forth. While thus engaged, they are difficult to arouse and appear to be in a trance. I didn't see how this bizarre activity could bring knowledge. . . . "Suppose I stare at this piece of paper and jerk my eyes back and forth," I said, grabbing a page from his desk. "Will that make me wise?" "No," he replied, growing annoyed at my skepticism. "It takes many years of practice to become a proficient reader. Besides, that was written by a Dean."

As with pressing a lever or opening a door, "reading" is defined not by how it looks, but by what it does. Reading aloud occurs when the audience can hear it. Silent reading occurs when the reader can demonstrate comprehension afterward by answering questions or otherwise acting in accord with the text.

Typically, we assign a particular act to a functional class on the basis of both its effect and its context. A rat presses a lever in the context of the experimental chamber in which lever-presses have many times in the past produced food. Lever-presses in another context—say a chamber in which they produced water—would belong to a different operant. The two operants could be labeled "lever-press for food" and "lever-press for water," as long as we remind ourselves that "*for* such-and-such" here means "which has produced such-and-such on many occasions in the past." We may consider "compliance with a threat" an operant because its members occur in a certain context (a "threat") and have historically had a certain effect (removal of the threat). Handing my wallet to my wife for her to remove money is a different operant from handing my wallet to a mugger.

"Hunting for an item in stores" defines a functional category that occurs in a certain context—the item's allowing further action that will ultimately be reinforced. Someone telling you to read *Moby Dick* sets the context for you to hunt for the book, because having it allows reading it, which is likely to be reinforced.

Whereas in behavior analysis we speak of history as defining the context and consequences of an act, in everyday talk we would say that different acts have different purposes. We turn now to the ways in which behavior analysis addresses the various uses of the word *purpose*.

❖ THREE MEANINGS OF PURPOSE

Everyday English has a rich vocabulary for talking about behavior in relation to its consequences. We not only use the word *purpose,* but a host of other terms related to it, such as *intention, expectation, want, wish, try,* and so on. These are what philosophers call "intentional terms" or "intentional idioms." Despite all their variety, intentional terms can be grouped, for the most part, into three types of uses: function, cause, and feelings.

■ Purpose as Function

One use of *purpose* and its cousins meshes readily with scientific talk. If I say that the purpose of this paperweight is to hold down these papers, I have pointed out nothing about the paperweight other than what it does, other than its function. No controversy arises because this use of purpose is really like a definition. That is what a paperweight is—something that holds down papers.

Applied to behavior, this use of purpose points to effects. The purpose of a lever-press is to depress the lever. One could say in this sense that operant classes are defined in terms of their purposes. "Walking home" is a class of behavior that gets me home.

In this context, home is also spoken of as the goal of my walking. When we are aware of a long history of action that typically leads to a certain outcome (home), we use *goal* to mean the usual reinforcer for that action. Speaking this way, one could say that the goal of a lever-press is food.

One could even interpret a statement like "I am trying to get home" this way, if by "trying to get home" I meant "engaging in behavior that usually gets me home." Seen this way, "The rat is trying to get food" might simply mean that the rat is pressing a lever that has produced food in the past, and "The rat wants food" might only mean that it is behaving in ways that might have preceded food in the past.

All these ways of speaking might apply to your hunting in bookstores for *Moby Dick.* The goal is obtaining the book, but obtaining the item is the usual effect of hunting and the usual reinforcer for that activity. You are "trying to find the book" and you "want the book" mean that you are engaging in behavior that often produced required items in the past and is likely to produce the book now.

People usually consider goals and desires to involve something more than simply naming customary reinforcers. They often say that the person or rat has something "in mind" on these occasions. This brings us to the next major use of intentional terms.

■ Purpose as Cause

Terms like *try* and *want* seem to refer to some event in the future that will be produced by behavior. "I am trying to open the door" suggests that my efforts are directed toward a future event, the open door.

Of course, a future event cannot cause behavior. That would violate a basic rule of science: only events that actually have happened can produce results. The variables on which my behavior depends must be in either the past or the present.

The common way of addressing this problem is to move the cause from the future to the present. Since the open door of the future cannot cause me to work the latch, it is said that the behavior is caused by a mental representation of the goal or purpose (the open door). Since you have yet to find *Moby Dick,* it is said that your hunting for the book is caused by a mental representation of it.

However, mental representations of future events are examples of mentalism and fall prey to all the problems that we discussed in Chapter 3. Where is this inner purpose? What is it made of? How could this ghostly open door cause me to work the latch? How could an inner representation of *Moby Dick* cause you to hunt for it? This is no explanation; it only serves to obscure the relevant facts about the environment: working the latch usually leads to an open door and hunting for an item usually produces the item. These natural facts explain the behavior without any need to bring in an inner purpose.

Purposive Behavior   What is it about behavior like working a latch that leads people to call it purposive? William James wrote that purposive behavior consists of "varying means [varying behavior] to a fixed end [customary reinforcer]." If you've ever had trouble opening a door, you know what James meant. Say the key doesn't turn all the way in the lock. What do you do? You turn the key several more times, turn it quickly, turn it slowly, push it in, pull it out, jiggle it in and out, and so on. These are varying means. Eventually the door opens (the fixed end), and the behavior ceases. In our *Moby Dick* example, if the book is not at one store, you go to another store and another until, having found the book, you stop hunting.

Perhaps even more than the variation in action, the action's ceasing when the reinforcer occurs seems to compel the word *purposive.* In James's definition, this aspect is contained in the preposition *to* before *fixed end.* We are inclined to say that the behavior was directed toward the goal (future reinforcer) because it stops when the goal is attained (reinforcement occurs). This seems particularly true of behavior like hunting for something. Say I am at a point in cooking a dish where the recipe calls for salt. I go to the place where the salt is usually found, but it is gone. I look on other shelves, on the table, all around the kitchen, in the dining room. I ask anyone I see where the salt is. Eventually I find the salt, stop looking for it, and go on with cooking. The salt is not only the reinforcer for the behavior that we call "looking for the salt," it is also the occasion for proceeding to other action; that is why the behavior ceases.

What might seem troublesome about this account of "looking for the salt" is that I may never have hunted for the salt before. We often search for things that we have never searched for before, and it might seem that there could be no history of reinforcement to explain the behavior.

We have already seen the solution to this sort of problem; it is the same as the problem with handing over one's wallet to a robber for the first time. This particular act may never have occurred before, but others like it have. I may never have complied with this exact threat before, but I have a long history of complying with threats. I may never have searched for *Moby Dick* before, but I have searched for other books and other things. The details may vary—I search in bookstores for the book and around the house for the salt—but "searching for household items" and "searching for items in stores" might be considered functional categories of behavior, just like compliance with threats. Children are often taught explicitly how to hunt for things around the house. They get better at it only after many experiences of searching and finding. In some cultures, learning how to hunt for animals, roots, or berries may be an essential part of growing up. Hunting for berries is learned in part because of instances of finding berries in the past.

One can think of examples of apparently purposive behavior in which the stated goal is never attained. Suppose my cause is to "rid the world of poverty" or "save the whales." I may have no experience with poverty or whales, so what history of reinforcement could maintain the behavior involved? The answer requires us to consider our social environment, particularly the types of reinforcement available to people as a result of living in a culture. People are taught by other people to pursue socially useful activities. The reinforcers the teachers use are usually right at hand, in the form of smiles, affection, and approval. We shall take this up in Chapters 8 and 13.

Purposive Machines   The uselessness of making up inner purposes to explain purposive behavior becomes especially clear when we look at purposive machines—that is, known mechanisms that can be said to behave purposively. A house's heating system is an example. If the air temperature falls below the setting on the thermostat (say, 68 degrees), the furnace comes on and heats the air. When the air temperature rises to 68 degrees, the furnace goes off. It is as if the system tries to keep the temperature at 68 degrees. When it attains this goal or purpose, it ceases its efforts.

More complicated purposive machines seem to lend their actions even more readily to intentional talk. A chess-playing computer might be said to choose moves that it expects will help it toward its inner purpose of winning. It seems to intend to win and know whether it has succeeded or failed.

Since the heating system and the computer are machines whose workings are understood, talking about them in intentional terms may be fun or poetical, but it is unnecessary. The thermostat contains a switch that is operated by the temperature to turn the furnace off and on; that is all there is to its purposiveness. The computer is programmed to make calculations on each move based on the positions of all the pieces, and each move depends only on the outcome of those calculations. The game ends when the result of the calculation coincides with checkmate. There is no inner purpose—only changing action in response to changing piece positions (i.e., environment).

If the purposiveness of the heating system and the computer can be illusory, it must be equally true that the purposiveness of a person can be illusory. The difference is that the mechanism underlying the person's behavior is unknown. If we knew exactly how the nervous system allows the environment to be sensed and turned into action, we could point to our insides the same way we can point to the insides of the thermostat and the computer.

Even without a thorough knowledge of how the thermostat or the computer works, we can still avoid talking about them in intentional terms. The thermostat may be just a box on the wall to me, but its apparent purposiveness still consists only in its being so constructed that one environmental variable (temperature below 68 degrees) initiates action, and another (temperature above 68 degrees) turns it off. The chess-playing computer is built to respond to a set of environmental variables—the positions of all the pieces. Some computers are programmed to "learn," too; the program records the results of past moves in similar circumstances. These programs include the past outcomes when calculating the next move. Whatever the complexity of the program, each action (move) is still a response to the present environment and the past history of reinforcement (winning).

Similarly, no special knowledge of the workings of the human body is required for me to avoid intentional idioms when discussing its actions. A satisfactory scientific account can be constructed from a knowledge of present circumstances and consequences of behavior in similar circumstances in the past.

Selection by Consequences   Inner purpose is no more necessary or helpful to understanding the behavior of a person than to understanding the behavior of the chess-playing computer. Whether I am hunting for a book or struggling up a mountain, I have hunted before and I have struggled before; the past consequences of those actions in those situations determine that those actions (action categories) will be likely to occur again in those situations (situation categories).

Selection by consequences invariably implies history. Over time, successful outcomes (reinforcement) make some actions more likely, and unsuccessful outcomes (nonreinforcement or punishment) make other actions less likely. Gradually, the behavior that occurs in such circumstances is shaped—transformed and elaborated. Although neurophysiologists know little about the mechanism by which the accumulation of successes and failures changes behavior, behavior analysts can study the dependence of behavior on that accumulation. What history of reinforcement determines that a person will look for something that is lacking? What difference in history determines that one person will climb a mountain while another will photograph it?

Creativity   What history of reinforcement leads someone to write poetry? Critics of behaviorism often point to such creative activity as an insurmountable challenge. When an artist paints a picture or a poet writes a poem, the whole point of the activity is to do something never done before, something original. Seemingly, past consequences could never account for works of art, because each work is unique and novel. The originality of each work seems to suggest that somehow the artist is free of the past, that some inner purpose guides the work.

By emphasizing the uniqueness and novelty of each work, such a view obscures an equally obvious fact about creative activity: the relatedness of an artist's works to one another. How do I tell that this painting is by Monet and that one by Renoir? No two paintings by the same artist are exactly alike, but paintings by Renoir resemble one another more than they resemble paintings by Monet. An expert, who is especially familiar with an artist's works, can usually tell a painting by that artist from even a careful forgery.

No painter, poet, or composer ever created a work of art in a vacuum. Each new poem may be unique, but it also shares much in common with the poet's previous efforts and stems from a long line of poetry writing by the poet. Along the way, poetry writing was maintained by at least occasional reinforcement—praise, approval, money—from family, friends, and other audiences. In other words, poetry writing, like any operant behavior, is shaped by its history of reinforcement.

Seen in the context of all the artist's works, the uniqueness of the individual works appears as variation within an action category. Mozart composed many symphonies—composing symphonies was a prominent activity in his life—but to say that each symphony represented a unique creative act would be like saying that each time a rat presses a lever in a new way the rat has engaged in a unique creative act. Within the category of symphony composing, each symphony may be unique, just as within the category of lever pressing each press is unique.

This sort of variation within a category occurs in the behavior of inanimate systems, too. Each snowflake is unique, just as each lever-press is unique. If one were to insist that some special force (genius or free will) lies behind each new press or each new work of art, one would have to allow that such a force lies behind each new snowflake. It seems absurd to suggest that clouds possess genius or free will. Logically, it is equally absurd to insist that human creativity can be explained only by genius or free will. At the least, we can conclude that if such a force is unnecessary to explain snowflakes, it is unnecessary to explain art.

A composer differs from a cloud or a rat in that people say the composer creates something new *on purpose*. Creative activity aims for novelty. This means that each new work is composed with an eye toward those before it. The earlier works set a context in which the new work may resemble them, but not so much as to be the "same old thing." Monet did a series of paintings of the same hayricks at different times of day: the color scheme of each painting sets it apart from the others. Seen in relation to earlier works, being creative "on purpose" requires no postulated inner purpose; it requires only that variation within the category depend partly on work that has gone before (i.e., that has been part of the history). Viewed in this light, porpoises and rats have been trained to be creative "on purpose." Karen Pryor and her associates at Sea Life Park in Hawaii arranged that reinforcement was available only for a new response (trick)—something the porpoise had never done before. Within a few days, new tricks begin to appear with regularity. The researchers reported that one porpoise, Malia,

> began emitting an unprecedented range of behaviors, including aerial flips, gliding with the tail out of the water, and "skidding" on the tank floor, some of which were as complex as responses normally produced by shaping techniques, and many of which were quite unlike anything seen in Malia or any other porpoise by Sea Life Park staff. It appeared that the trainer's criterion, "only those actions will be reinforced which have not been reinforced previously," was met by Malia with the presentation of complete patterns of gross body movement in which novelty was an intrinsic factor (Pryor, Haag, & O'Reilly, 1969, p. 653).

My colleague Tony Nevin and some undergraduates at our university used a similar criterion to train rats on a tabletop on which several objects—a box, a ramp, a little swing, a toy truck—were placed. The experimenters reinforced actions with respect to the objects that they had never seen before. Soon the rats began to display novel responses to the objects. Should we conclude from these observations that porpoises and rats possess creative genius?

Novelty may be reinforceable because past behavior can set a context for present behavior. We remember what we have done previously, and that may incline us to behave either similarly or differently, depending on what is reinforced. Having failed to find *Moby Dick* at one bookstore, you go to a new one. One need postulate an inner purpose to explain the novelty no more for you or Monet than for the porpoise or the rat.

■ Purpose as Feeling: Self-Reports

The third way in which people talk about purpose is as part of private experience. When we speak of the purposes of others, we can say nothing of private events, but when we speak of our own purposes, it seems we are referring to something present and private. Every day we ask one another questions about purposes and reply to one another as if the questions were perfectly reasonable. "Did you intend to make Zack feel badly?" "No, I was only trying to help." Such self-reports seem to say that my intentions are part of my experience of my behavior ("trying to help"). How can I be so sure? We commonly use the verb *feel* in this context, as when I say, "I feel like having some ice cream" or "I feel like taking a walk." What do I "feel"? What am I talking about?

Talking About the Future   Self-reports of purpose present a challenge to scientific explanation because they seem to talk about the future. What do I mean when I say I want to go to the beach tomorrow? Since being at the beach lies in the future and may never happen, one looks instead for something in the present to account for my saying this now. If I know what I want, does that mean some inner feeling is talking to me?

Sometimes private cues to self-reports of intention are obvious. If my stomach is growling or my mouth is parched, I may report that I feel like eating or drinking. Other times the cues are less clear. I might find it difficult to say just why I feel like going to a movie. The cues may be no less real, but I have less experience with them than with a growling stomach and a parched mouth.

Some of the cues to intentional self-reports may be public. If I cut myself badly, I may say, "I want to go to the hospital." Other people can see the cut and understand the statement without bothering about any private events. I may say, "It's Friday night, and I feel like a movie." To other people, the connection is obvious.

The set of all the cues, public and private, that go together to define the context make it likely that I will make intentional self-reports like "I want," "I wish," "I feel like," and so on. What do these mean?

An intentional statement makes a prediction. "I want some ice cream" means I would eat some ice cream if it were set in front of me, and I would go to some trouble (drive to the store, clean up my room) to have ice cream. In other words, I am saying that right now ice cream would act as a reinforcer for my behavior. "I feel like taking a walk" might mean that taking a walk would act as a reinforcer for my behavior or it might mean that under these circumstances taking a walk is behavior that is likely to be reinforced. On the basis of present cues, intentional statements make predictions about what events will be reinforcing and what behavior will be reinforced. "I want to read *Moby Dick*" means I am likely to read it. "I intend to take the bus" means I am likely to take the bus.

Talking About the Past   Predicting behavior is like predicting the weather. The weather forecaster cannot be absolutely sure it will rain today any more than I can be absolutely sure I will go to a movie, but we both say, "In circumstances like these, such an event is likely." We do this on the basis of our past experience with such circumstances. In the past, when a cold front met a warm front this way, it often rained. In the past, when I had nothing else to do on Friday night, I often went to the movies. Cues in the present determine statements in the present because of their relations to events of the past.

Apart from including a role for private events, self-reports of intention differ in no way from intentional statements about others. All intentional statements, including self-reports, although they appear to refer to the future, actually refer to the past. Words like *intend, want, try, expect,* and *propose* can always be paraphrased by, "In circumstances like these in the past. . . ." When the layperson says that a rat presses a lever because it wants food, the statement can be rephrased, "In these circumstances in the past, pressing the lever produced food and food was a reinforcer." "I propose we go to the beach" means, "In circumstances like these in the past, my going to the beach was reinforced, and it is likely that your going will be reinforced as well."

In everyday speech, intentional idioms are convenient, but in behavior analysis they constitute mentalism. In everyday speech, intentional statements ease many a social interaction, but for behavior analysis they are worse than useless because they direct inquiry toward a shadow world instead of toward the natural world. Scientific explanation both of apparently purposive action and of self-reports about felt purpose relies on present circumstances coupled with past reinforcement in similar circumstances, both of which are natural and discoverable. We shall never understand or prevent an unmarried teenager's getting pregnant and going on welfare as long as we say that she felt like it or was trying to satisfy a need. Such "explanations" only divert us from understanding the history and changing the environment that would lead to the pregnancy. Blaming the teenager or her parents may be convenient, but it interferes with effective remedy.

Feelings as By-Products   When feelings act as cues for intentional statements, they constitute private events of the sensing sort that we discussed in Chapter 3. This type of private event, which includes hearing a sound and feeling a pain, includes also feeling your flesh crawl and feeling your heart racing.

Feelings as private events, however, tend to be elusive. If I say I feel afraid, I will probably be able to tell you little about private events that might make me say that. A physiologist might be able to measure bodily changes that accompany a report of feeling afraid, but the person usually has little idea of them.

We usually find it much easier to point to the public circumstances that account for the feeling. Why do I say I feel afraid? Because I am hanging from a cliff or about to go for a job interview. Why do I feel happy? Because I just won the lottery or I got the job I applied for.

Seen in the light of public circumstances, the feelings and the statements about them arise from past history with similar circumstances. Directly or indirectly, they can be traced to experience with the phylogenically important events discussed in Chapter 4. Sometimes feelings arise simply because of genetic programming. We need no special training to find standing at the edge of a cliff frightening, nor to find sexual stimulation enjoyable. Most of the time, however, feelings arise in a situation because that situation has been correlated with some phylogenically important event—a reinforcer, a punisher, or an unconditional stimulus. In other words, feelings and statements about feelings arise because of classical conditioning that occurs along with operant learning.

English includes a rich vocabulary for talking about the feelings that accompany situations in which reinforcement and punishment have occurred in the past. In a situation in which positive reinforcement is likely, we report feeling happy, proud, confident, eager, ecstatic. If we are referring to a history of negative reinforcement, we are likely to report relief. Cancellation of a reinforcer—negative punishment—results in reports of disappointment or frustration. Situations in which positive punishment has occurred in the past give rise to reports of fear, anxiety, dread, shame, and guilt.

Since feelings arise from the same history of reinforcement and punishment that accounts for apparently purposive behavior, feelings are by-products, rather than causes, of the behavior. When you finally find *Moby Dick* in a bookstore, you are happy because now you have the book, you can read it and obtain further reinforcement, such as being able to talk about it to other people and the enjoyment of good writing. Finding the book makes you happy because buying recommended books and taking recommended actions led to reinforcement in the past. You buy the book and you are happy; you do not buy the book because it makes you happy. The athlete who is happy after scoring a goal is happy because that situation has often accompanied approval and other reinforcers. It would be a mistake to say that the athlete tries to make goals because goals lead to happiness. The behavior that has often resulted in goals occurs because making a goal is a conditional reinforcer; the feeling of happiness is a by-product of the same reinforcers (approval and status) that support the conditional reinforcer. The man who feels guilty after having yelled at his wife brings her flowers, not because this will relieve his guilt, but because, in the past, bringing her flowers (and other acts of kindness) have prevented punishment and restored reinforcement—that result, of course, also dissipates the feeling of guilt.

The one type of exception to the general rule that feelings are only by-products may be the reports of the feelings. The report, "I feel happy," may be viewed as operant (verbal) behavior partly under the control of private events. Since a full discussion requires that we first address stimulus control in Chapter 6 and then take up verbal behavior in general, we shall discuss this more fully in Chapter 7.

❖ SUMMARY

Population-thinking and historical explanation go hand-in-hand because the composition of a population is explained ultimately by its history of selection—whether that be natural selection operating on a population of organisms or reinforcement and punishment operating on a population of actions. Although it is commonly recognized that events in childhood can affect one's behavior as an adult, in everyday talk there is a tendency to represent the past with fictions in the present. This is mentalism and in no way helps with the scientific understanding of the behavior.

The temptation to this sort of mentalism arises from a prejudice toward explaining behavior by causes present at the moment the behavior occurs. The way to avoid the mentalism is to overcome the prejudice and allow that events in the past can affect behavior in the present, even if past and present are separated by a gap of time. The gap in no way diminishes the usefulness of understanding present behavior in the light of past history.

Particular actions in the present belong to populations—functional categories—that have a common history because of their common function. Functional categories are often treated as units. Species and operants are examples of such units. Actions belong to the same functional category if they share similar context and consequences. Even though each particular act has never occurred before, each belongs to some functional unit that has a history of occurring in a certain type of context with certain types of consequences.

Most uses of *purpose* and related intentional idioms belong to one of three types, referring to function, cause, or feelings. When the purpose of an action is equated with its function, with its effect in the environment, no problem arises for a scientific account. When purpose is viewed as an inner cause, a ghostly representation of consequences is imagined to be present at the moment of action. A future event cannot explain behavior, but inventing an inner cause fails, too, because it constitutes mentalism and falls prey to all the problems of mentalism. A proper scientific explanation of purposive behavior, such as looking for a book, refers to the history of reinforcement of such behavior. Creative behavior, too, such as writing poetry, is shaped by a history of reinforcement for such behavior.

Self-reports of feelings of purpose or intention are cued by present environment and private events. They consist of predictions about what events are likely to be reinforcing and what behavior is likely to be reinforced. Such predictions are always based on reinforcement in the past. Although self-reports about felt purpose may seem to refer to the future, they actually refer to one's past, just as statements about another person's intentions actually refer to that person's past. When feelings act as cues to self-reports, the feelings are private sensing events. They are by-products, due to classical conditioning, of the same history of reinforcement and punishment as the operant behavior that the statements are about. They have no causal relationship to that operant behavior, although they may be part of the context that explains a verbal report of felt purpose.

❖ FURTHER READING

Skinner, B. F. (1969). The inside story. *Contingencies of reinforcement* (Chapter 9). New York: Appleton-Century-Crofts. This paper contains a summary of Skinner's objections to mentalism.

Skinner, B. F. (1974). Operant behavior. *About behaviorism* (Chapter 4). New York: Knopf. Here Skinner argues for operant behavior as an effective concept for replacing traditional, ineffective notions about purpose.

Dennett, D. C. (1978). Skinner skinned. *Brainstorms* (Chapter 4). Cambridge, MA: MIT Press. A philosopher defends mentalism and attacks Skinner's accounts of behavior in terms of histories of reinforcement. The essay is interesting for its misunderstanding of Skinner and behavior analysis.

Pryor, K. (1985). *Don't shoot the dog.* New York: Bantam Books. A nice presentation of reinforcement for everyone's use.

Pryor, K. W., Haag, R., & O'Reilly, J. (1969). The creative porpoise: Training for novel behavior. *Journal of the Experimental Analysis of Behavior, 12,* 653–661. This is the original report of the use of reinforcement to train novel responses.

CHAPTER 6

STIMULUS CONTROL AND KNOWLEDGE

All behavior, whether induced or operant, occurs in a certain context. I salivate when I sit down to dinner, and less so at other times. With such induced behavior, the context is the set of environmental circumstances that induce it (the dining room, the set table, the smell and sight of the food). Species-specific responses to food, predators, potential mates, and other phylogenically important events are induced by the contexts in which these events are likely. In the context of the silhouette of a hawk passing overhead, quail crouch; otherwise they go about their business.

Operant behavior, too, occurs only within a context. The laboratory rat trained to press a lever does so only in the experimental chamber. When placed in the chamber, the experienced rat goes immediately to the lever and starts pressing. I carry my umbrella only when the weather looks threatening. I drive to work only on weekdays.

Up to now, we have made only passing mention of context. A history of reinforcement, for example, consists not only of certain actions resulting in certain consequences, but also of those relations occurring over and over in a certain context. "Compliance with a threat" has no meaning apart from its context—the presence of the threat, the raised voice, the raised fist, the gun. To see how behaviorists can offer a scientific account of what it means to know something, without resorting to mentalism, we need to understand and then apply the concepts that behavior analysts use to explain the effects of context. As we shall see, to know something is to behave in context.

❖ STIMULUS CONTROL

Behavior changes as context changes. I stop when the traffic light is red and go when it is green. My stopping and going are under *stimulus control.* Here, *stimulus* means "context" and *control* means "changes the frequency or likelihood of one or more actions."

I often show students a classroom demonstration in which a pigeon has been trained to peck at a red key and not to peck at a green key. In the first step of training, the key is lit red, and every peck operates the food dispenser. The number of pecks required to produce food is gradually increased to 15 pecks. The second step introduces the green key, with the contingency that if two seconds go by without a peck, food is made available. At first, the pigeon pecks at the green key without success. Sooner or later it pauses long enough for the food to be presented. As it pauses more and pecks less, the pause required for food is gradually lengthened to ten seconds. At the end of training, in the demonstration, I control the color of the key by a switch on the apparatus. As long as the key is lit red, the pigeon pecks rapidly. As soon as I switch the color to green, the pigeon ceases pecking. As I switch the color back and forth, the pecking switches on and off with it.

The demonstration illustrates stimulus control. The red and green colors on the key control the pecking in the sense that changing the color changes the likelihood of pecking.

Behavior analysts usually distinguish stimulus control from stimulus-response elicitation. When the traffic light turns green, it becomes likely that I will go, but I am not compelled to go the way I am compelled to sneeze when my nose is tickled. Changing context affects operant behavior more like modulation than like compulsion.

Most important, elicited or induced behavior appears to depend on context alone (if an itch in the nose can be called a context), whereas operant behavior depends on consequences occurring in a certain context—that is, it depends on the combination of consequences and context. The itch-context by itself suffices to make the sneeze likely; in the pigeon demonstration, pecks become likely in the context of the red key because pecks produce food only in the context of the red key.

▮ Discriminative Stimuli

To distinguish it from stimuli that elicit or induce behavior, the context of operant behavior is called a *discriminative stimulus.* In the pigeon demonstration, the red and green key lights are discriminative stimuli because key-pecks can be reinforced only in the context of the red key and cannot be reinforced in the context of the green key. As a result of the difference in contingencies from one context to the other, pecks are more likely when the light is red.

Even in the laboratory, more complicated discriminative stimuli are common. Suppose I have two keys side by side for the pigeon to peck, and either key can be lit red or green. I can train the pigeon to peck at a green key when it is presented along with a red key, and regardless of whether the green key is on the left or the right, by reinforcing only pecks at the green key. In an experiment like this, the discriminative stimulus for pecking is "green key, regardless of position." In the task called *matching to sample,* the pigeon is presented with a sample stimulus (e.g., red or green) on a center key and choice stimuli (red and green) on two keys on either side of the sample key. Only pecks at the side key that matches the sample are reinforced. The discriminative stimuli controlling pecking in matching to sample are compounds, such as "red sample plus red side key" and "green sample plus green side key."

In the world outside the laboratory, discriminative stimuli are usually compound like this. If you are driving on a two-lane road and you come up behind a slow-moving vehicle, you only pass when the center line is broken on your side *and* there are no oncoming cars in the opposite lane. The discriminative stimulus for passing consists of at least three elements: (1) the slow-moving vehicle ahead, (2) the broken center line, and (3) the clear opposite lane. If any one of those elements were absent, you would be unlikely to pass. The combination sets the context; it defines the discriminative stimulus in the presence of which the operant behavior (passing) is likely to be reinforced.

In still more complicated contexts, part of the context or discriminative stimulus may have occurred some time before the occasion for the behavior. In a matching-to-sample experiment, the sample can be presented to the pigeon and turned off several seconds before the choice keys are turned on. Even though the sample is no longer present, pigeons still peck the matching side key. Human beings can bridge much longer time gaps. If I tell you on Monday I will meet you in my office at three o'clock on Friday, your behavior of going to my office depends on: (1) its being Friday, (2) its being three o'clock, and (3) what I said on Monday. All three elements are required for your going to my office to be likely to occur and to be reinforced, but one of those elements was only present four days earlier. (See Chapter 5 for more discussion of time gaps.)

■ Chains and Conditional Reinforcers

Often in life we engage in sequences of behavior, doing one thing in order to be able to do another. I put gas in the car so I can go on a trip. Sometimes the sequences are long. A college student goes to classes so she can prepare for exams, so she can succeed in courses, so she can graduate after four years.

The result of putting gas in the car—say, the gas gauge reading *full*—serves two functions. On the one hand, it serves as a conditional reinforcer for the operant behavior (putting in gas) that produces it. On the other hand, it serves as a discriminative stimulus for further operant behavior (going on the trip) that occurs only in its presence.

Similarly, in the laboratory we can train a rat to pull on a chain to turn on a light in the presence of which pressing on a lever is reinforced with food. We begin by training the rat to press the lever by arranging for each press to operate a dispenser containing food pellets. Next, we reinforce the presses only when a light above the lever is lit, turning the light off and on every minute or so. After an hour or two, the light is established as a discriminative stimulus—presses are frequent when it is on and rare when it is off. Then we leave the light off, and suspend the chain from the center of the chamber. We wait until the rat approaches the chain, turn the light on, and let the rat press the lever and get food. When the light is again turned off, the rat returns to the chain, and a pull on the chain is required before the light will turn on. Before long, the sequence of pulling the chain followed by pressing the lever is occurring regularly. The light both conditionally reinforces chain-pulling and sets the occasion for lever-pressing.

When sequences are held together by the conditional reinforcer for one action serving as the discriminative stimulus for the next, the sequence is known as a *behavioral chain*. The "links" in the chain are the actions performed one after the other. The links are joined together by the discriminative stimuli.

The whole chain is maintained by the ultimate reinforcement at the end. In our laboratory example, if the food is discontinued, both chain-pulling and lever-pressing cease. The light loses its abilities as a conditional reinforcer and as a discriminative stimulus. When American continentals lost their value as currency, they not only ceased to work as conditional reinforcers, but also ceased to serve as discriminative stimuli for the further operant behavior of going to shops. If the weather is rainy and cold, I do not put gas in the car for a trip to the seashore; the full tank only serves as a conditional reinforcer and discriminative stimulus if the weather is fine.

■ Discrimination

When behavior changes as discriminative stimuli change, behavior analysts call that regularity a *discrimination*. In the rat experiment, the change from light off to light on depended on the rat's pulling the chain, whereas in the pigeon demonstration, the pigeon's behavior in no way affected the change from red to green key. (I switched the color.) Either way, whether stimuli change in a chain or whether stimuli change regardless of behavior, the change in behavior with the change in discriminative stimuli constitutes a discrimination. When behavior shifts from working to visiting the mall as a result of the shift from being broke to having money, that is a chain and a discrimination. When behavior shifts as day turns to night, that is not a chain, but it is a discrimination.

Since discrimination means a change of behavior with a change of stimuli, every discrimination involves at least two stimulus conditions—two contexts. In the simplest laboratory example, lever pressing occurs when the light is on—one discriminative stimulus—and not when the light is off—a second discriminative stimulus. If Sarah behaves differently with her parents and her peers, we say that she discriminates between these two discriminative stimuli—parents and peers.

Every discrimination results from a history. If unlearned, it results from an evolutionary history. A baby quail behaves differently in the presence of a hawk than in its absence because of phylogeny. If learned, the discrimination arises from a history of reinforcement. A rat presses a lever when a light is on and not when it is off because lever presses have been reinforced when the light was on and not when it was off. I visit the store when I have money and not when I am broke because going to the store was reinforced when I had money and not when I was broke. In general, one type of behavior occurs in the presence of one discriminative stimulus and another type occurs in the presence of another discriminative stimulus because the one type of behavior is reinforced in the presence of the one stimulus and the other type in the presence of the other stimulus.

That is the whole explanation: Discrimination arises from history. Nothing mental—usually nothing even private—figures into the account. If we say that a rat discriminates between the presence and absence of a light, we imagine no inner event inside the rat. If, for example, someone were to say that the rat discriminates because it "attends" to the light, we might point out that the attending adds nothing to the account because it only restates the observation that behavior changes when the light is turned on and off. It is an example of mentalism.

Stimulus control means that a stimulus exerts control over behavior; that behavior changes in its presence. It would be incorrect to say that the stimulus exerts control over the rat or person, in which case the rat or person would have to engage in some ghostly mental action, like attending, to go from the stimulus to the behavior. The idea in stimulus control is that the stimulus affects the behavior directly.

Discrimination refers only to the change in behavior with the change in setting. It would be incorrect to say that the rat discriminates and presses only when the light is on or that the rat presses then because it discriminates. "The rat discriminates" or "The light is a discriminative stimulus" means only that the frequency or likelihood of lever pressing changes when the light is turned on and off. Likewise, "Sarah discriminates between parents and peers" means only that Sarah's behavior is different in the presence of those two discriminative stimuli. In other words, it would be a mistake to think of discrimination as a private event that precedes and then causes the public change in behavior. In general, discrimination is never a private event; the one exception lies in the way some behavior analysts treat self-knowledge, which we shall come to shortly.

❖ KNOWLEDGE

Everyday talk about knowledge is mentalistic. A person is said to *possess* knowledge of French and to *display* it by speaking and understanding French.

A rat is said to press a lever *because* it knows that pressing produces food. As with purpose and intending (Chapter 5), knowledge and knowing in no way explain the behavior that supposedly results from them. What is a knowledge of French that it is "displayed" when I speak French? Where is it, and what is it made of that it could cause the speaking of French? As with all mentalisms, it seems to be some ghostly thing hidden away inside, invented as an attempt at explanation, but really saying nothing beyond what is already known: that the person speaks and understands French. How does the rat know about pressing and food? Does saying it knows say anything but that in the past presses have produced food in this situation?

Rather than taking knowledge and knowing as explanations of behavior, behaviorists analyze these terms by focusing on the conditions under which they occur. When are people likely to say someone "has knowledge" or "knows something"?

Philosophers and psychologists commonly divide knowledge into *procedural* and *declarative*: "knowing how" and "knowing about." A great deal has been written about the distinction, speculating about imagined inner schemes and meanings that might underlie it. To the behaviorist, if the distinction is useful at all, it must be based on behavior and environment, externals available to any observer.

Tradition also distinguishes between other people's knowledge and one's own knowledge, particularly *self-knowledge*—one's own knowledge of oneself. Traditionally, it has seemed to many thinkers that, because I am specially privy to all my doings, public and private, in a way that I cannot be privy to anyone else's doings, there must be something special and different about self-knowledge. Indeed, it has often been asserted that only self-knowledge can be certain, because all knowledge in others can only be based on inference. Supposedly, I can know for sure that I know French, whereas Tom's knowledge of French is for me only an inference based on my observation of his speaking and understanding French. Since the division between self and other cuts across the distinction between procedural and declarative knowledge, we shall take up procedural and declarative knowledge in self and others and then turn to self-knowledge in particular.

■ Procedural Knowledge: Knowing How

Figure 6.1 summarizes the four types of knowing and the tests that lead to speaking of knowing or knowledge. The first column treats procedural knowledge. When do we say that Tom knows how to swim? When we see him swimming. The test of Tom's knowledge is whether he has ever been seen swimming. To say that he knows how to swim simply means that he does swim.

Similarly, when do I say I know how to swim? When I have swum. The test of my knowledge parallels the test of Tom's knowledge: whether I have ever observed myself swimming. To say that I know how to swim simply means that I do swim.

	Knowing How	Knowing About
Other	Does she/he?	S^D: Appropriate behavior
Self	Do I ?	S^D: Appropriate behavior

Figure 6.1 Tests of knowing how and knowing about in others and oneself.

Ryle, whose views we discussed in Chapter 3, treated knowing and knowledge as dispositions or category labels. Knowing French, for example, is a complex case of knowing how. We can list various actions that might result in saying "Tina knows French":

1. Tina responds in French when addressed in French.

2. She reacts appropriately when she receives a telegram written in French.

3. She laughs and cries at the right places in a French movie.

4. She translates from French into English and English into French.

5. She reads French newspapers and discusses the news afterward.

This list could be expanded indefinitely because the category of actions that comprises "knowing French" is indefinitely large. Once we have seen several of these actions, however, we guess that the others are possible, and we say, "Tina knows French."

The category can be thought of also as a behavioral disposition. Tina can be said to know French even when she is not speaking it, even when she is asleep. The meaning of the statement resembles the meaning of the statement "Tina is a smoker." Tina smokes only some of the time and never when asleep; she is said to be a smoker because she smokes often enough. Similarly, "Tom knows how to swim" means he swims sometimes, and "Tina knows French" means that she acts occasionally in some of the ways that are encompassed by the category "knowing French."

A person asserts "I know French" or "I know how to swim" for much the same reasons as the statements might be made about Tina and Tom. The means by which I observe myself swimming are a bit different. Whereas I see Tom swimming, I rarely see myself swim, except in a home movie, but I feel it and see the water and some of my body moving, and other people tell me I was swimming. Similarly, with speaking French: I hear myself, observe myself reading, and so on.

All these events, whether of Tom swimming or of myself swimming, stand in relation to my statements that Tom knows or I know how to swim as discriminative stimuli stand in relation to operant behavior. As the rat is likely to press the lever only when the light is on, so I am likely to say "Tom knows how to swim" only after having seen him swim. Similarly, I am likely to say "I know how to swim" only after the stimuli associated with that have occurred. Just as with the rat's lever pressing, my utterances of this sort must have been reinforced in the past by people around me. Chapter 7 shall delve more deeply into verbal behavior; for now, the point to bear in mind is that utterances such as "Tom knows X" and "I know X" are examples of operant behavior under stimulus control.

Our shorthand name for such utterances under the control of environmental stimuli will be "verbal reports." "Tina knows French" or "I know French" is a verbal report under the control of French-speaking events and arises from a long history of reinforcement for making such verbal reports.

■ Declarative Knowledge: Knowing About

Knowing about differs from knowing how only in that it involves stimulus control. When do we say, "The rat knows about the light" or "Aaron knows about birds"? The rat is said to know about the light if it responds more when the light is on. Aaron is said to know about birds if he correctly names various specimens, explains their nesting habits, imitates their songs, and so on. The conditions for these utterances are a bit different than for knowing-how utterances, because the behavior comprised in knowing about must be appropriate to some discriminative stimulus or some category of discriminative stimuli. The thing known about is the discriminative stimulus or the category.

Figure 6.1 indicates that the test of knowing about is appropriate response to a discriminative stimulus. If I claim to know about the American Civil War, you might test that claim by asking me questions like, "Why do you suppose Pickett didn't argue with Lee instead of going ahead with his charge at Gettysburg?" or "What did Grant do when Lee arrived at Appomattox Court House?" If I can give you answers that agree with other things you have heard and read, it will become more likely that you will say that I know about the Civil War. The more I talk about it, the more likely you will be to say that I know. My speeches are operant behavior under the stimulus control of you and your questions. Figure 6.1 suggests also that my original claim to know has a similar basis. My own behavior of talking and answering questions about the Civil War constitute the discriminative stimulus that controls my saying "I know about the Civil War." If I had no answers for your questions, I might be inclined to take it back or say I know a little about the Civil War. The only difference between my test and your test is that your test is probably based on a smaller sample of my behavior than my test.

All of this leaves open an important question: How do we decide whether the knowing-about behavior is appropriate? Going back to our simplest example, the rat might be said to know about the light if it presses the lever more when the light is on. The lever-presses are appropriate because they have been reinforced in the presence of the light in the past. Similarly, my talk about the Civil War in response to questions has been reinforced in the past; in particular, my correct responses were reinforced and my incorrect responses were punished. *Appropriate* turns out to mean "reinforced and not punished."

Pigeons have been taught not only to peck at a red key and not at a green key, but also to peck at slides containing pictures of human beings and not to peck at slides containing no human being. The slides containing humans constitute a category of discriminative stimuli that controls the pigeons' pecking. Since they peck only at the slides with people, we could reasonably say that the pigeons know about people in slides. We say this even though they cannot talk. Their "knowledge" is "displayed" in their pecking. They peck appropriately—they discriminate, or peck when their pecks may be reinforced and not when they will not be—and that is the context for our saying they "know about."

Once we understand that discrimination and reinforcement are the observations that set the occasion for our talking of knowing about, we have two choices. We can go on talking about knowing about while admitting that it really only means "discrimination and reinforcement," or we can stop talking that way and talk about discrimination and reinforcement instead. When trying to be precise, behavior analysts use the technical terms because mentalistic talk about knowledge usually results in confusion.

For example, some philosophers and zoologists argue that if a nonhuman creature can be shown to deceive one of its comrades, then the creature must have consciousness (Cheney & Seyfarth, 1990). The following type of example is offered as evidence. A dominant monkey and a subordinate were in a conflict. The subordinate made an alarm call that would normally accompany sighting a predator, but no predator was present. As a result, the dominant monkey fled. These theorists consider that the threatened monkey must have privately put itself in the other monkey's shoes, knowing from its own past behavior that the dominant monkey would flee when it heard the alarm call. Thus, the subordinate lied to the dominant monkey by making the alarm call even though it knew there was no predator.

What is wrong with such an explanation? The behaviorist approaches the question "What is a lie?" by asking under what conditions people are likely to say that someone is telling a lie. People try to distinguish between a lie and a mistake. It is common to say that the two differ in that a lie is made "on purpose." In Chapter 5, we saw that one way to understand doing on purpose is to relate the act to a history of reinforcement. If Shona tells you that the post office is on Congress Street, and you find it is really on Daniel Street, you guess that she simply made a mistake, because there was no reason (i.e., no reinforcement) for her telling you the wrong street. If, however, it was almost time for the post office to close, and you were rushing to mail an entry into a contest in which you and Shona were both competing, you might suspect Shona of telling you the wrong street "on purpose," because there was reinforcement for her doing so.

The first condition that makes it likely to say someone is lying, then, is reinforcement for the action. Lying is operant behavior. Probably every child lies at some time. Whether the child's lying becomes common depends on the consequences, whether it is reinforced or punished. The reinforcement for lying is often avoiding punishment ("Did you eat that cookie?" "No, I never touched it."), sometimes gaining a reward ("Have you had any sweets today?" "No, none all day." "Good, then you may have dessert.") The monkey that was said to have lied made an alarm call that was reinforced by the removal of the threatening dominant monkey.

The second condition for calling an action a lie is inconsistency. You may have no idea of a person's motives (i.e., of the reinforcers) for the lie, but if Gideon tells you one day that he saw a robbery and tells you the next day that he saw no robbery, you may become likely to say he is now lying. You will be particularly likely to say this if he has been acting in several ways consistent with his having seen the robbery—having acted fearful, having related the events, having described the robber, and so on. As we saw in Chapter 3, Ryle or Rachlin would say that all of these belong in the same functional category, "having seen the robbery." The behavior that is inconsistent with the category—the denial in our example—is called a lie. The alarm-calling monkey was probably said to have lied on grounds of inconsistency also, because the researchers had observed it to call on other occasions when a predator was present. Since the other monkeys quickly learn to ignore unreliable callers (i.e., discriminate on the basis of who is calling), the reinforcement for the deceptive alarm-calling must soon disappear.

One question remains: Where did the deceptive alarm call come from in the first place? The temptation to mentalism arises just from the absence of this information. As we saw in Chapter 5, when we are ignorant of the past history of reinforcement, it is no help to make up stories about ghostly inner origins. Most likely, the subordinate monkey made alarm calls on earlier occasions when a predator was present, and on some of those occasions the calling was reinforced by the removal of the dominant monkey. It may have been a small step to alarm-calling when the predator was absent. Further research might reveal that such progressions occur. This would explain the monkey's action without any reference to its mental life and without giving any special significance to its "lie."

■ Self-Knowledge

According to the conventional view that we grow up with in our society, discussed in Chapter 2, there is an inner, subjective world and an outer, objective world. The thrust of modern behaviorism is away from this distinction.

According to the conventional view, we might ask, "Which do I know better, my inner world or the world outside?" The question itself makes little sense to a behaviorist. Two types of response are possible. One is to paraphrase into more understandable terms: Which exerts more control over my behavior, public or private stimuli? The other is to determine the circumstances under which someone is said to have self-knowledge. We now take up each of these.

Public Versus Private Stimuli   If we ask about public and private stimuli, the first point to recognize is that only public stimuli are available to significant others in a growing child's environment. The verbal reports of a child (operant behavior, remember!) are reinforced by those significant others. It is a relatively easy matter to reinforce appropriate verbal reports, like naming objects or colors, when the stimuli are public. The child says "dog," and the parent says, "Yes, that's right, that's a dog." "What color is this ball?" "Red." "Yes, wonderful, that's right."

Special problems arise when we try to teach the child to report on private events, because these are unavailable to significant others to set the context for reinforcement. We focus earlier on those that allow reasonable guesses because of collateral public cues—pain, for example. We see the child crying. "Did you hurt yourself?" A "yes" is followed by sympathy and care-giving (reinforcement), but also by "Where does it hurt? Did you bump your knee?" Visible signs of an injury may help. If we put together training to name parts of the body with questions about hurting, we eventually manage to train the child to make verbal reports of the general form, "My X hurts."

Training someone to report on private events without such reliable public accompaniments is much harder. That is why "getting in touch with your feelings" seems to be so slow and difficult. Am I angry or afraid? Am I doing this out of love or guilt? These are difficult judgments.

Their difficulty arises, however, not from lack of information, but from uncertainty about how to interpret the information. Restated in the behaviorist's technical language, the difficulty arises not from any lack of discriminative stimuli—public, private, past, and present—but from the lack of an adequate history of reinforcement for the discrimination between one verbal report and the other. The lack of the history of reinforcement results from the lack of public cues to control the behavior of those around who might reinforce the correct verbal report. If there were public discriminative stimuli indicating whether you were angry or afraid—say, you turned red for the one and green for the other—then you would have no difficulty saying whether you were afraid or angry because people around you would have no difficulty reinforcing the correct verbal report. The actual public cues, however, are complex and unreliable. Only someone with unusual training can tell fear from anger with certainty. That is why the therapist who helps you get in touch with your feelings may be able to tell you how you feel—fearful, angry, loving, or guilty—better than you can yourself.

Thus, our situation is exactly the reverse of the conventional view: private events are less well known than public events (Skinner, 1969). Since verbal reports, like other operant behavior, depend on reliable reinforcement, and reliable reinforcement depends on public cues for others to deliver the reinforcement, verbal reports occur readily only in the presence of public cues.

Whether learned readily or with difficulty, verbal reports based partly on private stimuli can be learned only if accompanied by cues, however subtle or unreliable, that are public. As with other forms of knowledge, the public cues that control the verbal reports that constitute my self-knowledge are much the same ones that control other people's verbal reports that constitute their knowledge about me. I know that I am angry in much the same way that someone else knows that I am angry: Here is a situation in which people in general behave angrily, in which I have behaved angrily in the past, and in which I have an angry expression, a red face, and clenched fists. The only difference, of course, is that I may also be able to report angry thoughts and a tightness in my chest. Someone else, however, might notice my angry expression and red face when I cannot. The stimuli that control my verbal report about myself may differ from those that control someone else's verbal report about me, but they are neither necessarily more abundant nor necessarily more reliable.

This idea that self-knowledge depends on the same sorts of public observations as knowledge about others flies in the face of the conventional view that self-knowledge depends on privileged information unavailable to others. It has some laboratory research to support it, however. Daryl Bem (1967) and his students, for example, conducted several experiments that tested whether people's self-perceptions might be under the control of their own public behavior. In the late 1950s, a psychologist named Leon Festinger put forward a theory about self-perception called dissonance theory. Since it was supposed to explain people's attributions about themselves—that is, their responses to questions about their beliefs and attitudes, usually on paper-and-pencil tests—dissonance theory quickly became part of more general attribution theory. It stemmed from observations that if experimental subjects could be persuaded without any good excuse to say things with which they initially disagreed, their attributions would change afterward to be more in keeping with what they had said. For example, in one experiment subjects first participated in two boring tasks and then were asked to lie to a woman waiting in another room (actually a confederate in the experiment), telling her that the tasks were fun and interesting. Half the subjects were paid a dollar to do this, and half were paid $20 to do this. Subsequently, when the subjects filled out a questionnaire, the ones that were paid only a dollar rated the tasks as interesting, whereas the subjects paid $20 and a comparison group that had not lied rated the tasks as boring. According to dissonance theory, the subjects paid only a dollar changed their self-perceptions because they experienced a need to reduce the dissonance between their inner knowledge that the tasks were boring and their outer behavior of saying the tasks were interesting.

Bem argued against this mentalistic theory. He suggested that the subjects simply observed their own behavior as they would another person's and concluded that the things said by a person paid only a dollar were more likely to be true than the person paid $20. For one of his experiments, Bem created a recording that could have been one of the original subjects lying convincingly to the confederate, who responded politely. All of Bem's subjects listened to a description of the tasks and to the recording. They were then divided into three groups, one group told nothing, one group told that the speaker was paid a dollar, and one group told that the speaker was paid $20. On a questionnaire that they filled out afterward, they rated the tasks as to whether they were interesting or boring, as had been done in the dissonance study. The results were the same as in the earlier study, except, of course, the ratings (attributions) were based now on observations of another person. Bem concluded that the person who is paid less is more credible, regardless of whether it happens to be someone else or oneself.

Like other forms of mentalism, dissonance theory serves only to distract us from the ultimate explanation of judgments of credibility, our earlier social experience. Just as our demonstration pigeons discriminate between a red key and a green key, most people discriminate between people who are paid to say things and people who are not. Like the pigeons, people discriminate as a result of a history of reinforcement depending on context. Behavior in accordance with the utterances of people who are paid is less likely to be reinforced. We are more apt to act in accord with the utterances of a person who is not paid. In the terms of Ryle and Rachlin, we are more apt to display those actions that belong to the category "believing what the person said." In these experiments, it made little difference whether the unpaid liar was another person or oneself.

Self-knowledge about inner beliefs and attitudes often depends on discriminations that involve many events over long periods, but the events are more public than private. The parent who wonders whether he or she spends time with a child because of love or guilt is said to be wondering about motives. Motives, of course, are mental fictions. Where do these supposed motives come from? Discriminating whether I act out of love or guilt requires access to the history of reinforcement for the behavior. Is it a history of positive or negative reinforcement? Do I spend time with my child because in the past my wife has threatened disapproval and withdrawal of affection if I did not? Or do I spend time with my child because in the past my child and my wife have reinforced the behavior with hugs, kisses, and other tokens of affection? If we say a therapist knows the difference between your guilt and your love better than you yourself do, it is because your therapist is better able to discriminate the one history of reinforcement from the other.

Introspection   Conventional ideas about self-knowledge are tied closely to the notion of *introspection*. According to this idea, one acquires self-knowledge by looking within the theater of the mind to see what thoughts, ideas, perceptions, and sensations might be there. In Chapter 3 we reviewed some of the problems with notions like this—that the mind would have to be a nonnatural space, that it is unclear who does the looking or how, and so on.

Ryle's account of self-knowledge differs from Skinner's only in the criticisms of introspection. Ryle rejects introspection on logical grounds. "Observing a robin" is a label for the category of behavior that includes talking about the robin, pointing to it, describing it, mentioning when it moves, and so on.

When you observe a robin, you do not do two things, observe it and talk about it, because logically all that is meant by observing a robin is that you do things like talk about it. Observing a thought seems to imply just what observing a robin does not, that the observing is some second behavior distinct from the thought. If that were true, then we should be able to observe ourselves observing, observe ourselves observing ourselves observing, and so on. In other words, the idea of introspection leads to an *infinite regress,* an outcome that is generally considered absurd.

Skinner takes the more pragmatic approach of looking for the circumstances under which someone might speak of introspection. If observing a thought were like observing a robin, then we would talk about the thought as we talk about the robin. Talk about one's own behavior, particularly about one's private behavior, seems to be the occasion on which we might say someone is introspecting. Accordingly, Skinner focuses on the verbal report. The only difference between a verbal report about a robin and a verbal report about a thought is that the discriminative stimulus is entirely public for the robin and partly private for the thought. Both verbal reports are examples of operant behavior under stimulus control. We shall examine how it is possible to treat verbal reports this way in Chapter 7.

❖ SUMMARY

People speak of "knowing" and "knowledge" when a person or other creature behaves with respect to the natural world, public and private, in ways that are reinforced (are "appropriate"). Procedural knowledge or *knowing how* means that some particular behavior or category of behavior has been observed. "Tom knows how to swim" means that Tom sometimes swims. "I know how to swim" means that I sometimes swim. Statements about knowing how to speak French are similar, except that the category "speaking French" includes more varied behavior. Declarative knowledge or *knowing about* means that the behavior referred to is under stimulus control. Whereas a rat might be said to know how to get food by pressing a lever simply because it presses the lever, it might be said to know about a light if it only presses the lever when the light is on. Knowing about refers to discrimination. In the special case of knowing about in which the behavior under stimulus control is verbal behavior, a person is said to know about a subject if the person makes statements that have been reinforced (are "correct") under the control of discriminative stimuli in the environment (talking about birds with birds around), particularly stimuli provided by others, such as questions. ("What color are robins' eggs?") Self-knowledge belongs to the same general category of "talking about under stimulus control." It is scarce and weak when it concerns private events, because private discriminative stimuli are inaccessible to the person's significant others, who train the discriminations that comprise declarative knowledge. The result is the opposite of what would be expected from the conventional view: Public (external) events exert better control over behavior (are better known) than private (subjective) events.

❖ FURTHER READING

Bem, D. J. (1967). Self-perception: An alternative interpretation of cognitive dissonance phenomena. *Psychological Review, 74,* 183–200. In this article, Bem reports several experiments, criticizes the mentalism of dissonance theory, and gives behavioral accounts of self-perceptions.

Cheney, D. L. & Seyfarth, R. M. (1990). *How monkeys see the world: Inside the mind of another species.* Chicago: University of Chicago Press. This book is about vervet monkeys observed in the wild, full of mentalistic interpretations such as the treatment of "lying" discussed in this chapter.

Dennett, D. C. (1987). *The intentional stance.* Cambridge, MA: MIT Press. Dennett is a philosopher who argues in favor of mentalism and who inspired many of the mentalistic interpretations of Cheney and Seyfarth's observations of monkey behavior. See especially Chapters 7 and 8.

Rachlin, H. (1991). *Introduction to modern behaviorism* (3rd ed.). New York: Freeman. See Chapter 5 for a discussion of cognition in relation to stimulus control.

Ristau, C. (1991). *Cognitive ethology: The minds of other animals.* Hillsdale, NJ: Erlbaum. This book is a collection of essays by zoologists, psychologists, and philosophers, full of mentalistic interpretations of animal behavior and discussions about the validity of such interpretations.

Ryle, G. (1949). *The concept of mind.* Chicago: University of Chicago Press. See especially Chapters 2 and 6 on knowing and self-knowledge.

Skinner, B. F. (1969). Behaviorism at fifty. *Contingencies of reinforcement.* New York: Appleton-Century-Crofts (Chapter 8.) This article includes a discussion of introspection and self-knowledge.

CHAPTER 7

VERBAL BEHAVIOR AND LANGUAGE

Much of what we discussed in Chapters 3, 4, 5, and 6 assumed that talking is a type of operant behavior. Many people—laypeople, philosophers, linguists, and psychologists—consider speech and language to be separate and different from other behavior. Indeed, language is often said to be what separates our species from other species. Behavior analysts, however, in keeping with their reliance on evolutionary theory, seek to understand all species and all types of behavior within the same general framework. They offer an account of speech and language that cuts across traditional categories, emphasizing the resemblance of speech to other types of behavior. In this chapter, we shall see that talking is one type, and not the only type, of verbal behavior, and that the notion of verbal behavior replaces many traditional ideas about talking and language.

❖ WHAT IS VERBAL BEHAVIOR?

Verbal behavior is a type of operant behavior. It belongs to the larger category of behavior that could be called "communication," except that *communication* suggests a mentalistic theory foreign to the behavioral point of view. As we shall see, the behavioral view would either redefine *communication* or replace it with other terms.

■ Communication

When a bird gives an alarm call and all the other birds in the flock hide from the predator, we could say that an act of communication occurred. In a behavioral view, the example illustrates all that there is to communication. "Communication" occurs when the behavior of one organism generates stimuli that affect the behavior of another organism.

The conventional view holds that in communication something passes from one person to another. By its derivation, *communication* means "to make common." What is made common? An idea, a message, a meaning. Some psychologists embellish this everyday conception by adding that an idea is encoded by the sender, passed in code to the receiver, and then decoded by the receiver, who then possesses the message.

Like all mentalistic notions, the everyday idea of communication adds nothing to what we observe and keeps us from a better understanding. Where is the message? What is it made of? Who does this encoding and decoding? The message, the encoding, and the decoding are fictions of some mental world forever beyond our reach.

The calling bird behaves—moves its pharynx and lungs—and this results in an auditory stimulus that changes the behavior of other birds within earshot. Adding that the caller sends a message which the others receive cannot clarify the account. Is it any different when one person talks to another?

■ Verbal Behavior as Operant Behavior

There is a crucial difference between alarm-calling and talking. The bird's alarm call is a fixed action pattern, whereas talking is operant behavior. When a fixed action pattern generates auditory or visual stimuli that affect the behavior of others (as in defense, aggression, and courtship), that can be called communication. However, it is not verbal behavior. Even the human eyebrow flash of greeting, although it affects the person who sees it and therefore is communicative, is not an example of verbal behavior.

"Communication" is the larger category. All verbal behavior could be called communication, but the reverse is not true. Fixed action patterns depend only on antecedents (sign stimuli), whereas verbal behavior, because it is a type of operant behavior, depends on its consequences.

Speaking Has Consequences   Suppose Bob and Jane are eating dinner. Bob's potatoes lack salt, and the salt is over by Jane. Bob says *Please pass the salt.* The consequence of this utterance is that Jane passes the salt. Bob behaves—he moves his larynx, lips, tongue, and so on. This generates an auditory stimulus, which Jane hears. Bob's saying *Please pass the salt* is reinforced by his receiving the salt.

We know that Bob's utterance is under the control of this reinforcer because if he were alone, or the potatoes were sufficiently salty, or the salt were next to his plate, the utterance *Please pass the salt* would not occur. Verbal behavior, like other operant behavior, tends to occur only in the context in which it is likely to be reinforced.

The Verbal Community   Those around who hear and reinforce what a person says are members of that person's *verbal community*—that group of people who speak to one another and reinforce one another's utterances.

An experiment by Rand Conger and Peter Killeen (1974) illustrated how the verbal community works. Four people sat around a table, having a conversation about a topic of interest. Three of the people were confederates of the experimenters, unbeknownst to the fourth person, who was the subject and was told only that the experiment was about social interactions and would be videotaped. Occasionally, on variable-interval schedules, two small lights behind the subject lit up to cue the persons to the subject's left and right to say something approving like "Good point" or "That's right" at the next appropriate opportunity. The person sitting opposite the subject served to facilitate the conversation. As the schedules on the left and right varied, the frequency of these reinforcers from the left and right varied. The subjects' verbal behavior shifted as the reinforcement shifted. If the person on the right delivered more reinforcers, the subject spent more time talking to that person; if the person on the left delivered more reinforcers, the subject spent more time talking to that person.

■ **Speaker and Listener**

Skinner (1957) defined verbal behavior as operant behavior that requires the presence of another person for its reinforcement. This other person, who reinforces the speaker's verbal behavior, is the *listener*. Operant behavior such as opening the refrigerator or driving a car cannot be called verbal behavior, because no listener need be present for it to be reinforced.

The Verbal Episode   Figure 7.1 diagrams the events that go into a complete episode of verbal behavior. In the example of Bob asking Jane for the salt, the initiating context or discriminative stimulus (S_S^D) for Bob's request is the situation that he and Jane are at the table, the potatoes lack salt, and the salt is out of reach over by Jane. Bob engages in the verbal behavior of moving his larynx, tongue, lips, and so forth (B_V; the utterance is written in Figure 7.1 with brackets around it). This verbal act generates an auditory discriminative stimulus (S_L^D written in Figure 7.1 with quotation marks around it). In the presence of "Please pass the salt," it becomes likely that Jane will pass the salt. Bob's receiving the salt reinforces the verbal act of asking for it and also serves as a discriminative stimulus (S_R^D) for Bob to reciprocate in some way. He moves his larynx, tongue, lips, and so on to form *Thank you* (in brackets), which generates an auditory stimulus, "Thank you," which serves as a conditional reinforcer for Jane's passing the salt.

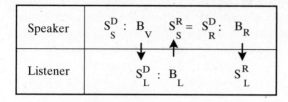

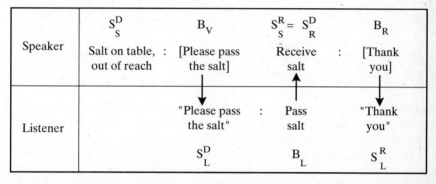

Figure 7.1 A verbal episode. S_S^D is the context for the speaker's verbal behavior (B_V), which generates a discriminative stimulus (S_L^D) that sets the occasion for the listener to act (B_L) so as to provide the reinforcement (S_S^R) for the speaker's behavior (B_V). The speaker's reinforcement serves also as a discriminative stimulus (S_R^D) setting the occasion for a reciprocating response (B_R) on the part of the speaker. This provides reinforcement (S_L^R) for the listener's behavior (B_L).

Reinforcement of Verbal Behavior   The crucial event in Figure 7.1 that makes B_v verbal behavior rather than another type of operant behavior, is S_S^R, the reinforcement delivered by the listener. If Bob obtained the salt in some other way that excluded Jane—perhaps getting up and fetching it himself—we would not call such behavior verbal behavior. For action to count as verbal, its reinforcement must be delivered by another person, the listener.

Most verbal behavior depends on social and conditional reinforcement. If Bob warns Jane *There is a tiger behind you,* the reinforcement for this verbal act comes from Jane's jumping to safety and her profuse thanks. When you and I are in conversation, we take turns as speaker and listener, my verbal acts serving to reinforce your verbal acts and vice versa. In terms of Figure 7.1, the listener's action, B_L, in a conversation is as much verbal behavior as B_V. If I say *Did you hear the news?* you hear "Did you hear the news?" and respond, *No, what is it?* I hear "No, what is it?", which reinforces my first act of asking, my further response reinforces your act of asking, and so on.

The shaping of conversational turn-taking may begin early. Catherine Snow (1977) recorded two mothers' interactions with their babies. She found that when the babies were only three months old, the mothers played listener to the babies' vocalizations. At this age, Snow observed, 100 percent of the babies' "burps, yawns, sneezes, coughs, coo-vocalizations, smiles, and laughs were responded to by maternal vocalizations" (p. 12). The mothers, of course, contributed far more to these "conversations" than did the babies, but by the time the babies were seven months old, their contributions had increased and the frequency of turn-taking increased accordingly. Here is an example that Snow recorded (p. 16):

Mother	Ann
Ghhhhh ghhhhh ghhhhh	
ghhhhh	
Grrrrr grrrrr grrrrr grrrrr	(protest cry)
Oh, you don't feel like it, do	
you?	*aaaa aaaaa aaaaa*
No, I wasn't making that noise.	
I wasn't going aaaaa aaaaa	*aaaaa aaaaa*
Yes, that's right.	

The babies' contributions increased steadily until at 18 months the frequency of turn-taking had gone up about tenfold.

Like other operant behavior, verbal behavior requires only intermittent reinforcement to be maintained. If Jane were angry with Bob, or busy with something, or hard of hearing, Bob might have to try several times before he got the salt. He might even fail altogether on this occasion, get up, and get the salt for himself. When the situation repeats itself on another day, his request will occur again. After several failures, the verbal behavior might extinguish, but probably only with respect to Jane. If Bob is at the table with Mary, he would ask for the salt. In other words, he would discriminate. Generally, verbal behavior is highly persistent and often reinforced only intermittently.

As with other operant behavior, verbal behavior requires less reinforcement to be maintained than to be acquired. For a child's first verbal acts, reinforcement is frequent and lavish. What is more exciting to a parent than the child's first words? No matter if the child says *da-ee* for *daddy, lee* for *milk, pee bur* for *peanut butter*—praise and affection are heaped on. The situation changes, of course, as the child gets older. Parents accept *da-ee, lee,* and *pee bur* in a two-year-old, but the same verbal acts in a four-year-old would be corrected and possibly mildly punished. Like much other operant behavior, verbal behavior is shaped over time by successive approximation.

Ernst Moerk (1983) studied tape recordings made by Roger Brown (1973) of a mother interacting with her daughter, Eve, who was between 18 and 27 months old. The mother–child "conversations" were extremely lopsided, with the mother uttering four or five sentences for every utterance of the child. Moerk estimated that Eve's mother generated more than 20,000 model sentences every day. At about 18 months of age, Eve responded to her mother's talk by imitating parts of it. Her mother would say something like, "Now you can have a cookie. Do you want a cookie?" Eve would respond *cookie,* which her mother would reinforce with comments like "That's right, you want a cookie" and with giving her a cookie.

Human children appear to be so constructed as to be likely to imitate speech sounds they hear from significant others. Between that genetically pro-grammed predisposition and the reinforcement provided by these significant others as listeners, verbal behavior is acquired and shaped.

The Listener's Role For the child learning to speak and for the adult speaking fluently, the listener plays a crucial role. Without listeners, or the verbal community, verbal behavior could not be acquired. As listeners, Snow's mothers massively reinforced every vocalization of their babies. The babies, on their part, provided reinforcement for the mothers' vocalizations; although they were just beginners, they were starting to play the role of listener. Each of us, growing up and partaking of the culture shared by those around us, learns to be a listener.

We learn, in other words, to respond to the heard utterances of others as verbal discriminative stimuli. We discriminate between vocalizations and noises and between one vocalization and another. By the age of 18 months, a child normally behaves differently to "Would you like a cookie?" and "Would you like some juice?"

Our actions as listeners provide reinforcement for the utterances of speakers around us. We frequently do this unconsciously; it would be a rare listener who would report "I am reinforcing this speaker's verbal behavior." However, we might be said to do it "on purpose," in the sense developed in Chapter 5, that our behavior as listeners is shaped and maintained by reinforcement—that is, arises from a history of reinforcement.

Along with speaking, listening is frequently and lavishly reinforced in small children. In the studies by Snow and Moerk, when the mothers responded to the infants' vocalizations, the mothers were reinforcing both speaker-behavior and listener-behavior because the children spoke in the context of hearing whatever their mothers had just said.

As time goes on, differential reinforcement refines the child's listening (i.e., the child's responding appropriately in a verbal context). A parent says "Pick up the red ball," and when the child picks up the red ball rather than one of another color, delight, praise, and affection follow. Thus our listener-behavior is reinforced and shaped. The teenager is admonished to "listen when I talk to you" and eventually learns to give those signs of truly listening: making eye contact, nodding, smiling, and so on. These signs, along with the results of the listener's other actions, such as picking up the red ball or passing the salt, reinforce the speaker's behavior, but the listener's actions must be reinforced to be maintained just as much as the speaker's actions. Hence the all-important "thank you" (S_L^R) in Figure 7.1.

■ **Examples**

The very notion of verbal behavior contradicts the conventional view of speaking and listening. To say there is such a thing as verbal behavior is to say that speaking and listening are not special and different from other behavior, but are continuous with it. In other words, verbal behavior is like other operant behavior.

In keeping with this continuity, examples abound of operant behavior that might or might not be called verbal. The category "verbal behavior" is a fuzzy category, one that is poorly defined around the edges. The fuzziness presents no problem because it underscores the similarity between verbal behavior and other operant behavior. Even if some of our behavior is clearly nonverbal and some may or may not be verbal, the concept of verbal behavior includes a lot of what we do. To understand the scope of the concept, we turn now to some examples that are either clearly verbal or nonverbal or are ambiguous.

The Importance of History   Suppose a stranger begins speaking to you in Russian, and you don't understand a word. There is no possibility of this behavior being reinforced. Is this verbal behavior? Are you a listener?

Even though the stranger's speaking cannot be reinforced in this situation, it can be called verbal behavior because it was reinforced in past situations by the stranger's verbal community. That it cannot be reinforced on this occasion in no way disqualifies it, because verbal behavior often goes unreinforced on particular occasions. This sort of behavior qualifies as verbal because it arises from a history of reinforcement by a community of speakers and listeners.

The answer to the question of whether you are a listener even though you cannot understand a word of Russian depends not only on a history of reinforcement, but also on perspective. From your perspective, you cannot be a listener because you cannot reinforce the stranger's behavior. From her perspective, however, you are being treated as a member of the stimulus class "listener." She will soon discover her mistake and discriminate—that is, she will go elsewhere or speak to you in another language. Her speaking to you in Russian can be thought of as an instance of generalization. As a discriminative stimulus, you look enough like a Russian listener for her behavior to occur. Your inability to reinforce the behavior insures that it will extinguish in your presence, but the initial action arose from a history of reinforcement in the presence of listeners a lot like you. From the perspective of that history, you are initially a listener, or at least a potential listener.

Sign Language and Gestures   Suppose you and the stranger share no common language, and she resorts to gestures. She points to her wrist and looks at you questioningly. You show her your wristwatch, and she nods and smiles. Do her gestures count as verbal behavior?

According to our definition, they do. Her pointing to her wrist is operant behavior, the reinforcement of which depends on your presence. (This makes you a listener, even though you may be deaf!)

According to our definition, verbal behavior need not be vocal behavior, and it can even be written. The great Indian mystic Meher Baba (1894–1969), who kept silent for 44 years, initially wrote with chalk on a slate, then spelled out words by pointing to letters on an alphabet board, and finally switched to a system of hand gestures (Purdom, 1971). All of this would qualify as verbal behavior—operant behavior that requires the presence of another person (the listener) for its reinforcement.

The best example of nonvocal verbal behavior is sign language. The silent signer acts as speaker, and the one who responds to the signs, though deaf, is the listener. A group of signers who alternately play speaker and listener roles constitutes a verbal community.

Nonhuman Animals   My cat comes to me at dinner time, meows, and rubs against my leg. He does this every day, and every day I feed him when he does this. Is my cat's meowing verbal behavior?

According to our definition, it might be. The meowing is operant behavior because it arose from a history of my reinforcing it by giving him food. It requires my presence for it to be reinforced. That would make me the listener and my cat the speaker.

However, you might disqualify my cat's meowing as verbal behavior because my cat and I cannot reasonably be called a verbal community. We never exchange our roles of speaker and listener. I never ask him for food, nor does he ever feed me. He sometimes comes when I call, but that seems too flimsy a reason to call us a verbal community.

Yet this example makes a point: The definition of verbal behavior in no way excludes nonhuman animals. Chimpanzees have been taught to communicate with humans by means of sign language. Although my cat and I may fail to qualify as a verbal community, when a chimp and a human sign back and forth, they do qualify. Just as two humans signing back and forth alternate as speaker and listener, so do chimp and human. Instances have been reported in which two trained chimps signed back and forth to each another. According to the definition, this might qualify as verbal behavior if the two chimps could reasonably be considered members of a verbal community.

Many thinkers have argued that language is uniquely human. Whether this is true depends entirely on the definition of *language*. If it is defined in terms of speech so as to exclude gestures, then of course it belongs only to humans. The definition of verbal behavior could be similarly narrowed so as to exclude nonhuman animals. Such definitions, however, would deny language and verbal behavior to signers. The present definition, by requiring that speaker and listener be able to exchange roles, rules out trivial cases like my cat and me, but because it includes gestures, allows the possibility of verbal behavior in nonhumans.

The human species is unique—every species is unique—not because of any particular characteristic, but because of a unique combination. By definition, no other species can share the whole constellation of characteristics that make us human, but any one of the characteristics can be shared with another species. From the perspective of evolutionary theory, humans are one species among many (and not necessarily superior to any other species) and are not divided by some insuperable barrier from "the animals." The thrust of behavior analysis is away from distinctions based on species membership and toward distinctions based on relations between behavior and environment, such as operant versus induced behavior (Chapter 4) and speaker versus listener.

Talking to Myself   When I talk to myself, is that verbal behavior? Behavior analysts disagree about this. Their answers depend on whether they accept the idea that the speaker and listener in a verbal episode can be the same person.

From Figure 7.1, we see that if the same person can be listener and speaker, then the verbal behavior of the speaker, B_V, is reinforced by a change in behavior, B_L, on the part of the same person (viewed as listener). This might happen, for example, when I instruct or command myself. In driving to an unfamiliar house, I might say to myself at an intersection, *Now, here I should turn left.* If I as a listener then turn left, that reinforces the verbal act (the self-instruction to turn left), particularly if I successfully reach my destination.

My self-instruction could be said aloud, or it could be said privately or covertly. It appears possible that I can say things to myself without detectably involving the speech apparatus. Such covert verbal behavior corresponds to one use of the word *thinking,* as when someone sitting still is said to be thinking to himself or herself.

Whether covert or overt, my talking to myself would have to result in a change in my behavior (as listener) before it could be called verbal behavior. Self-instructions and self-commands (*Hold your tongue!*) qualify. Even a self-declaration, such as *That is a beautiful painting,* would qualify if I then took some action like looking up the artist's name or asking the price.

What about singing or reciting a poem to myself, as we say, just for enjoyment's sake? Would this qualify as verbal behavior? According to our definition it doesn't because no one is playing the role of listener. Reciting a poem may be reinforced by the sound produced, but the reinforcement requires no other listener-behavior on the reciter's part. We know that not all verbal behavior is vocal (sign language). Now we see that not all vocal behavior is verbal.

Behavior analysts who reject the idea that talking to oneself constitutes verbal behavior regard it as part of an extended unit of action. Such extended or molar units play a large role in Rachlin's approach to operant behavior, discussed in Chapter 3. In this view, my driving to the unfamiliar house would constitute a unitary act, a functional category. The act might occur in a variety of ways, following different routes, with or without self-instruction, but all the variations could be considered members of the same functional category. If driving with self-instruction gets me to my destination (i.e., is reinforced) more often, then I will do that more often. Most likely, I will drive that way the first few times I drive to that particular place, and as the route becomes familiar, driving without self-instruction will take over. When behavior is thought of in these molar terms, an act cannot qualify as verbal unless the listener differs from the speaker.

▇ Verbal Behavior Versus Language

Verbal behavior differs from language. The word *language,* when used in phrases like "the English language" or "American sign language," seems to be a thing. Language is often spoken of as a possession, something that is acquired and then used. The common idea that language is used like a tool raises all the problems of mentalism. Where is this tool? What is it made of? Who uses it, how, and where? How does this tool cause speech?

Verbal behavior comprises concrete events, whereas language is an abstraction. The English language, as a set of words and grammatical rules for combining them, is a rough description of verbal behavior. It summarizes the way a lot of people talk. It is rough, because people often use poor English. Neither the explanations in a dictionary nor the rules in a book of grammar exactly coincide with the utterances of English speakers.

Although talk of "using language" is mentalistic and misleading, when we say a person is doing this, that person is usually engaging in verbal behavior. Instances of "using language" that might not be considered verbal behavior, as we saw earlier, could be events like writing a book or reciting a poem to oneself. Conversely, some instances of verbal behavior, such as waving and pointing, might not be considered "using language."

Figure 7.2 illustrates the relationships among verbal behavior, vocal behavior, and "using language." Each circle represents one of the categories, and particular events can be thought of as points inside the circles. The circles overlap, so particular events can lie in more than one circle, meaning they belong to more than one category. The shaded central subset indicates those events that belong to all three categories: people speaking to other people. The areas where two circles overlap indicate events that belong to those two categories but not to the third: A person or nonhuman animal might emit cries or other sounds (vocal behavior) that could be considered verbal behavior, but would not be considered "using language." Signing would be verbal behavior and could be called "using language," but cannot be called vocal. Reciting a poem aloud to oneself would be vocal behavior and "using language," but probably would not be called verbal behavior. Finally, there are events that can be categorized in only one of the circles. An alarm call that is a fixed action pattern would be vocal, but neither verbal nor "using language." Gestures like waving and pointing are verbal behavior only. Writing a book in the privacy of one's study, an instance of "using language," is not vocal, and because no listener need be present for its reinforcement, neither is it verbal behavior.

❖ FUNCTIONAL UNITS AND STIMULUS CONTROL

Like other operant behavior, verbal behavior consists of acts that belong to operant classes that are (1) defined functionally and (2) subject to stimulus

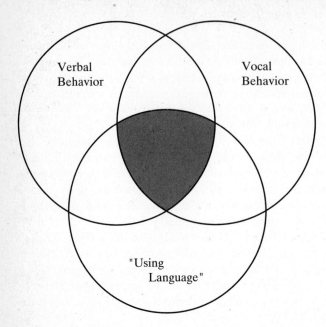

Figure 7.2 The relationships among the categories verbal behavior, vocal behavior, and "using language."

control. These two ideas set the concept of verbal behavior apart from traditional views of language and speech.

■ Verbal Operants as Functional Units

In Chapter 5, we distinguished structural units from functional units. Every event can be said to have a structure, and probably each event has a unique structure. A rat probably cannot press a lever twice in exactly the same way, using exactly the same muscles to exactly the same extent. (Even if a rat could produce two structurally identical presses, they would still be unique events because they occurred at different times.) In contrast, functional units are not particular events, but *classes* of particular events, and are defined by their effects in the environment.

Just like the rat's lever-press, each utterance has a certain structure, a certain sequence of motions of various muscles in the throat and mouth. When a novelist represents an utterance in writing, the novelist is making only a crude description of what an actual utterance is like. The reader has to imagine the timing and intonation of the utterance. Phonetic systems of notation represent utterances more accurately. For instance, the phonetic spelling of a word in a dictionary gives us some idea of how to pronounce the word. However, no representation can truly capture a particular utterance, because each particular utterance is unique. Even if you try, it is virtually impossible to make the same utterance twice in exactly the same way. Something will change—your inflection, your tone, your timing. Since we rarely even try to repeat an utterance exactly, naturally occurring verbal behavior varies a lot.

A verbal operant is a class of acts, all of which have the same effect on the listener. Just as all the structurally different ways of pressing a lever belong to the same operant because they all have the effect of getting the lever pressed, so all the structurally different ways of requesting the salt belong to the same operant because they all have the same effect on the listener—getting the salt passed. Think of all the different ways that Bob could ask for the salt: *May I please have the salt?*, *Please pass the salt*, *I would appreciate it if you would pass the salt*, and so on. To a linguist, these might seem fundamentally different utterances: the first is a question, the second an imperative sentence, the third a declarative sentence. Varied though they may be structurally, they all belong to the same verbal operant because they all have the same effect on Jane (she passes the salt). Some members of the operant may even lie outside of "using language"; it may suffice for Bob to catch Jane's eye and point at the salt. If we were to list all the structurally different ways that Bob could request the salt, the list would be long and varied, yet all variants would be instances of the same verbal operant because they would all function equivalently.

Linguists describing the structure of possible utterances point to units like words and morphemes (e.g., final -*s* on a plural noun and final -*ed* on a past tense verb). For instance, the sentence *The cats moved* is analyzed into three words and five morphemes (*the, cat, -s, move,* and -*ed*). Sentences can be broken down like this to analyze their structure, but such an analysis says nothing about the sentence's function. Structurally, *There is a tiger behind you* and *There is a child behind you* differ by just one word. They have the same pattern or *frame* (*There is X behind you*), but the two utterances belong to different operants because they have different effects. Many verbal operants include an utterance structured like this, but that structure is only one among many possible structures. Think of all the other ways I could warn you about a tiger.

Thus, just as the rat's lever-press structurally consists of many small muscle movements, each necessary to the functioning of the whole, so an utterance structurally consists of words and morphemes, each necessary to the functioning of the whole. Although necessary, however, structure tells nothing about function. Function can be understood only from circumstances and effects.

■ Stimulus Control of Verbal Behavior

As with other operants, a verbal one becomes more or less likely to occur depending on circumstances—that is, depending on discriminative stimuli. One reason that a word cannot constitute a functional unit is that the same word can serve different functions, depending on the circumstances. Think of all the different situations in which the utterance *water* might occur: I am desperately thirsty. "What is that puddle on the floor?" "What do you get when you combine hydrogen with oxygen?" "What should we add to the recipe now?" Since in each context the utterance *water* would have a different effect on the listener, in each context *water* would belong to a different verbal operant.

The relation of circumstances to the likelihood of the verbal operant is the relation of stimulus control (Chapter 6), not elicitation (Chapter 4). No strict one-to-one correspondence exists between a discriminative stimulus and a verbal operant, the way there might be between a tap on the knee and a jerk of the leg. The discriminative stimuli only modulate and make it likely that instances of certain verbal operants will occur.

Among the most important discriminative stimuli modulating verbal operants are auditory and visual stimuli generated by another person acting as speaker. Having played listener for the other person, I may play the role of speaker and generate discriminative stimuli that affect the other person's behavior.

As we noted in Chapter 6, all operants occur within a context, and the enabling effect that the context has on the operant arises from the history of reinforcement associated with that context. As with other operants, so with verbal operants. When I am lost, I ask directions because I was taught to do so, and such verbal behavior was reinforced in the past by my reaching my destination. Context can make a difference to the exact structure of my requests. In asking directions of a stranger, I am more polite than in asking directions of my brother. Asking directions in rural New Hampshire, I will be careful how I phrase my question. If I say, "Does this road go to Newmarket?" I am apt to get the reply, "That road don't go nowhere; it just sits there." I have to say, "Please tell me the way to Newmarket." Then you will either get directions or, after some thought, "No, you can't get there from here."

Like other operants, verbal operants cannot be defined solely in terms of their consequences. The context usually needs to be specified also. Requesting directions from a stranger differs from requesting directions from a familiar person. Are these two different operants because of the contexts in which they occur? If you were studying politeness theory, which concerns the way that verbal behavior depends on the person addressed, you might want to make the distinction. For other purposes, "requesting directions" or even "making requests" might be fine enough. Warning someone about a tiger differs from warning someone about a mosquito, but for many purposes "warning someone of danger" might do as a verbal operant. The "someone" and the "danger" (tiger or mosquito), part of the context, are part of the definition.

◼ Common Misunderstandings

The idea of verbal behavior emphasizes the similarity of speaking and gesturing to other types of operant behavior. Conventional views try to set language-related behavior apart, to define it as special and different. Three characteristics that have been urged as unique to language-related behavior are (1) that it is *generative*—that people constantly generate novel utterances; (2) that speaking, unlike other behavior, can refer to itself; and (3) that speaking, unlike other behavior, can refer to events in the future. Let us see if these really set language-related behavior apart from other behavior.

The Generative Nature of Language Every day you generate utterances you have never made before. Probably most sentences you speak are novel in this sense. In fact, each utterance is unique, because you cannot make two exactly the same. When we discussed novelty in Chapter 5, we saw that nonrepeatability characterizes all operant behavior. It is not that verbal behavior is varied and other behavior is fixed, as the conventional view would hold, but that all operant behavior is just as varied as verbal behavior. Each lever-press is unique, just as each request for salt is unique. Requesting salt is just as much a functional category as pressing a lever.

Critics of this view point to the importance of grammar in generating utterances. Grammar is a part of any language, and grammatical structure is often a feature of verbal behavior. But the best we can say about grammar is that it offers a rough description of the structure of some verbal behavior. Real speech is frequently (and sometimes mostly) ungrammatical. Our "sentences" often break the rules of sentence construction, and we often leave sentences unfinished.

Still, spoken English generally follows the order subject-verb-object, and there are other such regularities. But the rough structural regularities that characterize verbal behavior also characterize other behavior. A regular sequence of motions goes into each of a rat's lever-presses. Each lever-press could be equated with a sentence, and we could write a grammar of lever-presses. Only certain sequences of motions result in the lever being pressed; those would be the permissible "sentences." As before, the characteristic that is supposed to set verbal behavior apart can be seen as shared by other behavior. (We shall return a little later to a separate discussion of the notion that speakers follow the rules of grammar while speaking.)

Talking About Talking Linguists and logicians make much of statements called *meta-statements,* which refer to themselves or other statements. Meta-statements form the basis of some arguments that the ability of language to refer to itself sets it apart from other behavior. When I was a boy, my friends and I enjoyed the paradox "This statement is false." From a logical point of view, this meta-statement has a sort of magical quality because it seems to be true and false at the same time. Viewed as an utterance—as verbal behavior—however, there is nothing magical about it. It conforms to the standard English sentence frame of subject-verb-attribute. The only unusual aspect of this particular utterance is that the subject is an utterance.

To the behavior analyst, meta-statements are talk about talking—that is, verbal behavior under stimulus control of other verbal behavior. Talk about talking occurs all the time. If you didn't hear what I said, you ask me what I

just said and I repeat it. Your question plus what I said, which I heard perfectly well, constitute the discriminative stimulus for my repeat utterance. My
ability to do this derives from a long history of reinforcement for this sort of
repetition; we are trained from an early age to repeat utterances for effect and
on cue.

Repeating an utterance on request is an example of a verbal self-report,
which is verbal behavior partly under the control of one's own behavior as discriminative stimulus. In Chapter 3 we noticed that if someone can report on
his or her own behavior, we are inclined to say the person is "conscious" of it.
In Chapter 6, we noticed that one's own behavior can relate to a verbal report
in the same way as a light to a rat's lever-pressing—as a discriminative stimulus
to an operant act. You can ask me what I did this morning, and I can report *I
went to the store.* You can ask me what I said at a meeting yesterday, and I can
report *I said, "We need to plan a budget for the coming year."* Either way, my
present verbal behavior is under the control of a stimulus provided by my own
previous behavior, verbal or nonverbal.

We can report also on private verbal behavior, as when you ask me what I
am thinking, and I say *I was thinking how nice it would be to go to the beach
today.* My verbal behavior then is partly under control of a private discriminative stimulus.

Sometimes we talk about talk that never actually occurred, but only might
have occurred. We make utterances like *I felt like telling him to do it himself.*
This is a report, not on actual verbal behavior, but on an inclination toward
certain verbal behavior. It resembles reporting on a purpose or any other
behavioral tendency. It is equivalent to saying, "In the past, in circumstances
like those, I often behaved so."

We talk also about talk that never occurred but might occur now. I may
say *Let me tell you what I heard today.* In part this is a request for you to
serve as listener, and in part it is a report on my inclination to engage in the
verbal behavior of reporting on something I heard. As with other reports of
inclination or purpose (Chapter 5), although it may sound like a reference to
the future, it really arises from a history of reinforcement for such verbal
behavior in such circumstances (having heard something the repeating of
which will be reinforced by the listener) in the past.

Talking About the Future   When you talk about verbal behavior you are
inclined to engage in, it sounds as though you are talking about the future.
Since future events cannot affect present behavior, people are tempted to
invent a cause in the present—an inner purpose or meaning—and even to insist
that talk about the future proves the existence of mental images. Supposedly,
pigs in your mind cause you to say *I am going to tell you about pigs.* As we
saw in Chapter 5, such imaginary inner causes only distract us from the environmental events that led up to the utterance, your past experiences with pigs
and listeners who reinforced verbal behavior under the control of such past
experiences.

Nothing need be going on in my mind or anywhere inside for me to make utterances that seem to refer to events in the future or, for that matter, any other events that have never occurred. I have never seen a purple cow, but I have pronounced *purple* and *cow* and put adjectives together with nouns. My utterance including the phrase *purple cow* in no way requires that I have a purple cow in my mind or anywhere else. It only requires that I have a history of reinforcement for the sort of verbal behavior that people often call *imaginative*.

Similarly, if I talk to you on Monday about an appointment we will have on Friday, I need have no ghostly image or meaning in mind. Making and keeping appointments is operant behavior arising from a long history of reinforcement. You tell me you want to see me. Hearing this auditory discriminative stimulus, I write in my appointment book and say *I'll see you on Friday at 3:00.* Doing and saying this sort of thing has been reinforced many times in the past. (The reinforcement for the behavior on Monday may only occur on Friday; gaps in time were discussed in Chapter 5.)

❖ MEANING

In the conventional view of language-related behavior, words and sentences have meaning, and the meaning contained in an utterance is passed from speaker to listener. To a linguist interested in a formal analysis of the structure of English (not natural spoken English, but "correct" English), such a view might do little harm. As a theory of the behavior of speaking or verbal behavior, however, it suffers all the shortcomings of any mentalistic theory.

▣ Reference Theories

Philosophers and psychologists, trying to turn the rough everyday notion of *meaning* into a more definite theory of language, invented theories that rely on the notion of *reference.* The word *dog,* for example, whether spoken, written, or heard, is said to refer to the sort of four-legged mammal that barks. Speakers and writers are said to use the spoken or written word *dog* in place of the actual dog. Listeners and readers are said to use the heard or seen word *dog* to understand something about the actual dog. Such a view leaves completely unanswered the question of why the speaker or writer spoke or wrote the word in the first place, and what the listener or reader does as a result of hearing or seeing the word. Does it add any useful idea to the observation that one person speaks and the other does something as a result?

Symbols and Lexicons   The notion of reference suggests that the different forms of the word *dog*—spoken, heard, written, seen—are symbols for the category of actual dogs. How can all these symbols be recognized as equivalent? All the different symbols are somehow connected to something inside. Since actual dogs cannot be inside the person (available for use), some representation of the category is supposed to exist somewhere inside, and all the symbols for dog are said to be linked to this representation.

Where is this representation? It is said to be in a *lexicon*, a collection of such representations of objects and events of the real world. The speaker is said to look for the representation in the lexicon, find it there connected to its symbols, and then use the appropriate symbol. The listener is said to hear the symbol, look up the symbol in the lexicon, find it connected with its representation, and then understand it.

The mentalism of this theory is apparent. Where is this lexicon? What is it made of? What is its origin? Who does all this looking up and using? Do these complicated mental events really shed any light on speaking, hearing, writing, and reading?

The idea of reference was probably invented to explain equivalences. How is it possible for me, on seeing or thinking of a dog, to act in a variety of ways, speak or sign or write *dog*, all with equivalent effects on the listener? How is it possible for me to hear "dog," see the written word or the sign, and treat these different stimuli equivalently? Add to this variety the words for *dog* in different languages, and you may see how tempting it is to suppose that all these acts and stimuli are equivalent because they are all somehow tied to some representation or meaning somewhere inside.

It is altogether too easy to suppose that the observed equivalence arises from some ghostly inner equivalence. But where did the observed (or ghostly) equivalence come from? That question needs to be answered before we can say we understand the equivalence. No one comes into the world behaving the same way on hearing the sound "dog" and on seeing a dog, on hearing "dog" and hearing the French "*chien.*" We come to do this over time, after exposure to these different stimuli, and after a history of reinforcement for the appropriate response. Behavior analysts have begun studying the ways in which stimulus equivalence is learned in animals and children. Creatures can be trained to behave differently with two different stimuli and to behave the same. What are the conditions necessary for the learning of the equivalence? The temptation to posit some ghostly inner equivalence to explain the observed equivalence will disappear when the observed equivalence can be understood as the result of a history of reinforcement in context.

The Importance of Context Not only do reference theories offer no account of speaking, they fail even at the task for which they were invented—making sense of meaning—because they cannot take account of context. If the meaning of *water* were truly just an attachment to that sound or configuration of letters, as the idea of looking it up in a lexicon would suggest, then how is it possible for the utterance *water* to take on different meanings in different situations? It can be, among other things, a request, a question, the naming of a liquid on the floor, and the naming of an ingredient, depending on the context.

If context determines the meaning of concrete nouns like water, how much more fundamental it is to the meaning of abstract nouns and utterances composed of many words. Consider the meaning of the word *weed*. Most people in the United States regard poison ivy as a weed, but people in some Scandinavian countries consider it an attractive plant for landscaping. Whether we call it a weed depends on whether we like it or not. The word *weed* depends as much on the circumstances as it does on the plant. Many words are like this. You might capture the meaning of a concrete noun like *dog* in a list of characteristics—mammal, four legs, barks, and so on—but try doing this with *joke* or *justice*. The same story that Bob finds hilarious strikes Jane as a gross miscarriage of justice.

Reference theories have an even worse time with actual utterances containing several words. Suppose my son and I are building a brick wall. My job is laying the bricks, and his job is handing me bricks. Again and again, I ask for a brick. I say, *Hand me a brick, Let's have a brick, Brick!, I need a brick, Give us a brick,* and many other variations. Sometimes I just turn and look or hold out my hand. All of these acts have the same "meaning." You could not find the meaning by looking in a lexicon because their "meaning" lies in what the acts accomplish: getting my son to hand me a brick so that we can proceed with the wall.

■ **Meaning as Use**

As with other mentalistic terms, like *consciousness, purpose,* and *knowledge,* the term *meaning,* strictly speaking, has no place in behavior analysis. The question, "How does one know the meaning of a word?" is a pseudo-problem. It asks after the meaning as one would ask after the spelling, as if meaning were an attribute of the word. Instead of talking about meaning, behaviorists talk about the use or function of an act or utterance. Roughly speaking, that is the "meaning" of *meaning.*

Consequences and Context   Suppose I put a rat in a chamber with a lever and a chain. Pulling on the chain produces food; pressing on the lever produces water. The rat pulls and eats, presses and drinks. You could say that the "meaning" of a chain-pull is "food" and that the "meaning" of a lever-press is "water." A person in the same situation might make the sound *food* and receive food, make the sound *water* and receive water. Are these situations fundamentally different? The behaviorist says "no." The rat has had no food for a time—it pulls the chain and gets food. John has had no food for a time—he says *food* and gets food. The rat has had no water for a time—it presses the lever and gets water. John has had no water for a time—he says *water* and gets water. Either way, the use of the act consists of its consequences (getting food or water) in the context (having had no food or water for a time, being in the chamber, being with a listener).

The "meaning" of verbal behavior is its use, its consequences in the context. Why do we bother to learn the names of people we meet? So that we can get them to play listener (consequence) when we are near them (context) or so that we can converse about them with other listeners (consequence) when they are absent (context). The "meaning" of a name is the context and consequences of its occurrence.

This idea of meaning as use underlies much of our previous discussion of difficult everyday terms: *consciousness, purpose, knowledge,* and so on. For each term, we asked after the conditions (context) in which it is likely to occur. The context in which someone would emit an utterance including the word *meaning* tells us the "meaning" of *meaning.* To ask after the meaning of any term is to ask after the context and consequences of its occurrence.

As with other operant behavior, verbal behavior depends on a history of reinforcement. To say that the use or meaning of a verbal operant is its consequences in the context is to say that its occurrence depends on a history of such consequences in such contexts. My children learned to say *please* when they made a request because again and again reinforcement was available only for a request including that word.

Mands and Tacts   In everyday terms, verbal operants serve a variety of purposes. Two of the most important are to request and to inform. The verbal episode diagrammed in Figure 7.1 exemplifies a request, and it belongs to a larger category in which the verbal operant specifies its own reinforcer. Skinner (1957) named such an operant a *mand.* Mands include not only requests, but commands, questions, and even advice. The army sergeant who says *Left face!* emits a mand, the reinforcer of which is left-facing. My asking you *What time is it?* is a mand, the reinforcer of which is hearing or seeing the correct time. If a parent tells a child *You should take algebra this year,* that is a mand, the reinforcer of which is the child's taking algebra. The exact setting in which the request, question, or advice may be emitted can vary widely, and yet we still recognize it as the same mand—whether Bob asks Jane for the salt or whether he asks Tom, Dick, or Harry—because the reinforcer is the same. When the reinforcer of a verbal operant is well-specified, the operant is a mand.

Verbal operants that might be considered informative specify no particular reinforcer; rather, they occur in the presence of some particular discriminative stimulus. The whole point of the utterance *There is a tiger behind you* is the tiger; the reinforcer that the listener will provide (profuse thanks perhaps) remains unspecified. Skinner (1957) called such verbal operants *tacts.*

The warning about the tiger might have some of the quality of a mand, especially if we grant that the listener's avoiding the tiger might be a reinforcer for the speaker's utterance. A more pure example of a tact might be one person saying to another *What a beautiful day.* Exactly how the listener may reinforce this act remains to be seen; the main factors for understanding its occurrence are the setting (sun, blue sky, listener) and the history of reinforcement for such utterances in such settings.

Tacts include a wide variety of utterances. Opinions and observations are tacts. Replies to questions are often tacts: You look at your watch and tell me the correct time. What we have been calling verbal reports are all examples of tacts: *My son is wearing a blue shirt. I have a pain in my shoulder. You can get a ticket at window number two.* The first of these is a straightforward verbal report occasioned particularly by the blue shirt. The second is unusual in one way; it may be partly controlled by a private discriminative stimulus (pain in the shoulder). The discriminative stimulus for the third is more involved, because it depends on a history of events: my having gone to window number two and gotten a ticket. It is said to "point to" or "tact" (as a verb) a contingency: Going to window number two is reinforced by getting a ticket. Seen this way, the third tact is an example of a *rule,* an important concept that we shall take up in Chapter 8.

Dictionary Definitions If words and utterances cannot be understood by their inherent "meaning," then why should we bother with dictionary definitions? Let us rephrase the question. How are dictionary definitions helpful? When I come across an unfamiliar word and consult a dictionary, I do not learn the meaning of the word; I get a summary of how the word is used, usually with one or more examples and some synonyms (different words that might occur in similar circumstances or have similar effects) and antonyms (different words that occur in contrasting circumstances or have contrasting effects). All of this helps to guide my behavior as reader, listener, speaker, and writer.

Thus, dictionaries do not contain meanings. They exemplify the general way that we learn how to use words, by hearing and seeing them used. How did you learn *jump, run, talk, car,* and *baby?* Most of the words we use we never look up in a dictionary, and no one ever defines them for us. If this were not so, dictionaries would be useless, because they explain how to use a word in terms of other words that are supposed to be familiar already. When I was thirteen and wondered about the word *fornication,* the dictionary related it to terms that (I thought) I understood.

Technical Terms What is true of everyday words you might look up in a dictionary is doubly true of technical terms invented by scientists and other professionals. A term is always defined in terms of others. Sometimes a set of interrelated terms are equally familiar (or unfamiliar) yet are still all defined in terms of one another. Consider the terms *trait, gene,* and *inherit.* None can be defined without using the other two. So, too, with the terms of behavior analysis: *reinforcement, operant, discriminative stimulus.* What is operant behavior? Behavior that is more likely in the presence of a discriminative stimulus because of a history of reinforcement in the presence of that stimulus.

This interdependence of definitions only seems to be a problem if we insist that each term must have its own separate meaning, suitable for storage in a ghostly lexicon. It poses no real problem for scientists; it is simply a feature of scientific vocabularies. Interdependence of terms just means that they tend to be used together.

❖ THE BEHAVIOR OF SCIENTISTS

Since a scientist is a behaving organism, we should expect that the concepts of behavior analysis can be applied to the behavior of scientists as much as to anyone else. We can reasonably ask, "What are the activities that someone must engage in to be called a 'scientist'?" Those activities should be understandable in the light of our concepts of operant behavior and stimulus control.

❖ OBSERVATION AND DISCRIMINATION

The physicist Ernst Mach and other writers have pointed out that the activities of science are the same as some activities of everyday life, only they are done with more care and precision. Scientists are said to gather data, which is to say they make unusually careful and precise observations, often with the aid of special instruments. In non-experimental sciences like astronomy, observation is the whole of data gathering, and new observations often occur by luck. In experimental sciences, special environments are built and manipulated. An experiment consists of manipulation combined with observation.

In the technical vocabulary of behavior analysis, scientific observation is the forming of discriminations. One of the most basic activities of science is naming. The astronomer looks at a star and says *That is a red giant.* The biologist looks at a shape in a cell body and says *That is a mitochondrion.* Similarly, measurement consists of saying or writing something (operant behavior) as a result of looking at or listening to some instrument (discriminative stimulus). The chemist reads a meter and writes "32 degrees" in a notebook. The behavior analyst reads a counter and writes "528 lever-presses." Analysis of data, too, consists of forming discriminations. We manipulate numbers in the form of tables and graphs, looking for patterns, finally drawing conclusions, spoken and written. The physicist sees that the points in a graph fall close to a line and says *These numbers conform to Boyle's law.* A sociologist calculates a correlation coefficient and says *Family violence increases in times of economic hardship.*

All these discriminations share a special feature: The scientist not only makes the discrimination, based on the shape, counter reading, or pattern of numbers, but also behaves so as to produce the discriminative stimulus. This combination of actions, producing stimuli and discriminating on the basis of the stimuli produced, prompts people to call science "creative." We manipulate instruments again and again, looking for some recognizable discriminative stimulus, until finally something can be said or written: *There, now you can see it is a mitochondrion. Now it is clear that the points lie along this line, not that one. If you pick out these numbers and those, there is an increasing trend.*

Scientists are especially rewarded for making novel discriminations, which are called "discoveries." Nobel prizes are given for discriminations like *The structure of the DNA molecule is a double helix* or *This is a vaccine that prevents polio.*

■ Scientific Knowledge and Verbal Behavior

Scientific knowledge, in the terms of Chapter 6, is a type of declarative knowledge or knowing about. A scientist is said to know about something when he or she can speak (and especially answer questions) correctly in context. If a paleontologist announces the discovery of a fossil of a new species of dinosaur, other paleontologists ask many questions. How can you be sure it's not this other species? How good are your measurements? Could your estimate of the age of the fossil be incorrect? Aren't those shapes actually feathers? The paleontologist's ability to supply adequate answers determines whether the discovery is accepted. To put it in behavior-analytic terms, the scientist's verbal behavior serves as a discriminative stimulus for others to say that he or she knows something. If enough scientists begin to say this, the discovery becomes part of the common knowledge—part of the verbal behavior—of that group of scientists. Scientific knowledge is the verbal behavior of scientists in scientific contexts.

The main point here is that scientists are behaving organisms and that science is a type of operant behavior that, like other operant behavior, is controlled by context and consequences. Perhaps we should include scientists' writings as part of their knowledge. Since writing articles and books might not be called verbal behavior, we might have to say "speaking and writing." But the point would remain: speaking, writing, doing experiments, making measurements—all are types of operant behavior controlled by context and consequences.

If the paleontologist's answers to questions persuade other paleontologists, they reinforce the verbal behavior about the discovery. If too many others reject the "discovery," or fail to reinforce the verbal behavior and even punish it, then the "discoverer" may change his or her verbal behavior, and give up or take back the claim. Or, the would-be discoverer's verbal behavior may persist for a time in the face of nonreinforcement. The persistence may eventually pay off, but some scientists have gone to their graves upholding an idea that was never accepted. Why some persist and others give up in the face of little or no reinforcement for their verbal behavior is not understood, but the answer will most likely be found in individual histories of reinforcement.

Pragmatism and Contextualism   The view that scientists are behaving organisms, that science is operant behavior, and that scientific knowledge consists of the verbal behavior of scientists, all under the control of context and consequences, conflicts with the realist's view of science we discussed in Chapter 2. It says nothing about a real world, nothing about "sense data," nothing about ultimate truth.

Instead, as Chapter 2 suggested, the behavior-analytic view of science follows in the tradition of pragmatism. Pragmatists like William James hold that the truth of a scientific theory lies in its usefulness. To the behavior analyst, this translates into *the likelihood of verbal behavior depends on its reinforcement.* Talk about a flat earth persisted as long as it was reinforced by listeners and practical outcomes. It ceased when listeners ceased to reinforce it and instead began reinforcing talk about a round earth. Round-earth talk was more reinforced by practical outcomes than flat-earth talk. In other words, the round-earth theory was considered "true" when it became socially acceptable and was recognized to be more useful in practical activities like navigating a ship.

The behavior-analytic view resembles an idea that historians of science call *contextualism.* According to contextualism, scientific theories and research must be understood within the context of their time and culture. It rejects the view of science as objective and value-free. Instead, contextualists assert that the theories and even the experiments that scientists come up with depend on the cultural environment in which they live and grew up. To contextualists, it is no accident that the theory of evolution was proposed and eventually accepted at the same time that the Industrial Revolution was proceeding.

The behavior-analytic view agrees with contextualism in a general way, but goes beyond it, specifying the means by which the social environment (i.e., the verbal community) shapes science. The verbal and nonverbal behavior of scientists, like the operant behavior of other organisms, is shaped by its consequences.

❖ GRAMMAR AND SYNTAX

Linguists and cognitive psychologists interested in language have tended to focus on grammar, the rules by which words are put together into sentences. We have been calling this order (syntax) the structure of verbal behavior. Although there need not have been a conflict between the behavior analysts' interest in function and the linguists' interest in structure, Noam Chomsky (1959), an influential linguist, wrote a bitter review of Skinner's book *Verbal Behavior* that discouraged many from exploring the behavior-analytic approach. The situation has recently begun to change as some linguists are taking an interest in the functional approach (e.g., Andresen, 1991). Yet the question remains: how do behavior analysts deal with syntax?

■ Rules as Descriptions

Every language has its regularities. In English, the usual order for a sentence is subject-verb-object. In the sentence "Jane kissed Ted," were it not for the regular word order, it would be unclear who kissed whom. Many variants occur in the place of subject and object. In "The book on the table caught Jane's eye," a noun phrase of the form noun-prepositional phrase serves as subject, and a noun phrase of the form adjective-noun serves as object. The overall structure of the sentence can be seen as a higher-order regularity, the structures of the constituent phrases as lower-order regularities. Regularities like appending 's for possession, -s for plurality, and -ed for past tense would be lower-order still.

The job of the grammarian is to invent rules that generate all the sentences that are considered correct by speakers of the language. A grammar, a set of rules, like this would offer a concise description of much spoken English. Grammarians debate over the best approach to grammar. There is no one English grammar; there are several candidates, each with its own advantages and disadvantages. Chomsky invented a particularly general approach known as *transformational* grammar that can apply to almost any language. It begins with a basic pattern like subject-verb-object and then lists all the rules by which this pattern can be transformed into acceptable sentences. For example, the passive transformation would be to interchange subject and object and insert the correct form of *to be* and the word *by*. Thus, "Jane kissed Ted" becomes "Ted was kissed by Jane."

Working out possible English grammars offers an interesting intellectual challenge, and creating a grammar could be useful in teaching English to adults. However interesting or useful, though, a grammar of English remains just a description of the regularities of English.

Having listed an apparently complete set of rules for English, Chomsky imagined that these rules are innate—built in somewhere inside the person. This, of course, is mentalism: having observed regularities in behavior, the mentalist imagines rules somewhere inside the organism. Where the regularities come from remains unanswered. Skinner's idea of verbal behavior allowed the possibility that English syntax might be partly or wholly learned.

Competence and Performance   Since grammarians treat only correct English, when they turn to English as actually spoken they perceive an uncomfortable mismatch between the ideal and the acutal. Their only response to "errors" in actual discourse is to correct them. They have no way to account for them, because a grammar is in no sense a theory of behavior. Grammatical rules are norms, showing how speakers generally behave and how, in society's eyes, they ought to behave.

Grammarians like Chomsky misperceive the nature of grammar because they fall into the mentalistic trap of supposing that the rules must exist in some form somewhere inside speakers and listeners. The mistake resembles the mistake one could make with a term like "team spirit," discussed in Chapter 3, and arises from the way people speak. We say the team *shows* team spirit, and that we *follow* the rules of grammar. Both statements are misleading in that one makes team spirit seem as if it were something separate from the behavior of the team, and the other makes the rules of grammar seem as if they were something separate from the person's speaking and writing.

Supposing the rules to be separate from the behavior, mentalists like Chomsky distinguish between *competence* (the ideal, the rules) and *performance* (the actual speaking and writing). Competence is the ghostly inner ideal. It is what people supposedly know, but don't always do. The difference between competence and performance is "error."

The notion of competence presents the same problems as other mentalistic explanations, and if we apply it to other examples, its uselessness becomes clear. If we say the planets follow elliptical orbits around the sun, do we mean that each planet has inside it a competence, an ideal elliptical orbit? If a planet's orbit deviates a bit from an exact ellipse, shall we call that "error"? Here is Skinner's example: When a dog catches a ball thrown high into the air, the dog can be said in a sense to "follow" the laws of physics concerning falling bodies. Should we say that it moves to the right place at the right time because it has the laws of physics somewhere inside? Similarly, should we say of a four-year-old child who generally speaks grammatically that she has the rules of grammar somewhere inside?

Grammar and Grammarians   Another way of thinking about competences in general and grammar in particular is to recognize that they are idealized descriptions of actual performance. An idealization is always a simplification and, hence, inaccurate. The error is not in the performance, but in the simplified description. The performance is accurate; the rules may be inaccurate.

Grammarians make up sets of rules, or grammars. As long as this is an interesting and useful thing to do, the grammarians' behavior will be reinforced. No matter how precise, however, a grammar tells us nothing about how and why people come to say the things they do. Once we recognize that speaking and writing are forms of operant behavior, we can begin to explain them.

Where Are the Rules?   If the rules of grammar are not inside the speaker, then where are they? One could argue that there need be no rules anywhere, but our discussion of the behavior of scientists leads to a different idea. Instead, we can say that the rules are in the verbal behavior of the observer—the scientist or grammarian. The grammarian, like the scientist, having made observations, summarizes them in a concise form. In other words, the grammarian verbalizes a set of rules. If we listen to those rules and follow them when they are spoken by an English teacher, it is because we are trained to listen and obey. These matters we shall go into more deeply in the next chapter.

❖ SUMMARY

Verbal behavior is operant behavior that requires the presence of a listener for its reinforcement. The speaker and listener must belong to the same verbal community—they must be able to switch roles. Verbal behavior exemplifies the everyday term *communication,* a situation in which the behavior of one organism creates stimuli that change the behavior of another. Like other operant behavior, verbal behavior is explained by its consequences and context. It has consequences as a result of the actions of the listener, who is a major part of the context. Bob asks Jane for the salt because utterances of this sort were reinforced by listeners like Jane in Bob's history of reinforcement. Verbal behavior appears to begin in imitation and then is shaped by consequences such as receiving cookies and parental attention. Apart from the roles of the listener and verbal community, verbal behavior is just like other operant behavior. According to the definition, gestures and sign language, even though nonvocal, would count as verbal behavior, and non-operant behavior, even though vocal, would not count. Although specific examples might be ambiguous, these are of little importance because behaviorists aim to bring out the similarity of "using language" to other operant behavior, not to set it apart. In contrast to verbal behavior, language is an abstraction. The idea that language is used like a tool is an example of mentalism.

Verbal operants, like other operants, are functional units. The same verbal operant contains many utterances, each one structurally unique. All the utterances that belong to the same verbal operant belong to it in part because each has the same effect on the listener. In this respect, all the structurally different ways that one might ask for salt or warn of a danger could be instances of one verbal operant—"asking for salt" or "warning of danger." Like other operants, verbal operants are subject to stimulus control; they become more likely in certain contexts. As with other operants, the second part of the definition of a verbal operant, besides its effects, is the context in which it occurs. Utterances that are similar from a structural standpoint can belong to different verbal operants, depending on context. Variation in context may modulate the structural variants of the operant that are likely to occur.

Some thinkers have suggested that language use differs from other types of behavior because it is generative, can refer to itself, and can refer to the future. The generative nature of speech appears to lie in the structural regularity and frequent novelty of utterances. Since these properties are shared by all other operant behavior, they do not set language use apart. That speech can refer to itself also fails to set it apart, because this only means that one verbal operant can produce a discriminative stimulus for another. Nonverbal operant behavior can both provide and be controlled by discriminative stimuli in the same way. The apparent ability of speech to refer to the future resembles the ability of other discriminative stimuli to affect behavior after their occurrence, after a gap in time. There is nothing special about it, and it can be understood without resort to mentalism.

Like other operant behavior, verbal actions tend to occur in certain contexts; they are subject to stimulus control. If there is any meaning to the "meaning" of a verbal action (e.g., an utterance or signing gesture), it consists of the conditions under which the action is likely to occur: the context and the reinforcement in that context. Some verbal operants, called *mands,* depend more on the particular reinforcement than on context. Other verbal operants, called *tacts,* depend more on the particular context than on reinforcement. Much scientific verbal behavior consists of tacts under stimulus control of observations and data. Scientific knowledge consists of the verbal behavior of scientists. It depends both on a context created by research and on its consequences in the behavior of listeners, usually other scientists.

Grammar receives the attention of linguists and psychologists because it describes regularities in structure. A grammar consists of a set of rules that can generate all the sentences considered correct by the speakers of the language. It describes the structure of that subset of verbal behavior, but tells nothing about ungrammatical verbal behavior or about function. Some thinkers fall into the mentalistic trap of imagining the rules of grammar to lie inside the person. The rules lie, however, in the verbal behavior of those who state them.

❖ FURTHER READING

Andresen, J. (1991). Skinner and Chomsky 30 years later or: The return of the repressed. *The Behavior Analyst, 14,* 49–60. A linguist discusses the growing appreciation among linguists for Skinner's *Verbal behavior* and their movement away from Chomsky's mentalism.

Brown, R. (1973). *A first language: The early stages.* Cambridge, MA: Harvard University Press. This book describes Brown's classic study of language acquisition. He and his colleagues gathered and analyzed a large body of data from three children.

Chomsky, N. (1957). *Syntactic structures.* The Hague: Mouton. This book describes transformational grammar, Chomsky's great contribution to linguistics.

Chomsky, N. (1959). *Verbal Behavior* by B. F. Skinner. *Language, 35,* 26–58. Chomsky's review of Skinner's book. It is reprinted in several books.

Conger, R. & Killeen, P. (1974). Use of concurrent operants in small group research: A demonstration. *Pacific Sociological Review, 17,* 399–415. This is the report of the experiment described in this chapter.

Day, W. F. (1969). On certain similarities between the *Philosophical Investigations* of Ludwig Wittgenstein and the operationism of B. F. Skinner. *Journal of the Experimental Analysis of Behavior, 12,* 489–506. Day was one of the first to recognize affinities between the ideas of Skinner and Wittgenstein.

Laudan, L. (1984). *Science and values. The aims of science and their roles in scientific debate.* Berkeley, CA: University of California Press. To learn more about contextualism, consult this book.

MacCorquodale, K. (1970). On Chomsky's review of Skinner's *Verbal Behavior. Journal of the Experimental Analysis of Behavior, 13,* 83–99. The first response to Chomsky's review of Skinner's book.

Moerk, E. L. (1983). *The mother of Eve—As a first language teacher.* Norwood, NJ: Ablex. A reexamination of Roger Brown's data on language acquisition, in which Moerk finds abundant evidence in support of Skinner's idea that verbal behavior is acquired similarly to other operant behavior.

Purdom, C. (1971). *The god man.* North Myrtle Beach, SC: Sheriar Press. This biography contains information about the life and teachings of Meher Baba, the great Indian spiritual master.

Skinner, B. F. (1945). The operational analysis of psychological terms. *Psychological Review, 52,* 270–277, 291–294. Reprinted in *Cumulative record* (New York: Appleton-Century-Crofts, 1961). Contains a discussion of meaning and definition.

Skinner, B. F. (1957). *Verbal behavior.* New York: Appleton-Century-Crofts. This chapter draws heavily on this classic work.

Snow, C. E. (1977). The development of conversation between mothers and babies. *Journal of Child Language, 4,* 1–22. This article provides some data on the course of turn-taking by mother and infant up to 18 months of age.

Wittgenstein, L. (1958). *Philosophical investigations* (2nd ed.). New York: Macmillan. Translated by G. E. M. Anscombe. This chapter's discussion of meaning as use draws partly on this book, in which Wittgenstein's thinking can be seen to overlap greatly with Skinner's. (See especially pages 1–21.)

CHAPTER
8

RULE-GOVERNED BEHAVIOR AND THINKING

E very culture has its rules. A child growing up in the culture may learn to obey some of the rules without explicit instruction. I cannot remember anyone ever telling me I had to wear clothes when I went out in public. Although I cannot remember, someone may have, and probably most rules are explicitly taught.

Learning rules from a speaker-teacher requires playing the role of listener. Most children first learn to play listener—to discriminate on the basis of speakers' verbal behavior—from their parents. Later this effectiveness of verbal discriminative stimuli generalizes to others: teachers, coaches, employers, and so on. Were it not for this docility, we would never become acculturated (Simon, 1990). This chapter is about the way behavior analysts understand teaching and following rules.

❖ WHAT IS RULE-GOVERNED BEHAVIOR?

To say that behavior is "governed" by a rule is to say that it is under stimulus control by the rule and that the rule is a certain type of discriminative stimulus—a verbal discriminative stimulus. When my father told me, "You must be home for supper by 6:00," that was a rule that governed my behavior because the consequences of being late were most uncomfortable. A rule can be written as well as spoken. A "no smoking" sign in an elevator constitutes a verbal discriminative stimulus, and the person who posted the sign constitutes the speaker because part of the reinforcement for posting the sign is the effect on those who read it (listeners).

■ Rule-Governed Versus Contingency-Shaped Behavior

Only some behavior that can be described by rules can be called rule-governed in the present sense. A pigeon trained to match to sample (Chapter 6) pecks at the key with the stimulus that matches the sample key. It could be said to be following a rule, but the "rule" is only a verbal summary, a brief description, of its performance. Whether a nonhuman animal's behavior should ever be called rule-governed remains debatable, but this pigeon's behavior cannot qualify as rule-governed because no verbal discriminative stimulus is involved. In Chapter 7, we made a similar point about the rules of grammar; insofar as a four-year-old's speech is grammatical, it "follows rules," but since the four-year-old cannot state the rules, and no one else states them for the child, in the present sense its verbal behavior cannot be called rule-governed.

Although people tend to say a person or animal is following a rule whenever they notice some sort of regularity in behavior, here we use the term to mean something more specific than just any complex discrimination. We focus on discriminations that involve verbal statements of rules, like the rules of a game, because historically people's ability to respond to the verbal behavior of others was considered evidence in favor of mentalism. Behaviorists maintain that a scientific account is possible, and try to show that rule-following can be explained by the concepts of behavior analysis (reinforcement and stimulus control).

To understand rule-governed behavior, it is useful to distinguish it from contingency-shaped behavior, which can be attributed solely to unspoken contingencies of reinforcement and punishment. Strictly speaking, all behavior—even rule-governed—is shaped by contingencies. The term *contingency-shaped* means behavior that is shaped and maintained directly by relatively immediate consequences, not dependent on hearing or reading a rule (as described in Chapter 4). An incident in an episode of *All in the Family* illustrates this: Archie Bunker argues with his son-in-law Mike over the correct method of putting on socks and shoes. Mike puts a sock and a shoe on one foot and then the other sock and shoe on the other foot. Archie puts on both socks and then both shoes. Probably neither one was ever actually told to do it the way he did it; the behavior of each was contingency-shaped.

Rule-governed behavior depends on the verbal behavior of another person (a speaker), whereas contingency-shaped behavior requires no other person, only interaction with contingencies. The difference between Mike and Archie might have arisen by chance; each one's way of putting on socks and shoes was reinforced by being able to do the next activity in a chain (Chapter 4). Rule-governed behavior is talked about, directed, instructed (under the control of verbal discriminative stimuli), whereas contingency-shaped behavior arises without instruction and frequently cannot be talked about. Ask someone how he or she catches a ball, ask someone who has just told a joke how he or she managed to tell it so well, or ask someone on a bicycle how he or she succeeds in staying upright, and often the only answer you will get is, "I don't know, I just do it." He or she can demonstrate the act, but not talk about it, which is a sure sign that the behavior is contingency-shaped.

It is difficult to think of pure examples of contingency-shaped behavior, because much of our behavior begins with instruction and shifts to being shaped by contingencies once it occurs in an approximation to the final form. Beginning gymnasts are told first how to perform a stunt, to carefully place hands and feet according to instructions, execute a crude version, and then practice and practice. During practice, the behavior is shaped by unspoken contingencies between body movement and correct form until the form is correct. Many of our skills conform to this pattern: writing, driving, good manners, playing a musical instrument, and so on. The first rough approximation is rule-governed, but the final product is contigency-shaped.

In the terms of Chapter 6, contingency-shaped behavior coincides with procedural knowledge—knowing how. Once the behavior is shaped, we know how to stay upright on a bicycle, even if we cannot explain it. If the behavior and its consequences can be talked about, that is a type of declarative knowledge—knowing about. John knows about the game of chess if he can explain its rules. Rule-giving nearly always constitutes knowing about.

Of course, we often both know how to do something and know about it, as well. We may learn to talk about contingency-shaped behavior before or after it is shaped. We may learn all the rules to a game before playing it, and after having acquired skill in it, may learn how to talk about strategy in order to teach others. The incident between Archie and Mike illustrates also how readily we make and justify rules. Archie stops Mike and tells him he should put on both socks before putting on a shoe. Mike objects. Archie says, "What if there's a fire? If you run out in the street, at least you won't be barefoot." Mike replies that at least he would have one shoe on and could hop around on one foot. The making of rules is part of our business as speakers. We discussed it implicitly in Chapter 7, and we shall return to it in Chapters 12 and 13 when we discuss values and culture. Right now we are concerned with the justification of rules, because justification is verbal behavior about contingencies (*at least you won't be barefoot*).

■ Rules: Orders, Instructions, and Advice

Skinner (1953, 1969) defined a rule as a verbal discriminative stimulus that points to a contingency. When people are playing a game together, they often generate such stimuli with utterances like *If the ball touches the line, it's out* or *Four of a kind beats a full house*. These utterances are reinforced by the behavior of the listeners (agreeing the ball is "out" and giving in to four of a kind). How do these rules point to contingencies?

When talking about operant behavior, as we are now, a contingency means a relationship between action and consequence. Planting seeds leads to crops—that is a contingency. We saw in Chapter 4 that every contingency can be summarized by a statement of the form, "If this action occurs, then this consequence becomes more (or less) likely." If you plant seeds, then crops become more likely.

To say that the verbal behavior of stating a rule points to the contingency is to say that the utterance is under stimulus control by the contingency. The statement *If you turn left at the corner, you will come to the bank* reflects the speaker's experience—turning left at the corner made coming to the bank more likely—a complex discriminative stimulus. Similarly, if we are playing tennis and I tell you that the ball is out if it crosses the line, my utterance is under the control of my having hit balls that crossed the line and were called "out." The implicit contingency is if the ball is hit so as to cross the line (action), then the punisher of losing the point becomes more likely. I would rarely state the rule exactly this way, but this is a precise summary of my experience and the discriminative stimulus for my utterance.

An example of a laboratory experiment may help to clarify the behaviorists' use of the term *rule*. Mark Galizio (1979) paid college students to work in an experiment for up to seventy-five 50-minute sessions. The apparatus they worked at is illustrated in Figure 8.1 The students were told that a maximum of two dollars could be earned in a session, that occasionally a loss of five cents, signaled by the flash of a red "loss" light and a tone, would occur, and that these losses could be prevented by turning the rubber handle 45 degrees (which would flash the blue "feedback" light). In periods when losses were scheduled, one would occur every 10 seconds unless a handle-turn occurred.

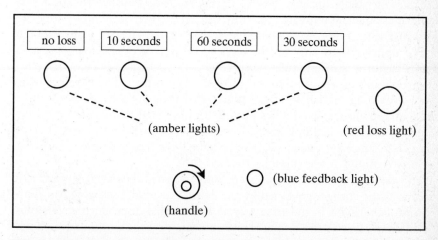

Figure 8.1 The apparatus used in Galizio's experiment. Each student sat in front of the panel shown. Turning the rubber handle 45 degrees avoided losses of money. Each completed handle-turn produced a flash of the blue feedback light. Losses were signaled by a flash of the red loss light and a tone. Each amber light signaled a different loss-avoidance schedule. The labels that sometimes served as instructions (rules) are shown in place.

Each experimental session was divided into four 12.5-minute periods, with the following arrangements: in one period, each handle-turn postponed a loss by 10 seconds; in a second period, each handle-turn postponed a loss by 30 seconds; in a third period, each handle-turn postponed a loss by 60 seconds; and in a fourth period, no losses were scheduled. In the 10-second postponement period, losses could be avoided if a handle-turn occurred at least once every 10 seconds; in the 30- and 60-second postponement periods, handle-turns were required at least every 30 and 60 seconds. The no-loss period required no handle-turning. The four periods occurred in random order. Each was signaled by one of the four amber lights shown in Figure 8.1.

In the first phase of the experiment, no additional information was given to the students, and only one out of four students displayed appropriate rates of handle-turning during the four periods: highest in the 10-second period, lower in the 30-second period, lower still in the 60-second period, and close to zero in the no-loss period. The other three students turned the handle at about the same rate in all four periods. In the second phase, instructions (i.e., rules) were added in the form of labels above the four amber lights, as shown in Figure 8.1. The label *10 SEC* meant "turn the handle at least every 10 seconds," and the *30 SEC* and *60 SEC* labels meant "turn every 30 seconds" and "turn every 60 seconds." The *NO LOSS* label meant "do not turn the handle." Two additional students began the experiment in this phase. Within three sessions, all six students displayed the appropriate rate of handle-turning in each of the four periods. All six students' handle-turning was now being governed by the labels. In technical terms, all six students displayed discriminations with respect to the verbal discriminative stimuli.

In the third phase, the labels were withdrawn. The amber lights were shuffled with respect to the four periods so the students would need to rearrange their rates of handle-turning. Two of the six students returned to turning the handle at about the same rate in all four periods. Whereas the other four discriminated with respect to the different amber lights as discriminative stimuli, the two discriminated only on the basis of the verbal discriminative stimuli. Their behavior was strictly rule-governed.

In Galizio's experiment, he was the speaker and the students were the listeners. Providing the labels constituted verbal behavior because it was reinforced by the changes in the listeners' behavior. (Had there been no effects, Galizio would have had nothing to write about and could not have published the article.) When the students' behavior came under control of the verbal discriminative stimuli, it was rule-governed.

The changes in behavior that were rule-governed, however, were exactly the same as the changes governed by the lights. A verbal discriminative stimulus controls behavior in the same way as a nonverbal discriminative stimulus. The difference lies in the origin of the control. Verbal discriminative stimuli depend on a long and powerful history of rule-following that begins soon after birth. It should come as no surprise that all the students in Galizio's experiment responded appropriately when the rules were introduced. It is striking, however, that some of them responded appropriately only to the rules.

Galizio's experiment illustrates also that experience with the contingency that occasions the rule need not be firsthand. Galizio need never have turned the handle to be able to say that handle-turns need to occur at least every 10 seconds to avoid losses. He could have said this on the basis of stimuli generated when he programmed the apparatus and when the students operated the apparatus. Similarly, I need never have played tennis to tell you that the ball is out if it crosses the line; I need only have watched other people play. The discriminative stimulus is still the contingency, only now it involves other people's actions and consequences.

There is one important type of exception: Sometimes a speaker has no experience, even secondhand, with the contingency, but is repeating someone else's utterance. Frequently we preface such statements with "I heard" or "They say." ("I heard that you can get a better price at the store around the corner.") This exception confirms our general rule, because even if I am only repeating what another speaker said, the discriminative stimulus for that speaker's behavior was experience with the contingency. Ultimately, the discriminative stimulus for any utterance we recognize as a rule is a contingency.

Everyday use of the word *rule* is narrower than the behavior analysts' technical meaning. Everyday rules fit into the category "verbal discriminative stimuli that point to a contingency," but this category also includes stimuli that would not ordinarily be called rules. For example, technically speaking many orders and commands are rules. When a parent tells a child, "Don't play down by the railroad tracks because you might get hurt," this verbal discriminative stimulus is a rule because the parent's verbal behavior producing it is under the control of (points to) the contingency "if a child plays by the railroad tracks, then the child is more likely to get hurt." When children are told to "just say no" to drugs, this rule points to the contingency "if you say no to drugs, then you are more likely to avoid the bad consequences of taking them." Often, as in this example, the rule points implicitly to the contingency because context makes it obvious. Even the drill sergeant's commands— "Attention," "At ease," "Left face," and so on—can be viewed as rules because they can be said to point to (can be said to be occasioned by) the contingency that if a soldier obeys the sergeant quickly and well, then that soldier is more likely to fight effectively in battle.

All instructions are rules. The clerical trainee is told, "Keep just one file open at a time; then you won't mix them up." When you buy a table that requires assembly, the written instructions are rules, implicitly pointing to the contingency that if you behave thus, then you are likely to have a useful table. Maps and diagrams count also. If I draw you a map of how to get to my house, that instructs you in the same way as if I told you the directions. Drawing the map constitutes verbal behavior, the map constitutes a rule, and map-following is rule-governed behavior.

Advice conforms to the definition of a rule. "Son, I think you should marry Mabel; she will make a good wife and you will be happy" is a verbal discriminative stimulus that points explicitly to a contingency between marrying women like Mabel and being happy. If the son generally follows his father's advice, the likelihood of the behavior of marrying Mabel will be increased. We pay a lot of money to brokers, lawyers, physicians, and other experts for advice because they can point to contingencies (produce verbal discriminative stimuli) that we cannot.

Offers of mutual benefit constitute rules. "If you will scratch my back, I will scratch yours" points explicitly to a contingency between your behavior and a likely consequence. As a discriminative stimulus it increases the chances that you will scratch my back.

All these examples share two features. First, since the rule implicitly or explicitly points to a contingency, it is always possible to restate the rule in the form "if this action occurs, then this consequence becomes likely." You can recognize a verbal discriminative stimulus as a rule by stating it explicitly in this form.

Second, the rule always points to some "larger concern." That is, the contingency pointed to is always relatively long-term, often perceivable only over a long time, perhaps even longer than a person's lifespan. People are advised not to smoke because of an association between smoking and illness that was perceived only gradually over several decades. Americans tend to insist on the superiority of democracy because of experience with alternatives over hundreds of years. The whole point of a rule is to strengthen behavior that will pay off in the long run according to the long-term, ill-defined, but all-important contingency pointed to. In this sense, it can be said that the person who makes the rule acts in part "for the good of" the person affected, an idea to which we shall return in Chapter 12.

■ Always Two Contingencies

Rule-governed behavior always involves two contingencies: a long-term, *ultimate* contingency—the reason for the rule in the first place—and a short-term, *proximate* contingency of reinforcement for following the rule. Delayed consequences and ill-defined contingencies tend to be ineffective: rarely does a smoker quit the habit after hearing that it may lead to lung cancer in 30 years. Something more immediate is needed to break the habit. The rule and the proximate reinforcement, both usually supplied by the speaker, get the listener to engage in the desired behavior, such as breaking a bad habit or picking up a good one. When a child follows instructions, the speaker—the parent or teacher—applies copious reinforcement. Later in life, when a person is being trained to do a job or perform in a sport, the trainer applies reinforcement for rule-following in the form of statements like "Good," "That's right," and "Way to go."

Figure 8.2 diagrams the two contingencies of rule-governed behavior—the proximate contingency on top, the ultimate contingency below. As explained in Chapters 4 and 6, each contingency includes a context (discriminative stimulus, or S^D) and a reinforcer (S^R) for the behavior. The notation $S^D:B \rightarrow S^R$ indicates that the S^D increases the likelihood of the behavior B because it sets

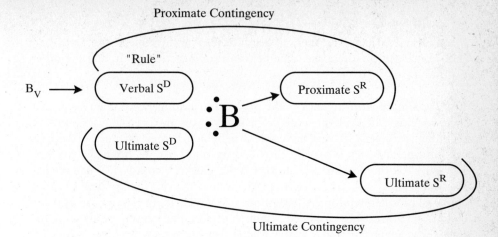

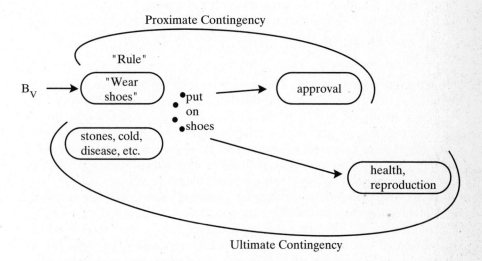

Figure 8.2 The two contingencies of rule-governed behavior. Top: Contingencies in symbols. Both contingencies conform to the pattern $S^D:B \rightarrow S^R$. In the proximate contingency, shown above, the S^D, or rule, is produced by the verbal behavior of a speaker, B_V, and controls the desired behavior of the listener, B, by virtue of its relation to the proximate reinforcement, which is usually social—that is, provided by other people, often the speaker. The ultimate contingency, shown below, is the reason for the proximate contingency because it involves consequences (ultimate reinforcement) that are important but delayed or obscure (symbolized by the longer arrow). The ultimate S^D constitutes the natural context of the ultimate contingency, the signs that should govern B if the ultimate contingency took over. Bottom: An example of the contingencies. The speaker (say, a parent) tells the listener (a child) to wear shoes when going outdoors. This produces an auditory proximate S^D (a rule), "Wear shoes." If the child puts on shoes, this results in the proximate reinforcer of approval (or avoidance of disapproval) from the parent. The ultimate contingency, which is important but obscure to the child, relates putting on shoes to the ultimate reinforcement of good health and, beyond that, likelihood of successful reproduction. The ultimate S^D, which should come to control wearing shoes, consists of conditions such as sharp stones, cold weather, presence of parasites (e.g., hookworm), and so on.

the context in which B is likely to produce ($\rightarrow$) reinforcement. Most notably, both contingencies affect the same behavior: one encourages it, and the other justifies it.

The Proximate Contingency   The proximate contingency is the reason that behavior B is called rule-governed. The speaker-supplied verbal discriminative stimulus is the rule. It sets the context in which B may produce proximate reinforcement, which is usually provided by other people, often the speaker. In Figure 8.2, the proximate reinforcer is the speaker's approval. When the listener complies with an order, request, or instruction, the speaker supplies approval or token reinforcers (e.g., money or vouchers) or removes an aversive condition (a threat). Even advice, although often called neutral, rarely is so; the father who advises his son to marry Mabel also approves when his son does so.

The proximate contingency is relatively obvious, because the reinforcement is relatively frequent and immediate, symbolized in Figure 8.2 by the shorter arrow pointing to the proximate reinforcement. Clear contingencies like this are especially important when behavior is being trained initially. Once the desired behavior is acquired, reinforcement can be less frequent and less immediate.

The Ultimate Contingency   The proximate contingency exists because of the ultimate contingency. Though ill-defined and long-term (symbolized by the longer arrow in Figure 8.2), the ultimate contingency justifies the proximate contingency, no matter how trivial or arbitrary the proximate contingency might seem, because it embodies a relation between behavior and consequences that truly matters. The relation is important because it touches long-term health, survival, and the welfare of offspring and kin.

In a word, the ultimate contingency concerns fitness. Why do people in the United States wear shoes? Why not go barefoot, as people do in so many places in the world? The practice seems arbitrary only as long as we overlook the relation to health. Protection from cold weather aside, the likely consequences of going barefoot are bruises, cuts, infections, and hookworm. Like other ultimate contingencies, the relation by itself would be ineffective, because any one person in any one year might suffer no ill effects of going barefoot; only on the average and in the long run can we perceive the insult to health. Consequently, our culture includes making and buying shoes for our children, instructing them from an early age about the need to wear shoes, and forbidding people to go barefoot in stores. If the ultimate context (Figure 8.2) takes over, shoes will be worn when dangers such as cold and disease are about. Yet people who wear shoes may have little idea of the connection to health because they need to know only what is socially acceptable (the proximate contingency). They only need to follow the rule.

When we examine rules in the light of the ultimate contingencies with which they make contact, the connection to fitness is usually clear, even if people in general never acknowledge it. We follow the rule "charity begins at home" because ultimately the welfare of children and close relatives commands top priority for advancing one's fitness. "Love thy neighbor as thyself" can be interpreted as encouraging cooperation among group members that benefits every member's fitness. Other rules, like "a penny saved is a penny earned" and "a stitch in time saves nine," concern the effective use of resources.

In Figure 8.2, the ultimate contingency is shown as having its own context (ultimate S^D) and consequence (ultimate S^R), separate from the proximate contingency. Health-threatening circumstances like sharp objects, hookworm larvae, snakes, scorpions, fungi, and thorny plants constitute the context—the ultimate S^D—for wearing shoes (B), because wearing shoes prevents injuries and illnesses that you may get by going barefoot. The reduced likelihood of injury and illness and the increased likelihood of surviving and reproducing constitute the ultimate reinforcement for wearing shoes. Children are told to "be nice to your cousins" because cooperating (B) with relatives (ultimate S^D) enhances the fitness of shared genes (ultimate S^R).

The relations to the proximate and ultimate contingencies give the verbal behavior of the speaker, B_V in Figure 8.2, the dual functions of commanding and informing. In the terms of Chapter 7, stating the rule (B_V) is a mand relative to the proximate contingency, but is a tact relative to the ultimate contingency.

Although Galizio's experiment (Figure 8.1) seems simple in comparison to real-world situations, it too conforms to the pattern in Figure 8.2. The proximate contingency was the relation between following the instructions on the labels and avoiding losses. The ultimate contingency was between following the instructions and earning close to the maximum of two dollars per session. (Avoiding excessive effort may also have been a factor.) The labels constituted the rules, and the experimental setting constituted the ultimate S^D.

The rule and the proximate contingency may be temporary. If behavior B is strengthened enough, it will come into contact with and be maintained by the ultimate contingency. Children would never learn that wearing shoes is a good thing if they never wore shoes. Once a child begins wearing shoes most of the time, the advantages of wearing shoes—the ultimate contingency—may take over. The situation is much like starting a car: The engine has to be going at some speed before it can run on its own. The proximate contingency is like the car's starter; it gets the behavior going at a rate sufficient for the ultimate contingency to keep it going. In Galizio's experiment, some of the students made the transition from the proximate to the ultimate contingency when they no longer needed the labels to tell them how to respond to the different loss contingencies. I tell my children to be honest with others in the hope that someday they will be honest without my having to tell them.

If occasions for the rule-governed behavior are too infrequent, then transition to the ultimate contingency may never occur. Perhaps that is why some of Galizio's students never made it; they might have eventually gotten free of the instructions with further training. When I buy a table that requires assembly, I slavishly follow the instructions, because this is the first and probably the only time I will assemble this table. In contrast, someone working in a factory assembling many tables every day soon ceases to consult the instructions. We have fire drills and boot camp drills so that when the ultimate S^D (fire or battle) actually arises, the appropriate behavior is likely to occur; the more realistic the practice situation, the better.

A question remains: People sometimes can say what to do but not why. If the speaker cannot verbalize the ultimate contingency—has no idea why the children should be good to their cousins—then where did the rule come from? Someone had to originate it, but only one person need ever have come into contact with the ultimate contingency, because members of a cultural group learn rules from one another. Once that person stated the rule and taught it to offspring, relatives, and neighbors, if the rule truly made contact with an ultimate contingency, it spread from person to person and group to group. Rule-making, just as much as rule-following, is an integral part of human culture. (More about that in Chapters 13 and 14.)

❖ LEARNING TO FOLLOW RULES

People exhibit a remarkable tendency to do as they are told. Sometimes we wish people would be less obedient and "think for themselves" more—especially soldiers and bureaucrats. Stanley Milgram's famous "obedience" experiment—in which people were willing to deliver near-lethal electric shocks to a stranger just on the say-so of a research psychologist—actions by Nazis in concentration camps, and actions by American soldiers in Vietnam have shown how this obedience can go too far. Despite these examples, it remains true that conformity generally pays; even the most rebellious teenager can usually be persuaded to wear sunscreen at the beach. Why do people follow rules so readily?

▧ Shaping Rule-Following

People may be so inclined to follow rules partly because they are exposed to so many different proximate contingencies from such an early age. Again and again children do as they are told and win cookies, affection, and approval. The rules are verbalized by mother, father, other family members, and then teachers. We even have games that teach rule-following, such as Simon Says and Mother May I?

As a result, rule-following becomes a functional category, a generalized skill—so much so that we unhesitatingly follow the directions even of strangers. As it generalizes, rule-following itself becomes partly rule-governed. Children are told, "Do as I say" and "Listen to your elders." We form discriminations, too. ("Don't listen to Jim, he's a liar.") In an old episode of the TV show *WKRP in Cincinnati,* one character tells another, "It's bad luck to take advice from crazy people."

In a sense, this generalized rule-following makes the world go around. Galizio capitalized on it in his experiment, assuming that the subjects would read and respond to the labels over the lights (Figure 8.1). Without generalized rule-following, the possibilities for culture would be limited indeed. With it, complex practices like sending children to public school or building jet airplanes can exist and be transmitted. (More about this in Chapters 13 and 14.)

■ Where Are the Rules?

Traditional explanations of rule-following have been mentalistic. As with grammar, rules in general are often spoken of as if they were possessions, as if people *have* them. Psychologists sometimes say rules are "internalized." As with other forms of mentalism, the rules that govern our behavior are supposedly somewhere inside, as if each of us possessed an internal rulebook in which rules were somehow recorded and could be looked up on appropriate occasions. The usual questions about mentalism arise (Chapter 3). Where are these inner rules? What are they made of? How could they cause behavior? Who looks them up and writes them down? Isn't the behavior of writing down and looking up rules just as complicated as the behavior that they are meant to explain? And so on.

If it makes sense to speak of rules as being somewhere at all, behaviorists place them in the environment. They are given, not just figuratively, but actually, in sound and sign. They are discriminative stimuli.

People are tempted to think of rules as being inside because the rule that strengthens behavior B may be absent when B occurs. There are two reasons for this. First, the gap-in-time problem discussed in Chapters 5 and 6 arises. Since the rule may have occurred earlier, there is a gap between the act and part of the context. I insist that my children be honest with me and hope that this behavior will generalize to their being honest with others. If my children are honest with teachers and friends, we might say that the children "remembered" the rule; but we need not. It is not necessary to suppose that the children state the rule publicly or even privately at the time. It is only necessary to recognize that part of the context for the act occurred at an earlier time.

Second, since control by the proximate contingency may be temporary, when the ultimate contingency takes over, the rule may be absent, perhaps for good. When people talk about rules being "internalized," they are probably talking about this transition. The students in Galizio's experiment who responded appropriately after the labels were removed might be said to have internalized the rules. The change, however, is not from an external to an internal rule, but from one external contingency to another. In Galizio's experiment, control switched from the labels to the amber lights. When my children are nice to their cousins, their cousins are nice to them back, with the result that my children continue to be nice. My children have not internalized the rule that they should treat their cousins well; instead, the natural and ultimate consequences now maintain their behavior.

❖ THINKING AND PROBLEM-SOLVING

People are especially likely to talk about someone "thinking" when that person is solving a problem. The architect who is seeking the best design for a living space or the motorist who has locked the keys in the car may "ponder" the situation, "consider" various solutions, or be "lost in thought." The mentalist sees in such situations justification for imagining complex inner processes because the person may sit still for a while, apparently doing nothing, and then suddenly act to solve the problem. Here is a challenge to behaviorists, then. Is it possible to discuss problem-solving without appealing to complex inner processes?

In Chapter 5, we discussed briefly the behavioral approach to problem-solving. Mentalistic accounts focus on the suddenness of the solution, on the "creative" or "inspirational" moment. They overlook the long history of reinforcement prior to any particular instance of problem-solving. Just as we learn to be listeners, we learn to be problem-solvers. It is an essential skill for getting along in life, and the parent or teacher who fails to help a child learn how to solve problems is considered derelict. The motorist who locks the keys in the car might call the police for help. This motorist has been instructed in this sort of solution before, and perhaps has called the police before on similar occasions of helplessness. The architect's design, too, no matter how seemingly original, derives from training, practice, and observation. No instance of problem-solving occurs in isolation; it is to be understood in the light of previous training, instruction, and reinforcement.

Although behaviorists agree on this general approach, they differ a bit in their accounts. Molar behaviorists regard problem-solving as fully integrated with previous history. We gain experience with certain types of situations and come to act in certain ways in those situations. Problem-solving in this perspective is only a step along the way, and not especially significant. Someone becomes a scientist by behaving and receiving consequences in the laboratory, in the field, in the office, and at conferences. Solutions occur to problems with apparatus, data, and theory, but that is all part of becoming and being a scientist. Such behavior is rule-governed only to the extent that it depends on previous instruction.

Skinner's (1969) more molecular account, on which we shall now focus, treats problem-solving as rule-governed in another, more immediate, sense. Since Skinner accepts the idea that talking to oneself can be considered verbal behavior (Chapter 7)—that a person can simultaneously play the roles of speaker and listener—his account relies on the concept of self-instruction: as speakers, we give ourselves rules as listeners.

▪ Changing Stimuli

As we saw in Chapter 5, situations that we identify as problems are those in which the reinforcer—the successful outcome—is apparent, but the required behavior—the solution—is obscure. The problem is removed when the solution occurs and obtains the reinforcer. When the architect sketches a design that works (matches the requirements), enormous satisfaction follows—not to mention money and praise from clients and colleagues.

While the architect is solving the problem, many sketches may cover the desk. One possibility is tried, then another and another. One sketch suggests the next, and features of several different sketches may be combined into the one that finally succeeds. The behavior (sketching) varies, but is far from random. Not only do the sketches depend on the architect's previous training and observations, but the sketches depend on one another.

To say that one sketch influences the next is to say that the first sketch acts as a discriminative stimulus for making the next. The architect makes a sketch, looks at it, concludes it doesn't work or almost works, and then tries another. All the sketches that go before may set the context for the final one. That they rule out some possibilities and suggest others means that, as discriminative stimuli, they weaken some further acts of sketching and strengthen others. The behavior of problem-solving produces stimuli that serve to change the likelihood of further behavior that might include the solution.

There is no mystery to where such behavior comes from. In the experienced architect, such "brainstorming" has been reinforced many times in the past. We discussed in Chapter 5 how discriminations in which past behavior serves as part of the context are trained in porpoises and rats as well as humans. Even though each new act may be unique, it still relates to those that went before.

When solutions need not be original to be reinforced, similar problems tend to be solved similarly as long as such solutions continue to pay off. Many psychology textbooks describe an experiment by A. C. Luchins, who had people solve a series of problems like that shown in Table 8.1. Each problem pre-

TABLE 8–1 A SERIES OF PROBLEMS USED BY LUCHINS IN HIS EXPERIMENT ON "MENTAL SET."

EACH PROBLEM PRESENTS THREE JARS OF DIFFERING CAPACITY (COLUMNS A, B, AND C). THE AMOUNT REQUIRED (COLUMN D) HAS TO REMAIN IN ONE JAR AFTER POURING WATER OUT OF IT INTO THE OTHERS.

PROBLEM	JAR A	JAR B	JAR C	AMOUNT REQUIRED (D)
1	14	163	25	99
2	18	43	10	5
3	9	42	6	21
4	23	49	3	20
5	14	36	8	6
6	28	76	3	25

sented three imaginary jars of water, with the capacities shown for Jar A, Jar B, and Jar C, and required for solution a sequence of pourings that would lead one jar to contain the amount shown in the last column. The first three problems are solved by subtracting one A and two Bs from C. Problems 4 and 5 can also be solved this way, but can be solved more simply by subtracting C from A. Problem 6 can be solved only by subtracting C from A. Luchins found that problems 4 and 5 were nearly always solved in the more complicated manner of problems 1–3, and that most of the people in the experiment failed to solve problem 6.

Mentalistic attempts to explain Luchins's results attribute them to a "mental set" or "cognitive set." Supposedly the person forms this set internally while solving the first three problems, and then the set causes the person to continue solving the problems accordingly. This set also supposedly prevents solution of the sixth problem. As we saw in Chapter 3, the behaviorist asks where the set is supposed to be, what it is made of, and how it affects behavior. The set only labels the observation that needs to be explained: the persistence of a certain pattern of behavior (here, B-A-2C). It is worse than no explanation because it gives an appearance of explanation that distracts from finding a true explanation (Chapter 3).

Behavior analysts, who seek explanations in the natural world of behavior and environment, see the situation another way. As each of the first three problems is solved, a pattern of behavior (B-A-2C) is reinforced. This pattern provides a discriminative stimulus—a verbal discriminative stimulus if the pattern is stated "B-A-2C" or a visual stimulus if the pattern is seen as a sequence of imagined actions. This discriminative stimulus controls behavior in the subsequent problems. The history of reinforcement of the B-A-2C pattern combined with the similar appearance of all the problems, ensures that for each new problem B-A-2C will be the first action to occur. Solutions that omit B (e.g., A-C) will be unlikely and will occur only after a lot of patterns involving B, if they occur at all.

The difference between Luchins's subjects, who got into a rut, and the creative architect lies in their histories of reinforcement. Problem-solving becomes stereotyped or creative and original depending on whether the same pattern is reinforced over and over or novel patterns are reinforced.

The only unusual aspect of these explanations is that the discriminative stimuli that strengthen possible solutions arise from the problem-solver's own behavior. Just as Luchins's subjects might have talked to themselves about the jar problems, the architect might also talk to himself or herself, saying things like, *What if the kitchen were here?* or *Suppose we move this bedroom upstairs?* Playing speaker, the architect is generating verbal discriminative stimuli (like the rule in Figure 8.2) that then change the likelihood of certain further behavior on his or her part as listener. The variation in action that eventually leads to the solution comes from the architect's own verbal behavior.

When I am trying to solve a problem, I may talk to myself out loud or privately. Talking to oneself inaudibly is commonly called "thinking." If my car fails to start, I may say to myself *Perhaps I should press on the accelerator.*

Whether I say it out loud or privately, the behavior generates a verbal discriminative stimulus (as in Figure 8.2) that makes it more likely I will press on the accelerator. The person who sits quietly and then "suddenly" solves a problem may have gone through a whole process of privately saying things and visualizing results, one after another. Regardless of whether the process went on overtly or covertly, it can still be understood as speaker-action alternating with listener-action.

■ Precurrent Behavior

Skinner (1969) called the speaker-action that generates discriminative stimuli *precurrent,* meaning that it goes before the solution. Precurrent action allows problem-solving (listener-action) to vary systematically rather than randomly. Although random variation may be helpful, as jiggling and twisting the key in a worn lock eventually opens the door, problem-solving is usually systematic in that attempts at solution follow patterns, particularly patterns that have worked before. I may never have been lost in this particular neighborhood before, but I have a history of consulting maps and deriving possible routes—I behave in ways that have been successful (were reinforced) in the past. The precurrent behavior involved is often called reasoning, imagining, hypothesizing, and so on. All of these share the property of generating discriminative stimuli that change the likelihood of further actions.

When you looked at the first three problems in Table 8.1, you might have said things to yourself like *The water has to be poured out of Jar B, because the amount required is larger than in A or C* and *What's the difference between B and D?* This would be precurrent behavior, because when you heard yourself, you likely behaved accordingly.

Like other behavior-analytic concepts, the idea of precurrent behavior cuts across traditional distinctions. Sometimes it coincides with what people call thinking or reasoning or brainstorming, but not always. If we accept the idea that the same person can act simultaneously as speaker and listener, then precurrent activity would conform to the definition of verbal behavior and the stimuli generated would be rules. Indeed, this almost seems obvious when we talk to ourselves out loud in attempting to solve problems. Precurrent behavior, however, can be private or public, vocal or nonvocal. When someone working on a jigsaw puzzle picks up a piece and turns it this way and that, eventually finding a place for it, that is precurrent behavior—public and nonvocal. If, when trying to decide on a color scheme for a house, I hold up color chips and imagine the house painted those colors, that could be called precurrent behavior, partly private and nonvocal.

The connection between precurrent behavior and rule-governed behavior lies in the discriminative stimuli generated. Precurrent behavior is like rule-making. We might stop short of saying they are exactly the same because, according to our definition, to qualify as a rule a discriminative stimulus must be generated by behavior under the control of (pointing to) an ultimate contingency acting as a discriminative stimulus. It may be stretching to say that a match of shapes generated by manipulating a puzzle piece should be called a rule.

The key insight gained by defining precurrent behavior is that problem-solving is like rule-governed behavior. No new principles need be invented to understand how people surmount everyday difficulties or how they act "creatively." The explanations we have considered are sketchy and require further research, but the point is made: scientific accounts of rule-making, rule-following, thinking, and problem-solving are all possible.

❖ SUMMARY

Making and following rules are two of the most important activities in human life and culture. The things called rules, whether spoken or written, are verbal discriminative stimuli. They govern our behavior in the same way that discriminative stimuli control our behavior. They are verbal because they are generated by verbal behavior on the part of a speaker. The one who follows the rule is a listener, and reinforces the speaker's making the rule. Rule-governed behavior can be distinguished from contingency-shaped behavior, which arises directly from contact with contingencies. Although people sometimes regard complicated contingency-shaped performances as rule-following, the rule being followed is really only a brief summary of the performance. In contrast, behavior analysts' more technical concept of rule-following excludes contingencies that are never spoken of, because they define a rule as a verbal discriminative stimulus that points to a contingency of reinforcement. *Points to a contingency* means "is under discriminative control by a contingency acting as a stimulus." This definition includes most examples that people would consider rules, but more besides. Requests and orders often qualify, particularly when they can be viewed as offers or threats. Instructions and advice also qualify.

The contingency pointed to (the ultimate contingency) is always long-term or ill-defined, but important in that it affects health, survival, and the welfare of children and relatives (fitness). The rule is associated with a more immediate contingency (the proximate contingency), involving reinforcers like approval and money, that helps to bring behavior into contact with the ultimate contingency. Children are taught to follow rules—to be obedient—because of ultimate contingencies, and acquiring this generalized skill is a part of growing up in a culture. When people learn generalized rule-following, however, they acquire only a discrimination—their actions come under control by a certain category of verbal discriminative stimuli from a certain category of speakers. To imagine that the rules somehow move inside is mentalism. The rules are in the environment.

If we accept the idea that talking to oneself is verbal behavior—that one person can simultaneously play the roles of speaker and listener—then it becomes possible to understand problem-solving as an example of rule-governed behavior. The person's behavior generates discriminative stimuli, often interpretable as rules, that increase the likelihood of further actions that may include the "solution"—the action that is reinforced. The behavior that produces the stimuli is called precurrent. It can be public or private, vocal or nonvocal, and it functions like self-instruction. In particular, the "thinking" that goes on during problem-solving can be understood as precurrent behavior, usually private and vocal.

❖ FURTHER READING

Galizio, M. (1979). Contingency-shaped and rule-governed behavior: Instructional control of human loss avoidance. *Journal of the Experimental Analysis of Behavior, 31,* 53–70. This article reports the experiment by Galizio described in this chapter.

Hayes, S. C. (1989). *Rule-governed behavior: Cognition, contingencies, and instructional control.* New York: Plenum. This book contains much up-to-date thinking about rule-governed behavior.

Simon, H. A. (1990). A mechanism for social selection and successful altruism. *Science, 250,* 1665–1668. The author, a well-known cognitive psychologist and computer scientist, makes the connections among docility (rule-following), culture, and fitness.

Skinner, B. F. (1953). *Science and human behavior.* New York: Macmillan. See Chapter XVI on thinking.

Skinner, B. F. (1969). An operant analysis of problem solving. Chapter 6 in *Contingencies of reinforcement.* New York: Appleton-Century-Crofts. This is Skinner's classic discussion of rules and precurrent behavior.

PART
THREE

SOCIAL ISSUES

The areas of application for behavior analysis and behavioral thinking are broad and diverse. Pick any aspect of human existence and you will find that behaviorism gives it a new perspective. Politics, government, law, education, economics, international relations, and environmentalism all take on a fresh appearance.

Our social problems are behavioral problems. They all concern getting people to behave better—to govern well, to obey the law, to learn in school, to recycle trash. How should we get people to behave appropriately, and what is appropriate behavior, anyway? Traditional approaches to these thorny questions have almost always been mentalistic and thus of little help. Can behavior analysts do better?

Part Three offers few definite answers, but instead offers a fresh approach—the behavioral approach. It aims to demonstrate that behavior analysis can help solve the world's problems. The absence of simple or definite solutions need discourage no one, for behavioral thinking allows us to frame our problems in ways that can lead to solutions. Half the work of solving a problem is seeing it in the right terms. Trying to change behavior without the concepts of reinforcement, induction, and stimulus control is like trying to create new chemicals and materials without atomic theory.

Behaviorists have written a great deal about social issues, and the results have been mixed. For instance, John B. Watson wrote prolifically for the popular press, but was probably of little help to his readers because relatively little was known about behavior in the 1920s and 1930s. However, much more is understood about behavior now. When B. F. Skinner wrote *Beyond Freedom and Dignity* in 1971, he had new concepts to draw on. Part Three covers much the same ground as Skinner's book, but expands and updates the discussion to include the thinking of the last two decades.

CHAPTER
9

FREEDOM

As we did with other terms, so we can do with the word *free*—to understand what it means, we will examine how it is used. As we saw in Chapter 1, only the notion of free will actually conflicts with behaviorism. Most uses of the word can be understood in behavioral terms.

❖ USES OF THE WORD *FREE*

There seem to be three types of use for *free*. First, people speak of freedom from restraint, as in becoming free from slavery. This is often spoken of as being free, suggesting that freedom is an attribute or possession. The extension of this idea is the notion of free will, which implies that a person has the freedom to behave without regard to past or present environment. Second, people speak of political and social freedom. Here the issue is not so much constraint as having to face unpleasant consequences for certain choices. Persecution for your beliefs means not that you cannot act in accordance with them, but that you are punished for doing so. That is when we speak of lack of religious or political freedom, and we say we do not feel free. Third, people—particularly religious people—speak of spiritual freedom. When a church advertises that "Jesus will free you from bondage," no lack of free will or political or religious freedom is suggested, but rather deliverance from a metaphorical prison. We shall take these uses up in turn.

■ Being Free: Free Will

Someone who is freed from jail has had a physical restraint removed. Locked in a cell, the person cannot go out. Opening the cell door is like opening a cage door; "free as a bird" means the person is able to move about totally unfettered.

This particular type of being free presents no problem for behavior analysis because it refers only to whether an action is possible. It is like saying that when the lever is removed the rat is not free to press, and when the lever is inserted the rat is free to press.

As constraints go, jails and cages are only the most obvious. You never chose freely to breathe, walk, or even learn to talk. These were constrained by your genes and environment. Were it possible to be free from such constraints, then we would have free will.

In Chapter 1, we discussed problems with the notion of free will. Apart from philosophical and aesthetic considerations, the results of public policies based on an assumption of free will usually range from poor to disastrous. The assumption is often used as a justification for doing nothing. If cocaine addicts are free to choose not to take the drug, then it seems that addiction is the addicts' fault, that they should just "pull themselves together," and that no help need be given.

It seems that we are slowly learning that wise policies cannot assume free will. It is useless and self-serving to say that people growing up in urban slums choose to be ignorant and unemployed. Some small-scale projects in urban high schools have succeeded in keeping students in school, and job-training has gotten people back to work and off the welfare roll. These projects succeeded because they created contingencies and backed them up with encouragement and explanations (rules in the sense of Chapter 8).

Behavior analysts argue that as long as we go on assuming free will, we will fail to solve our social problems. If, however, we move forward in a frankly behavioral framework and try to change problematic behavior, then our focus will shift to questions about which methods to use. Skinner argued in favor of positive reinforcement, for two reasons. First, it is highly effective. Second (and important to our discussion of freedom) when people's behavior is shaped and maintained by positive reinforcement, people do not feel coerced; they feel free.

■ Feeling Free: Political and Social Freedom

Another example of people who are said to lack freedom is slaves. Slaves' lack of freedom has less to do with physical restraint, for a slave can refuse to work. The likely consequence of such refusal, however, would be a beating. Someone who cooperates because of threatened punishment may in principle be free to defy the threat, but does not feel free to do so.

People who live in a police state are also said to lack freedom because many of their actions are prohibited by threat of punishment. They cannot feel free, as most of us who live in a democratic society do. We feel free to criticize our rulers in public because they cannot punish us for doing so.

The key obstacle to feeling free is coercion. People cannot feel free when they are coerced—that is, when their behavior is controlled by the threat of aversive consequences.

Coercion and Aversive Control   In Chapter 4, we defined the two types of aversive control, positive punishment and negative reinforcement. If speaking out results in a beating, then speaking out is positively punished. If lying avoids a beating, then lying is negatively reinforced. The two tend to go hand-in-hand; if one action is punished, there is usually some alternative that avoids punishment.

Figure 9.1 illustrates the relationship involved in coercion. When an over-seer holds a whip and tells the slave to work, the slave's working is negatively reinforced by preventing a whipping. The steps in between involve an interaction between overseer (controller) and slave (controllee). Waving the whip, or the threatening behavior (B_T), produces a discriminative stimulus for the slave (S_T^D), usually called a threat. The threat-stimulus sets the occasion for compliance (B_C)—working or "doing what the boss wants." The controllee's compliance produces a positive reinforcer (S_C^R)—getting the crops harvested—for the controller, so the controller's threatening behavior is positively reinforced as a result of the controllee's action. As long as the slave works and positively reinforces the overseer's threatening behavior, the overseer holds back on the whip. This means that the positive reinforcer—the controller's goal—acts also as a discriminative stimulus (S_C^D) that sets the occasion for the controller's not punishing (No B_P) or withholding punishment (B_W). The consequence for the controllee is no punishment (No S^P) or the negative reinforcement of avoiding it (S_W^R).

Figure 9.1 resembles Figure 7.1—the diagram of a verbal episode. The con-

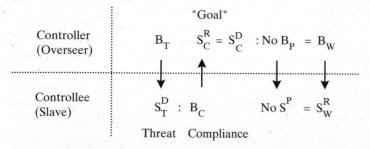

Figure 9.1 Coercion. The controller's threatening behavior (B_T) is positively reinforced as a result of the controllee's compliance (B_C), which produces the reinforcer (S_C^R) that constitutes the controller's goal. The controllee's compliance sets the occasion (S_C^D) for the controller to withhold punishment (B_W), and is reinforced by preventing the threatened punisher, by negative reinforcement.

troller's threatening behavior is like verbal behavior; to be reinforced, it requires a listener—the controllee. When two people reinforce one another's behavior, as shown in Figures 9.1 and 7.1, we can say that they have a *relationship*. We shall explore relationships more generally in Chapter 11.

Figure 9.1 shows the key defining features of coercion: positive reinforcement for the controller's behavior paired with negative reinforcement for the controllee's behavior. Whenever this asymmetry exists, the controllee is said to be coerced, to lack freedom, and not to feel free.

All sorts of relationships can be coercive. A parent may threaten spanking or disapproval to get a child to obey. A teacher may threaten a student with bad grades or public humiliation. One spouse may threaten the other with yelling or removal of affection or sex. An employer may threaten an employee with disapproval, humiliation, or job loss.

All these coercive relationships can be replaced with noncoercive ones. The parent can give affection or treats when the child obeys. The teacher can give good grades or approval when the student performs. Spouses can reward one another with affection, sympathy, and help. Employers can reinforce good performance with tokens of approval (certificates, badges, office furniture) and money. Why then do people so often resort to coercion?

The main reason is that coercion usually works. Those who suggest that coercion is ineffective are mistaken, for, trained properly, human beings are exquisitely sensitive to potential aversive consequences, particularly disapproval and social isolation. Every culture has its taboos, and most members of any cultural group learn to avoid transgressing on pain of disapproval and rejection. Even a threat as remote as jail suffices to keep most of us in line. The minority who wind up in jail usually lacked childhood training with positive social reinforcers and rules about long-term aversive consequences—that is, they received little affection or approval for good actions and no reinforcement for rule-following.

The trouble with coercion lies in its long-term consequences for the person controlled and, eventually, for the controller. In the long run, a family or a society that relies on coercion to keep some of its members in line will suffer nasty side effects. The most salient are resentment, anger, and aggression.

People who are controlled by aversive means not only cannot feel free, but tend to be resentful, angry, and aggressive. Evolutionary history probably has a lot to do with this because natural selection would favor individuals that responded aggressively to the two chief tools of coercion, pain and threatened loss of resources. One sure way to induce aggressive behavior in many species, including ours, is to inflict pain. Two peaceful rats begin to fight almost immediately when they are given electric shocks. Thus, it should come as no surprise that people in jail tend to be violent. Threatened loss of resources (loss of positive reinforcement) also induces aggression in many species, including humans. One has only to stop feeding one pigeon to have it attack another one standing near. Sibling rivalry can be vicious in families where affection is scarce.

As a way of dealing with people, then, coercion is bad because it makes people angry, aggressive, and resentful. In a word, it makes them unhappy, and unhappy controllees eventually behave in ways that are aversive for the controllers. Disaffection eventually leads to noncooperation and revolt. The child runs away or engages in self-destructive behavior. The marriage breaks up. The employee steals from the company, sabotages projects, or quits. Someone who feels trapped in a coercive relationship shows all the signs of unhappiness. Someone who feels free is happy.

Freedom and Happiness   Speaking of political or social freedom, people often say that freedom means having choices. To the behavior analyst, "having choices" has nothing to do with free will; it means only that more than one action is possible. Does social freedom consist of having choices—of being able to vote for the candidate of one's choice or attend the church of one's choice?

Our discussion of coercion suggests that social freedom consists not so much of having choices as of not being punished for one's choices. I may choose to belong to a political party or a religion that is outlawed; we say my political or religious freedom is restricted because I will be punished.

The conditions under which we feel free turn out to be identical with the conditions under which we feel happy. How much sweeter it is to work for wages than to avoid the whip! Most people would rather play the state lottery than pay state taxes. We feel both free and happy when we behave one way rather than another—belong to one group rather than another, work at one task rather than another—not because the unchosen action is punished, but because the chosen action is more positively reinforced.

Rarely, of course, does a choice result in unmixed agreeable results. Most social situations present a mixed bag. The person who says he or she feels trapped but happy in a marriage is saying that, on the whole, the positive reinforcement for staying in the relationship outweighs any aversive control (coercion) in the relationship. Citizens accept restrictions such as having to register cars and pay taxes if, on the whole, good-citizen behavior is positively reinforced. We shall discuss relationships and government further in Chapter 11. For now, we stop with the observation that the less our behavior is shaped by punishment and the threat of punishment—the more our choices are guided by positive reinforcement—the more we feel both free and happy.

Objections to the Behavioral View   Critics raise a number of objections to the behavior analyst's view of social freedom. We shall consider two that seem particularly relevant: (1) that the view cannot be correct because of the nature of desire and (2) that the view is naive.

The first objection is based on the idea that freedom consists of being able to "do what I want." In Chapter 5, we dealt with terms like *want*, which seem to refer to the future or some ghostly representation in the present, by pointing out that you say you want or desire something when you are inclined to act so as to have that thing. The something is a reinforcer, and the wanting—the inclination to act—occurs in a context in which reinforcement has been produced in the past.

One of the forms of verbal operant that children learn earliest is "I want X." As a mand, this is reinforced with X or the opportunity to act to obtain X. Eve tells her mother she wants a cookie, and her mother either hands her one or tells her to take one. Generally speaking, a person would say "I want X" when the listener is likely to assist somehow—say, with money or advice.

But you can desire things which you have never experienced, runs the objection. You can say you want a Caribbean vacation even if you have never been to the Caribbean. How could a history of reinforcement account for that?

Two factors account for wanting the novel thing: generalization and rules. You are only inclined to say you want something if you have had experience with similar things. You may never have been to the Caribbean, but you have been on vacations and other trips. You generalize across the category "vacations and fun trips." In addition, someone (perhaps a friend or a TV advertisement) is telling you about the Caribbean, saying "Go to the Caribbean and have fun." In other words, someone is producing verbal discriminative stimuli (rules) that make it likely you will behave with respect to Caribbean vacations as you do toward other "vacations and fun trips."

As with creativity and problem-solving, to understand desire behavior analysts point to histories of reinforcement rather than posit mental representations. After all, where did the inner desire itself come from?

The second objection to the behaviorists' account of social freedom—that it is naive—arises from a skepticism about the benignity of positive reinforcement. It would seem that granting controllers the means for positive reinforcement grants them power that is easily abused. After all, critics say, the power to confer is also the power to withhold. Just as an employer might coerce employees with the threat of losing their livelihood, a government with the power to reinforce behavior with the necessities of life could coerce citizens by threatening to withhold them.

The answer to this objection requires a more careful discussion of the difference between reinforcers and punishers. In Chapter 4, we noticed that sometimes the distinction seems arbitrary. Is getting sick a punisher or is staying healthy a reinforcer? Do I eat a good diet to avoid getting sick (negative reinforcement) or to keep healthy (positive reinforcement)? If I eat too much and feel ill, is my overeating punished positively by the illness or negatively by the loss of feeling well? Fining people for misbehavior would seem to qualify as negative punishment, and yet people behave as if a fine is an aversive event—maybe not as bad as breaking an arm, but along the same line.

These are all questions about *norms,* or the usual state of affairs in individuals' lives. Someone who is normally healthy regards a sore throat as an aversive event, whereas someone suffering from cancer would gladly exchange that illness for a sore throat.

Human beings show a remarkable ability to adapt to their normal circumstances. This is why rich people are no happier than anyone else. When we have money, we get used to it. Even if you live in excess, if you are accustomed to owning three houses and two yachts, losing one of the yachts still seems like a disaster. Once you have adapted to a certain affluence, having some of your wealth taken away seems a truly aversive event.

This adaptation to the norm can be understood as an establishing condition, akin to deprivation and satiation. In Chapter 4, we noted that reinforcers and punishers wax and wane according to the state of affairs prevailing in the recent past. Someone who is well fed is unlikely to find food a powerful reinforcer. In the same way, a rich person's behavior is less affected by the possibility of gaining or losing a hundred dollars than a poor person's, just as if the rich person were relatively satiated and the poor person relatively deprived. Loss of money (a fine) becomes aversive when a person gets used to having money, but the amount of the fine has to reflect the person's resources to be effective. If set too high, the fine is unrealistic because you can't get blood out of a stone; if set too low, it is insignificant. Thus, fines usually tend to a level at which, relative to people's accustomed resources, the threat of loss seems both realistic and nontrivial.

Control of behavior by threats of losing accustomed comfort constitutes coercion just as surely as control by threats of torture. It is true that the power to confer is also the power to withhold, and that such power can be abused. When it is abused, however, people will feel neither free nor happy.

Positive reinforcement means making available contingencies by which socially desirable behavior can lead to an improvement in an individual's lot. Some American industries are learning that the way to produce quality products is to reward workers for their efforts to improve quality. The extra cost is more than offset by the increased quality, and the workers are happier, too. Some communities have tried rewarding drivers for good driving instead of punishing them for violations. How differently we would feel about highway police if they occasionally pulled us over and gave us money for driving within the speed limit! It would save the state money because fewer clerks would be needed and less time would be taken up in traffic court, and people might well be more inclined to obey the speed limit.

One problem with positive reinforcement, however, is that it can be used abusively. Small, conspicuous reinforcers delivered immediately can be so powerful that people sacrifice long-term welfare for short-term gain. Such situations are known as *contingency traps*.

Contingency Traps and Self-Control   People recognize contingency traps when they talk about someone being a "slave to a habit." Bad habits, particularly addictions, are hard to give up, and when someone experiences the nasty effects of the habit, that person neither appears nor feels free. When Tom is smoking and appears relaxed, we may say that he simply enjoys smoking, but when he has run out of cigarettes in the middle of the night and is a nervous wreck, we are more inclined to say he is trapped in a bad habit.

Bad habits like smoking and overeating are said to require self-control. This seems to suggest controlling a self somewhere inside or a self inside controlling external behavior. Behavior analysts reject such views as mentalistic. Instead they ask, "What is the behavior that people call 'self-control'?"

Self-control consists of making a choice. The smoker who refrains from smoking exhibits self-control. The alternative, giving in to the habit, is acting impulsively. The smoker faces a choice between two alternatives: impulsiveness (smoking) and self-control (refraining). The difference between the two is that impulsiveness consists of behaving according to short-term reinforcement (enjoying a cigarette), whereas self-control consists of behaving according to long-term reinforcement (enjoying good health).

Figure 9.2 illustrates a contingency trap. The upper diagram shows the trap in general terms. Acting impulsively (B_I) leads to a small but relatively immediate reinforcer (S^R). The relative immediacy of the reinforcement is symbolized by a short arrow. The short-term reinforcement for smoking, shown in the lower diagram, lies in the effects of nicotine and social reinforcers such as appearing grown-up or sophisticated. The trouble with impulsive behavior lies in long-term ill effects, symbolized by the large punisher (S^P). The long arrow indicates that the punishment for impulsiveness is substantially delayed. It may be months or years before the bad habit takes its toll in consequences such as cancer, heart disease, and emphysema, shown in the lower diagram as the long-term effects of smoking. The large size of the symbol indicates that the long-term ill effects are much more significant than the short-term reinforcers.

The alternative to impulsiveness, self-control, is symbolized in Figure 9.2 by B_S. In the lower diagram this is shown as refraining from smoking, although it might consist of specific alternatives such as chewing gum. Like impulsiveness, the behavior of self-control leads to both short-term and long-term consequences. The short-term consequences, shown by the short arrow,

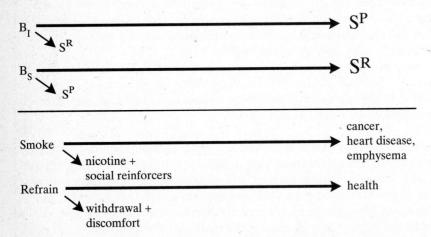

Figure 9.2 A contingency trap—a problem in self-control or a bad habit. Acting impulsively (B_I; smoking) produces short-term reinforcement (nicotine and social reinforcement) and long-term major punishment (cancer, heart disease, and emphysema). Using self-control (B_S; refraining from smoking, chewing gum) produces short-term punishment (withdrawal and social discomfort) and long-term major reinforcement (health).

are punishing but relatively minor: withdrawal symptoms (e.g., headaches) and possibly social discomfort. In the long run (long arrow), however, self-control leads to major reinforcement (large S^R). Refraining from smoking reduces the risk of cancer, heart disease, and emphysema; ultimately, it promotes health.

A second major category of contingency traps is postponement and procrastination. When someone with a small cavity postpones going to the dentist, the immediate discomfort of having the cavity filled prevails over the delayed greater punishment of eventually having toothaches and a root canal or loss of the tooth. In the terms of Figure 9.2, postponement constitutes impulsiveness and going to the dentist constitutes self-control. Postponement is reinforced immediately by avoidance of minor discomfort, but is punished ultimately by major discomfort. Going to the dentist is punished immediately by minor discomfort, but reinforced ultimately by avoidance of major discomfort.

A third common example of a contingency trap is the conflict between spending and saving. In the short run, spending (impulsiveness) is reinforced immediately by small purchases. In the long run, saving (self-control) produces much greater reinforcement, such as buying a car or making the down payment on a house. Compulsive spenders are people who have become trapped by the immediate reinforcement of spending. We regard compulsive spending as a bad habit or even an addiction because in the long run it is punished by the loss of major reinforcement.

Situations like those diagrammed in Figure 9.2 are called traps for two reasons. First, the person behaving impulsively is trapped by the immediate small reinforcement for impulsiveness and the immediate small punishment for self-control. Delay weakens the effect of any consequence. Small immediate consequences overpower even an outcome as big as dying from cancer if the outcome is in the distant future. Second, the large punisher for impulsiveness is recognized and talked about. More technically, the long-term punishment acts as a discriminative stimulus for verbal behavior including words like *trap* and *slave*. Before all the discussion of the connection between smoking and cancer, smoking was viewed more benignly; some people called it a bad habit, but nothing like today.

Recognition of the aversive consequences of impulsiveness explains why people caught in contingency traps are unhappy and do not feel free. Insofar as the long-term punishment acts as a threat and self-control is seen as avoidance of the threat, a contingency trap resembles coercion. If the trapped person hears someone, even possibly himself or herself, talk about the long-term dangers of smoking (S_T^D in Figure 9.1), then self-control becomes like compliance (although, of course, the punishment for failing to comply is delivered by the natural connection between smoking and disease, rather than by a controller). Contingency traps conform to the general rule that people feel trapped and unhappy when their behavior is controlled by the threat of punishment. Someone who escapes from a contingency trap, like someone who escapes from coercion, feels free and happy. Ask anyone who has kicked an addiction.

It is no accident that the long-term consequences in Figure 9.2 resemble the ultimate consequences discussed in Chapter 8 and diagrammed in Figure

8.2. Many of the verbal discriminative stimuli called rules and the proximate contingencies that go with them exist precisely to help people avoid contingency traps. When a parent tells a child to refuse illicit drugs when they are offered, the point of the order is to keep the child from suffering the long-term consequences of addiction. The proximate social reinforcement from the parent for rule-following offsets the relatively immediate reinforcement for taking the drugs that would draw the child into the trap. Viewed this way, many cultural practices appear to be trap-avoidance. Wearing shoes, the example in Chapter 8, resembles self-control because we tolerate the immediate inconvenience of putting on shoes for the sake of the long-term reinforcement of avoiding illness. Without cultural support in the form of rules, people might go barefoot (impulsively) for short-term convenience and suffer delayed dire consequences. We shall return to this point in Chapter 12 when we consider how behavior that produces long-term reinforcement is labeled "good," whereas behavior that produces short-term reinforcement is labeled "bad," and in Chapter 13 when we see how cultural practices evolve in response to ultimate consequences.

Without the protection of rules and rule-following, the ease with which controllees fall into contingency traps presents a temptation to controllers. The way for controllers to use positive reinforcement abusively is to set contingency traps for controllees. We all disapprove of the drug pusher who offers free samples to children, but what about governments that set contingency traps? Crafty state legislatures resort to lotteries to raise revenue knowing that people who hate taxes will happily play the lottery even though they can ill afford it. A government that takes advantage of a weakness like this is exploitive. Since the issues involved have more to do with management than with freedom, the discussion of exploitation will wait until Chapter 11.

The notion of a contingency trap helps us to understand some instances of failing to feel free and of getting free. It may help us also to understand another use of the word *free,* one that appears to differ from those we have discussed so far: *spiritual freedom.*

■ Spiritual Freedom

Religious figures throughout the ages have talked about spiritual freedom. Such talk has nothing to do with social freedom, such as being able to attend the church of your choice. Instead, the focus is on the *world,* worldly goods, and worldly comforts. People are urged to break free from bondage or attachment or slavery to worldly pleasures. The Indian spiritual leader Meher Baba (1987), for example, taught, "One important condition of spiritual freedom is freedom from all wanting" (p. 341). He continued:

> Man seeks worldly objects of pleasure and tries to avoid things that bring
> pain, without realizing that he cannot have the one and eschew the other. As
> long as there is attachment to worldly objects of pleasure, he must perpetually

invite upon himself the suffering of not having them—and the suffering of losing them after having got them. Lasting detachment . . . brings freedom from all desires and attachments . . . (pp. 391–392).

This idea of freedom from attachment to worldly things finds its place in literature also. In the novel *Siddhartha,* Hermann Hesse describes the central character's impressions on first seeing the Buddha:

> The Buddha went quietly on his way, lost in thought. His peaceful countenance was neither happy nor sad. He seemed to be smiling gently inwardly. With a secret smile, not unlike that of a healthy child, he walked along, peacefully, quietly. He wore his gown and walked along exactly like the other monks, but his face and his step, his peaceful downward glance, his peaceful downward-hanging hand, and every finger of his hand spoke of peace, spoke of completeness, sought nothing, imitated nothing, reflected a continuous quiet, an unfading light, an invulnerable peace (pp. 27–28).

Nor is this linking of spiritual freedom to escape from worldly desires confined to books about religion. In the novel *Free Fall,* by William Golding, the central character at one point finds himself on his bicycle near the home of Beatrice, with whom he is in love:

> And even by the time I was on the bike by the traffic light, I was no longer free. . . . For this part of London was touched by Beatrice. She saw this grime-smothered and embossed bridge; the way buses heaved over its arch must be familiar. One of these streets must be hers, a room in one of these drab houses. I knew the name of the street, Squadron Street; knew, too, that sight of the name, on a metal plaque, or sign-posted might squeeze my heart small again, take away the strength of my knees, shorten my breath. I sat my bike on the downward slope of the bridge, waiting for a green light and the roll down round to the left; and already I had left my freedom behind me (p. 79).

Here again the sense of freedom is opposed to the sense of wanting, attachment, or desire. Although Golding does not call the freedom "spiritual," it is clear he would equate it with the absence of desire for Beatrice.

"Worldly pleasures"—food, sex, nice cars, Caribbean vacations—these are reinforcers. In technical terms, the preceding writers seem to be talking about something beyond freedom from aversive control; they seem to be talking about freedom even from positive reinforcement. If one could be free of aversive control and positive reinforcement, what control would be left? Does talk of spiritual freedom necessarily imply that people can get free of all control? Can behaviorists make any sense of such talk?

A way to understand spiritual freedom becomes clearer when we consider not only what is being denigrated but also what is being advocated. If pursuing worldly pleasure is bad, then what is good? Answers vary, but they generally advocate values like kindness and simplicity. Help others even at your own discomfort. Eat to live instead of living to eat. Give up selfishness and excess.

From a behavioral perspective, such injunctions point to deferred aversive consequences. Selfishness and high living may pay off in the short run, but in the long run they lead to loneliness, illness, and remorse. In the long run, you'll be happier if you help others and live moderately. Such long-term contingencies are just the sort that have little effect on behavior without rules and rule-following. "Do unto others as you would have them do unto you" is a rule that makes it likely our social behavior will come into contact with the long-term advantages of helping others.

Kindness and simplicity pay off with more than just avoiding sorrow; they have their positive reinforcement, too. We benefit from mutually helpful relationships with others, and moderation usually leads to improved health, and advocates of spiritual freedom point also to less tangible rewards.

This is especially clear in the quote from Hesse. The word *peace* appears in the passage five times. The Buddha's detachment means attaining inner calm, tranquillity, relief from the anxieties of pursuing worldly aims, getting off the emotional roller coaster of despair and elation. Meher Baba was the one who said, "Don't worry, be happy."

In behavioral terms, advocating spiritual freedom can be seen not as arguing for freedom from all positive reinforcement, but rather as arguing for one set of positive reinforcers against another. It is about quality of life. "Eat to live" and "moderation in all things" do not mean give up food, sex, clothes, or cars; they mean that those reinforcers should not be the main or only reinforcers in life.

The argument resembles the reasoning about contingency traps illustrated in Figure 9.2. Worldly reinforcers for selfishness and self-indulgence, which would be analogous to impulsiveness, are relatively short-term. In the long run, they are offset by ultimate major aversive consequences such as illness, loneliness, and sorrow. In contrast, the reinforcement for kindness and moderation (analogous to self-control), though potentially large, is also relatively delayed. Seen this way, getting free from short-term worldly reinforcers (i.e., spiritual freedom) means only making a switch, coming under control of the long-term reinforcement for simple, moderate living and for kindness toward others. We shall return to the idea of behaving for the good of others in Chapter 12.

❖ THE CHALLENGE OF TRADITIONAL THINKING

Traditional thinking, based on free will, challenges the behavior-analytic view of freedom. If all behavior is determined by inheritance and environmental history, then how can an individual be held responsible for his or her actions? Wouldn't society fall apart if people could not be held responsible? Even if determinism were true, perhaps it should be opposed anyway, because it is a wicked idea that seems to undermine democracy and lead inevitably to dictatorship. When all is said and done, doesn't science tell us only *how* we behave?

Doesn't it still remain silent about how we *ought* to behave? C. S. Lewis put this especially well in his book *Mere Christianity:*

> There is one thing, and only one, in the whole universe which we know more about than we could learn from external observation. That one thing is Man. We do not merely observe men, we *are* men. In this case we have, so to speak, inside information; we are in the know. And because of that, we know that men find themselves under a moral law, which they did not make, and cannot quite forget even when they try, and which they know they ought to obey. Notice the following point. Anyone studying Man from the outside as we study electricity or cabbages, not knowing our language and consequently not able to get any inside knowledge from us, but merely observing what we did, would never get the slightest evidence that we had this moral law. How could he? For his observations would only show what we did, and the moral law is about what we ought to do (p. 33).

Lewis's argument is couched in terms of the "in here, out there" dualism that we criticized in Chapters 2 and 3. We dealt with having rules (Lewis writes of having a moral law) in Chapter 8. Still, the challenge stands: What can science tell us about how we *ought* to behave?

The remaining chapters in the book deal with such questions. In Chapter 10, we shall see how determinism still allows a notion of responsibility. Chapter 11 looks at how behavioral thinking could help us solve social problems without threatening our liberty. Chapter 12 considers how far science can go toward understanding how we ought to behave. Chapters 13 and 14 take up culture and how it changes, and how behavioral thinking might extend rather than curtail democracy.

❖ SUMMARY

The only use of the words *free* and *freedom* that conflicts with behavioral thinking is that which implies free will. Other uses have more to do with feeling free and happy. Social, political, and religious freedom consist of freedom from coercion, which we have defined here as freedom from the threat of punishment. When some of our behavioral alternatives are punished, we cannot feel free. Even if behavior is positively reinforced in the short run, if it leads to major punishment in the long run the person who falls into such a contingency trap cannot feel free. When our behavior is maintained instead by positive reinforcement (short- and long-term), and our choices are between different reinforcers, we feel both free and happy. Even spiritual freedom can be understood in behavioral terms when we see that its advocates encourage a shift away from short-term personal (worldly) reinforcement to larger long-term reinforcement from simplicity and service to others.

Although most uses of *free* and *freedom* can be interpreted behaviorally, such interpretation implies a change in how we view people, culture, government, law, education, and other social institutions. Free will aside, the other types of freedom serve useful social functions. They point the way to the more basic issue—happiness. Advocates of social freedom oppose the use of threats and punishment to control behavior, because people who are coerced are unhappy. Advocates of spiritual freedom strengthen the effects of long-term contingencies that bring greater happiness in the long run. When a society arranges positive reinforcement for desirable behavior and supports long-term contingencies, its citizens are productive and happy.

❖ FURTHER READING

Golding, W. (1959). *Free fall.* New York: Harcourt Brace. A novel about a young artist in a crucial period of his life, exploring freedom and responsibility.

Hesse, H. (1951). *Siddhartha.* New York: New Directions. A novel about a young man's spiritual journey in India at the time of the Buddha.

Lewis, C. S. (1960). *Mere Christianity.* New York: Macmillan. A collection of essays by this famous religious thinker. Lewis presents the challenge to the scientific world view clearly and in modern terms.

Meher Baba (1987). *Discourses,* 7th ed. Myrtle Beach, SC: Sheriar Press. A collection of discussions of spiritual issues by a modern Indian spiritual leader.

Sidman, M. (1989). *Coercion and its fallout.* Boston, MA: Authors Cooperative. This book treats at length the drawbacks of aversive control and the advantages of substituting positive reinforcement.

Skinner, B. F. (1971). *Beyond freedom and dignity.* New York: Knopf. Skinner laid out the basics of the behavior-analytic view about freedom in this book. The present chapter draws heavily on Skinner's Chapters 1 and 2.

RESPONSIBILITY, CREDIT, AND BLAME

In *Beyond Freedom and Dignity*, Skinner argued that mentalism not only interferes with attempts to find scientific explanations of behavior, but is impractical in the sense that it prevents us from solving social problems like war, crime, and poverty. One pair of mentalistic terms that he criticized was *credit* and *blame*. Although Skinner discussed credit and blame in connection with the concept of dignity, in my experience arguments about the social implications of behaviorism more often revolve around the related notion of *responsibility*. People are considered to have dignity when they can be considered responsible. In this chapter, we shall focus on the concept of responsibility, its philosophical underpinnings, and its practical implications.

❖ RESPONSIBILITY AND THE CAUSES OF BEHAVIOR

In many uses, the word *responsible* seems to be a way of talking about causes. When we say, "Bad wiring was responsible for the fire," we could just as well say, "Bad wiring caused the fire." There might be other factors, too, but we mean that bad wiring was the crucial factor.

But what do we mean when we say, "Tom was responsible for the fire"? Putting Tom in the place of bad wiring has two sorts of implications. First, there is the practical implication that Tom set the fire; this is a potentially important connection and might call for some action on our part. Second, there is the implication that Tom caused the fire in much the same way that faulty wiring might cause a fire. We shall return to practical considerations later; first we need to examine the notion that a person can be a cause.

■ Free Will and the Visibility of Control

The idea that a person can be responsible for an action, in the sense of causing the action, is based on the notion of free will discussed in Chapter 1. In the most common way of thinking, the difference between faulty wiring causing a fire and Tom causing a fire is that Tom chose freely to set the fire. The bad wiring is attributed to environmental factors like vibration and weather, whereas Tom's action is attributed to Tom himself.

Although it might seem almost common sense that Tom and faulty wiring should be treated differently, the distinction between them tends to vanish under closer scrutiny. The wiring worked fine when it was first installed. It became faulty over a long time—many winters, many summers, years of vibration. Finally it gave out and "set" the fire. Similarly with Tom, a combination of genetic factors and a history of environmental events (his upbringing) led Tom to be "faulty" and to set the fire. Tom, like the wiring, is only the instrument by which the fire came to pass.

This view of Tom's action may seem strange because we are accustomed to drawing a line between the behavior of things and people. The behavior of people seems different from the behavior of things for two reasons: the alternatives among which a person might choose seem obvious, and the factors determining the chosen action remain hidden. Few of us set fire to houses; it seems obvious that Tom could behave just like the rest of us.

But is it so obvious? We sometimes excuse someone's actions by saying the person "had no choice." Suppose someone was holding a gun to Tom's head when he set the fire; we might say he had no choice.

Now we have reached a contradiction. If Tom had a choice before, he has a choice now. He could refuse and risk having his head blown off. Either Tom has a choice both with the gun held to his head and when he acts on his own or he has no choice in either situation.

Tom seems to have no choice only because the reason (the gun) for his action is apparent. The more we learn about the reasons for Tom's setting the fire the less we say he chose freely. Say he was abused as a child or he is a pyromaniac. We begin to think of him as faulty in much the same way as the wiring, and we say he couldn't help it.

The temptation to invoke free will arises because we cannot see anything faulty about Tom, the way we can see that a wire is frayed. If no cause is clear and present, like a gun aimed at Tom's head, then we have to look to events in the past. These, however, can be difficult to discover. Invoking free will is an easy way out, but it is no explanation at all from a scientific point of view.

■ Assigning Credit and Blame

When responsibility is bound up with free will and the idea that people cause their own behavior, then it seems only natural to assign credit and blame to people for actions of which we approve and disapprove. Credit and blame are yet another way of talking about causes, but with the added element of approval and disapproval.

Creditable actions are reinforced; blamable actions are punished. We shall discuss good and bad actions further in Chapter 12, but for the present discussion we need to note only that people seek credit and avoid blame.

People make up all sorts of excuses when they are caught in some shameful act, everything from "The devil made me do it" to "my unhappy childhood." The point is to assign blame to something else—in other words, to put the causes for the behavior in the environment. Defense attorneys argue for compassion. They persuade judges to consider extenuating circumstances in the experience of people convicted of all sorts of crimes. From a behavioral perspective, *extenuating circumstances* mean environmental factors, and *compassion* means considering those environmental factors.

In contrast, when people have credit assigned to them for some praiseworthy deed, they often resist any suggestion that environmental factors may have played a role. Successful businesspeople frequently attribute their achievements to hard work and sacrifice, and rarely to luck. Artists, writers, composers, and scientists often evade or resent questions about where they get their ideas. No one wants to talk about the extenuating circumstances of their creditable actions (unless modesty is reckoned a greater virtue than the good deed).

If we are willing to assign the blame for punishable actions to the environment, then why resist assigning credit for reinforceable actions to the environment? The reasons are not far to seek. Assigning blame to the environment is operant (mostly verbal) behavior. It is reinforced by avoiding punishment. We get out of sticky situations by blaming environmental factors. People resist assigning credit to the environment because that would have an analogous effect, except that the loss would be credit instead of blame. The behavior of assigning credit to the environment would be punished by the loss of reinforcement. As long as the practice of linking reinforcement to the assigning of credit continues, people will tend to conceal the environmental factors to which credit could be assigned. If, instead, reinforcement for desirable actions were delivered without having to pretend the actions originated entirely from within, people would feel more free to acknowledge environmental factors, as Isaac Newton did when he said, "If I have seen so far, it is because I have stood on the shoulders of giants." Whereas separating punishment from personal blame makes for compassion, separating reinforcement from personal credit makes for honesty.

■ Compassion and Control

In the past, the idea that people choose according to free will was often bound up with the use of punishment to persuade people to avoid wrong actions. Thieves had their hands cut off; public hangings were common.

In the United States today such ideas and practices are giving way to a more compassionate approach to wrongdoing. The notion that there can be extenuating circumstances introduces the possibility of moving beyond blaming and punishing criminals. It allows judges more flexibility in deciding what consequences to impose. A teenager who steals a car to impress his friends can be treated differently from an adult who steals cars for a living.

From a practical standpoint, criminal behavior raises two sorts of questions: Can the behavior be changed? If so, what must be done to change it? (If the answer to the first question is "no," then the second question becomes how to protect the rest of society from an incorrigible criminal.) When we focus on how to change behavior, we raise practical questions, such as whether jailing the miscreant will serve any useful purpose, whether the person might benefit from job training, or whether counseling might help. The more we recognize that behavior is under the control of genes and environmental history, the more we feel free to be compassionate and practical about correcting wrongdoers.

If it is better to be practical about wrong behavior, it might also be better to be practical about right behavior. The advantages of practicality about right behavior have been slower to catch on, mostly because people retain credit for their correct actions only so long as the rewards for virtue remain obscure. When we learn that a philanthropist gets a break on income taxes, we give that person less credit for the donation. If people were rewarded for obeying the speed limit instead of fined for breaking it, those who obeyed would no longer be able to feel righteous and superior to those who speed.

People who cling to credit often call the use of rewards to strengthen desirable behavior "bribery," as if there were something ignoble about doing right for clear reasons. In 1991 Oprah Winfrey had a discussion on her TV talk show about a highly successful program to prevent teenage girls from getting pregnant and to encourage them to finish high school. A private organization was helping girls who had been pregnant once by paying them small amounts of money every week as long as they stayed in school, remained nonpregnant, and attended special classes on nutrition and child-rearing. Many members of the audience objected to the program on such grounds as "I cannot agree with paying people to do what they should do anyway." Ironically, these objections arose even though the program was saving U.S. taxpayers a lot of money. Most teenage mothers never finish high school and need welfare payments to survive. They often have one baby after another, and they stay on the welfare roll. The teenagers in the program, however, who had all been on welfare, were now having no more babies, were finishing school, and were getting off of welfare. Even if the program had been using federal funds (it wasn't), it still would have saved money, because its cost was trivial in comparison to the welfare payments. Insisting that people should do right for "their own" reasons (i.e., for hidden reasons) and calling reinforcement "bribery" only blocks us from using reinforcement to strengthen desirable behavior and save taxpayers' money.

The audience's reaction shows how much slower people have been to accept the idea of giving up personal credit in favor of arranged reinforcement. In deciding whether to punish the girls' behavior, these same people would probably have spoken of compassion and extenuating circumstances. When deciding on the appropriateness of reinforcing correct behavior, however, the people in the talk show never brought up extenuating circumstances. The program targeted teenage girls who already had babies, a population known to be at risk. Even though some women in the audience were single mothers who might well have brought up environmental factors, still the girls' likely fate if no action was taken failed to bring about acceptance of reinforcement. If decisions about social policy are to be more practical, we must consider environmental effects in decisions about reinforcement as well as punishment.

❖ RESPONSIBILITY AND THE CONSEQUENCES OF BEHAVIOR

Practically, responsibility comes down to a decision on whether to impose consequences. People trying to decide whether to punish a misdeed may talk about justice and morality, but in the end no punishment is given or some appropriate punishment is decided upon. As a behavior analyst, I tend to focus on this final, practical outcome. If my son breaks a window, my decision whether to punish him depends not so much on considerations of justice as on what I am likely to accomplish by punishing him. Will I reduce the likelihood of a repetition, or will I just make him resentful? The situation might be especially complicated if he has confessed to the misdeed; do I punish to prevent a repetition or reinforce to strengthen truth-telling?

If you say that you hold Tom responsible for an action (breaking a window or saving your life), that tells more about your behavior than about Tom's. It says that you are likely to impose consequences, to punish or reinforce Tom's behavior. If you believe in free will, that only tells some more about your tendencies; you are probably more likely to punish and less likely to reinforce. Your tendency to behave so, however, might have nothing to do with belief in free will. The lack of need for believing in free will becomes clear when we examine the way people use the word *responsibility,* to which we now turn.

■ What Is Responsibility?

The philosopher Gilbert Ryle argued that deciding whether an act is responsible resembles deciding whether it is intelligent. As we saw in Chapter 3, no single criterion governs the decision about the intelligence of a particular act; we look for clusters or patterns of action into which the particular act fits. Someone makes a brilliant move in a chess game; was it intelligent or lucky? Someone steals money from an employer; was it part of a pattern of sleazy and criminal action or was it an aberration?

The defense of an act on grounds of temporary insanity carries two implications. First, it implies that the act was uncharacteristic. Witnesses are called in to testify that a man who beat his girlfriend in a fit of rage hasn't a violent bone in his body, is kind to animals and children, helps elderly people across the street, and never even raises his voice. In the example of Tom setting the fire, we inquire whether he has always been a good citizen or whether he has engaged in other antisocial acts. Second, temporary insanity means that punishing the act would serve no purpose—if the behavior is unlikely ever to recur, there is no need to deter it. If setting fires is totally uncharacteristic of Tom, then we need have no fear of a repeat offense.

The idea of responsibility shares much with the ideas of intention and acting on purpose discussed in Chapter 5. When a particular act is part of a pattern and the reinforcement for it is obvious, we are inclined to say it was done on purpose and that the person should be held responsible for it. In a practical approach to wrongdoing, the reinforcement is the problem. The bank teller is tempted to embezzle because of the money. Bank managers usually try to deter such behavior by threatening to punish it and by following through with punishment if it occurs. The threat and the punishment are meant to offset the temptation and the reinforcement. We hold the person responsible in the sense that we make the threat and punish the behavior if it occurs.

Although it is usual to talk about responsibility in connection with reprehensible acts, such reasoning can be extended also to creditable acts. The question with desirable actions is whether to reinforce them. If a child does his or her homework regularly, there may be no need to impose any special reinforcement, but if homework is completed irregularly and only with reminders, then it may be essential to reinforce completion with praise and special treats. Is this wrong? Is it bribery? If there are good reasons (long-term reinforcers) for the behavior, then special imposed reinforcement should be necessary only to establish the behavior. Once homework is being completed regularly, the special reinforcers can be phased out. A policy of this sort would justify programs like the one of paying welfare mothers to avoid pregnancy and stay in school; once the woman has graduated and is supporting herself as we would normally expect, the payments can stop. (The payments must, of course, be small in comparison to the reinforcement for being self-supporting.)

When someone behaves "responsibly," that person is behaving in ways that society deems useful. Usually this means behaving in accordance with long-term contingencies; in the terms of Chapter 9, this use of *responsible* coincides with self-control (B_S in Figure 9.2). If Mary saves her money instead of squandering it, she is behaving responsibly. Similarly, if Mary stays in school in accordance with long-term reinforcement instead of dropping out in accordance with short-term reinforcement, she is behaving responsibly.

Responsible behavior needs to be maintained. If the long-term reinforcement for staying in school (B_S) is insufficient to maintain the behavior and it is desirable for students to remain in school, then private or public institutions must provide explicit short-term reinforcement for staying that will offset the short-term reinforcement for dropping out (B_I in Figure 9.2). That is why paying teenage mothers to stay in school may be both practical and necessary.

From a behavioral viewpoint, talk about responsibility is talk about the desirability or usefulness of imposing consequences. To say we hold someone responsible is to say we hope to change the person's behavior by punishing or reinforcing it. The contingencies that maintain it or ought to maintain it are clear, and we wish either to offset or augment them. To say Tom should not be held responsible is to say that either he is incorrigible (possibly insane) or the action will probably never happen again (it was a lucky or unlucky aberration). Either way, it would be useless to punish or reinforce the behavior. To say that we hold Tom responsible or that we wish to make Tom responsible is to say that it would be useful to punish his undesirable behavior or reinforce his desirable behavior. Behavior analysts usually recommend strengthening desirable behavior with positive reinforcement.

■ Practical Considerations: The Need for Control

Freedom-loving people oppose management by coercion because they recognize that it makes for unhappiness and rebellion in the long run. Many people who oppose coercion generalize and claim to oppose control in whatever form. They base their position on the idea that people should be allowed to choose freely.

In the behavioral perspective, there is no such thing as choosing freely in the sense of exercising free will, or choosing without explanation. In Chapter 9 we discussed choosing freely in the sense of choosing on the basis of positive reinforcement, the condition in which people tend to feel free and happy. And since, in the behavioral perspective, all actions are controlled—that is, are explainable—by genetic inheritance and environmental history, the question of escaping control cannot arise. The parent or manager who refuses to control the behavior of children or employees only leaves the control to others and to accident. Control will occur, but by other children, other employees, and strangers, with who knows what results. Parents and managers who refuse to control can be called irresponsible, in that *responsible* denotes behaving according to long-term contingencies. The responsible approach to management and social problems in general is to plan and design environments in which people will behave well. This idea raises two big questions that the remainder of the book addresses: Who shall control? How shall the control be accomplished?

Imposing Consequences   Whether or not we like it or recognize it, we are constantly reinforcing and punishing one another's behavior. Probably most of the time we remain unaware of the consequences we provide for the behavior of others. My thoughtless remark may cut you to the quick or buoy you up, though I know nothing of the result. Someone in a managerial position, however—parent, teacher, supervisor, or ruler—has to be aware of the consequences he or she provides: it is part of the job. To capture the sense of such deliberate providing of consequences, we can use the word *impose* and speak of imposing reinforcement and punishment.

Imposing consequences—one part of management—is itself operant behavior, and is under the control of long-term contingencies. Adequate parenting determines the success of children in adulthood. A skilled parent reads the signs of a child's ultimate success—school performance, friends, athletics— and behaves so as to produce them. In the same way, adequate supervision determines the profitability of a business. A skilled manager's behavior is under the control of signs that predict ultimate success—conditioned reinforcers like attendance records, quality control reports, and sales.

Many of the reinforcers and punishers that control the manager's behavior (attendance, school grades, and so on) come from those who are being managed. This fact should be significant to freedom-lovers, because it opens the door to recognizing and explicitly engineering mutual control not only in management, but in all human relationships. We shall take up mutual control in the next chapter. For now, we turn to the question of *how* to control.

What Kind of Control?   We saw in Chapter 9 that behavior analysts advocate using positive reinforcement rather than aversive means. When behavior is controlled by punishment and threats, people report feeling trapped, miserable, and resentful, and are likely to complain, avoid, and rebel. Coercion is a poor means of control because it usually backfires in the long run. Although it can be effective in the short run, sooner or later its accomplishments are outweighed by its nasty side effects.

When behavior is under the control of appropriate positive reinforcement, people report feeling free, happy, and dignified. They feel free because they are not punished for their choices, happy because their choices result in good things, and dignified because the reinforcers count to their credit. Something important, however is implied by saying *appropriate* positive reinforcement.

Management by positive reinforcement can backfire just as surely as coercion. When it does, there are usually two reasons: behavior-reinforcer mismatch and neglect of history. We discussed the idea of mismatch briefly in Chapter 4, when we noted that reinforcers often induce certain sorts of behavior and are also particularly effective at reinforcing those actions. Pigeons' keypecking is a good example; pigeons tend to peck, especially at shiny objects, in situations where they are likely to be fed, and if pecks at a key are reinforced with food, key-pecking is established extremely rapidly. Similarly, when a child interacts with a parent, displays of affection (touching, smiling, praise) become powerful reinforcers that readily strengthen behavior that produces them. Other reinforcers, like money and goods, may work, but not as well; without the affection, they may ultimately fail. Unless parents, teachers, and other caretakers back up token reinforcement (points exchangeable for goods and privileges awarded to reinforce desired behavior) with affection, their management is likely to fail.

For adults, an important factor in management is *affiliation.* Workers appear to function better when they belong to moderate-sized groups with stable membership. Over time, repeated interaction with the same people tends to make those people a powerful source of social reinforcement. The Japanese have long used the power of affiliation in their industrial management, and U.S. industry is beginning to follow suit, supplementing or replacing the isolation of the assembly line with "quality circles," groups that work as a unit to produce a product from beginning to end. For adults as well as children, monetary reinforcement works best if backed up by social reinforcement.

The second reason for failure, neglect of history, can be understood by analogy to momentum. Trying to change behavior that has been shaped by a long history of powerful reinforcement by superimposing some new artificial contingency may be like hoping to divert a speeding bus by hitting it with a rubber ball. Part of the skill of an effective therapist is recognizing old and powerful contingencies. This is a point about which psychoanalysts are right: To understand the behavior of an adult, you must often look to the events of childhood. For example, if a woman behaves inappropriately with men, a skilled behavior therapist tries to find out whether her father was affectionate, what sort of behavior he reinforced with affection, and what sort of behavior her mother displayed toward her father. The best way to prevent embezzlement is to provide a history of reinforcement for the behavior we call "respect for the property of others," or behavior incompatible with stealing. A bank teller who embezzles money most likely lacks such a history, and the bank manager who hopes to prevent a recurrence by threats or minor incentives would do better to remove the person from temptation. Interventions that ignore the history of reinforcement for present behavior are likely to fail.

Positive reinforcement can be the most powerful means to change behavior, but it has to be applied correctly. Naive enthusiasm cannot substitute for an understanding of induction, reinforcement, rules, and delayed consequences. Without understanding, positive reinforcement, like any technique, can go wrong in any number of ways and can even be abused. We shall see how behavior analysts approach the problem of correct and equitable management in Chapter 11.

❖ SUMMARY

The word *responsible* is often used to talk about causes, as when we say that an earthquake was responsible for damage. When applied to people, this usage raises all the problems of free will because the people are seen as the origin or cause of their behavior. People are viewed as the cause of their own behavior when their choices seem obvious and environmental causes remain obscure. When environmental factors become clear, it is often said that the person had no choice. As genetic and environmental determinants are understood, talk about free will and responsibility tends to give way to talk about extenuating circumstances.

From a practical point of view, creditable actions are ones the community reinforces; blamable actions are those the community punishes. Blamable actions are often attributed to genetic and environmental factors—extenuating circumstances—and treated with compassion, whereas creditable deeds are usually attributed to the person. People try to take credit for their actions to ensure they will be reinforced. Recognizing the effects of environment on praiseworthy actions makes for honesty. If we can be practical and compassionate about punishing undesirable behavior, we can be practical and honest about reinforcing desirable behavior. Whether someone is responsible or not in a practical sense comes down to a decision about whether or not to impose consequences. A plea of temporary insanity or aberration implies that no practical good can come of punishment. Calling an action "lucky" implies no use in reinforcement. Parents, teachers, supervisors, and rulers would manage behavior more effectively if they made decisions about reinforcement and punishment openly. They would manage most effectively if they strengthened desirable behavior with positive reinforcement. Control by threats and punishment can work in the short run, but makes for rebellion and disaffection in the long run.

Management by positive reinforcement, however, requires care and skill. Failures arise when reinforcement is inappropriate and history is neglected. Appropriate reinforcement for management in our species is at least partly social. Money and other token reinforcers appear to be most effective when backed up with reinforcement by approval and affection from significant others. Neglect of history results in failure when an assumed normal history is actually absent. A deficient or abnormal history of reinforcement can overwhelm even the best management contingencies. Correcting the effects of a long history requires therapy; until they are corrected, a manager does well to avoid contexts in which history is likely to produce bad behavior.

❖ FURTHER READING

Hineline, P. N. (1990). The origins of environment-based psychological theory. *Journal of the Experimental Analysis of Behavior, 53,* 305–320. This paper, which was written as a review of Skinner's classic book *Behavior of Organisms,* compares environment-based with organism-based explanations of behavior.

Skinner, B. F. (1971). *Beyond freedom and dignity.* New York: Knopf. Chapters 3, 4, and 5, on dignity, punishment, and alternatives to punishment, deal with themes similar to those treated in the present chapter.

CHAPTER
11

RELATIONSHIPS, MANAGEMENT, AND GOVERNMENT

Human beings are highly social creatures. Much of our stimulation, reinforcement, and punishment comes from one another. The give-and-take of stimuli and consequences leads us to form relationships with one another. We take it for granted that a normal person has relationships with parents, siblings, other relatives, spouse, friends, and neighbors. Such personal relationships are characteristic of our species, and can also be found in other species. The special relationships that we call management and government originated more recently, and we associate them exclusively with human culture. In this chapter, we shall examine the way that behavior analysts can treat relationships in general, with a special eye toward management and government. Critics of behaviorism have often claimed that it will lead to inhumane management and totalitarian government. This chapter shows why these accusations are false.

❖ RELATIONSHIPS

When do we say two individuals have a relationship? Isolated encounters widely separated in time cannot suffice. If the mail carrier and I greet each other once a month, we can hardly be said to have a relationship, although if we greeted one another on a daily basis, there might be some basis for the claim. Though the frequency of interaction required for saying two people have a relationship varies from speaker to speaker, the higher the frequency, the more likely is this bit of verbal behavior.

If a relationship consists of frequent repeated interaction, we still need to say what we mean by *interaction*. Figures 7.1 and 9.1 diagram two types of interaction: a verbal episode and a coercive episode. Such episodes might never repeat: I might ask the time of someone I never see again, and I might deliver my wallet to a robber I never meet again. When such episodes occur over and over, however, then the two individuals have a relationship. To understand what *interaction* means in behavioral terms, we must understand a feature that verbal episodes, coercive episodes, and other interactions have in common: *mutual reinforcement*.

◼ Mutual Reinforcement

We call verbal episodes and coercive episodes *social* because each person's behavior provides reinforcement for the other's. When one person watches another—a detective in a police investigation or a peeping Tom—nothing social occurs because the reinforcement goes only one way. Stage performances usually cannot be called social; they only become social when the performer's behavior is reinforced by the audience. For an episode to be called a social interaction and to count as the basis for a relationship, reinforcement must be mutual.

Figure 11.1 shows a general diagram of a social interaction. As in the earlier diagrams, a colon indicates stimulus control and an arrow connects a consequence to the behavior that produces it. One person initiates the episode with some operant behavior (B_I) under the control of the setting (S_S^D), which includes the other person, the responder. B_I could be stating a rule (making a threat or a promise such as "If you don't work I shall beat you" or "If you

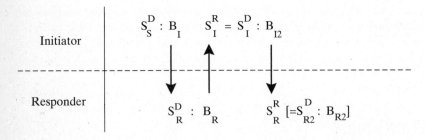

Figure 11.1 General diagram of a social episode, showing mutual reinforcement. Arrows indicate behavior producing consequences; colons indicate stimulus control. The initiator's behavior (B_I) produces reinforcement (S_I^R) as a result of the responder's behavior (B_R), which in turn produces reinforcement (S_R^R) as a result of the initiator's behavior (B_{I2}). When such episodes repeat often enough, the two individuals are said to have a relationship.

work I shall pay you"), smiling, or offering a gift. This produces a discriminative stimulus (S_R^D), making it likely that the responder will act (B_R; work, smile, give a gift) so that B_I is reinforced (S_I^R). This reinforcer functions also as a discriminative stimulus (S_I^D) for further behavior on the part of the initiator (B_{I2}) that provides reinforcement (S_R^R) for the responder's behavior.

At the point where both parties have acted and their actions have been reinforced, the episode could end. That could be called the *minimal* social episode.

The episode could continue, however, as when two people have a conversation. In Figure 11.1, when the initiator responds to the S_I^D provided by the responder's behavior, one could say they have switched roles. The roles could switch again. This possibility is indicated in Figure 11.1 by the notation in brackets showing that S_R^R could serve as a discriminative stimulus (S_{R2}^D) for further behavior (B_{R2}). The roles could switch back and forth until there was some sort of break. Sometimes an interaction may seem interminable for one of the parties, as when the responder is polite and the initiator is a persistent salesperson or a religious fanatic.

Let us consider a couple of examples. Zack works for a wholesaler that distributes lenses to opticians; Naomi is his supervisor. One interaction they have is occasioned by the arrival of a number of orders in the mail (S_S^D). Naomi hands Zack a stack of orders to fill (B_I). The stack of orders sets the context (S_R^D) for Zack to get busy searching through thousands of drawers for the correct lenses (B_R). The sight of Zack being busy reinforces (S_I^R) Naomi's original behavior (giving him the orders) and serves also as a discriminative stimulus (S_I^D) for her to say something like "Way to go" (or perhaps to withhold criticism; either would constitute B_{I2}), which serves to reinforce (S_R^R) Zack's working. At the end of the week, of course, in another interaction, Naomi's "Way to go" is backed up with a paycheck.

For a second example, we have a married couple, Bill and Liz. On weekday mornings, Liz gets ready to leave for work at 7:30 (S_S^D). She stands with her briefcase at the door and says, *Well, I'm off* (B_I), which produces the sound "Well, I'm off" that Bill hears (S_R^D), and which occasions his saying (B_R), *Have a good day, I'll see you tonight* and kissing her. Bill's affectionate behavior serves to reinforce (S_I^R) Liz's original announcement and also sets the context (S_I^D) for her to respond with something like *You have a good day, too—Don't take any wooden nickels* (B_{I2}). Bill's hearing Liz's affectionate reply reinforces (S_R^R) his affectionate behavior.

When such social episodes occur repeatedly between the same individuals, we say that they have a relationship. In certain limited relationships, the actions and reinforcers might always be the same. If Shona buys the newspaper from the same newsdealer every morning, one might say Shona and the dealer have a relationship. In other relationships, the actions and reinforcers vary widely. A husband and wife may cook for one another, shop together, discuss their children, make love. All of these can be diagrammed as in Figure 11.1, but the actions and reinforcers differ from one interaction to another.

We distinguish relationships between peers from relationships between unequals. Two brothers or two friends may be peers, but an employer and employee or my cat and me would be considered unequals. Two people can be called peers when their interactions include acts and reinforcers on both sides that are similar in kind. If two brothers are affectionate with one another, ask and receive money of one another, and lend toys and tools to one another, then we say they are peers. We might deny the brothers were peers if one is affectionate and the other is not or one always borrows money from the other but never the other way around.

In relationships between unequals, little or no overlap exists between the actions and reinforcers on the two sides. Naomi, the employer, gives work, pays wages, and receives part of the profits from the sales; Zack, the employee, works and receives wages. The patient presents symptoms and pays fees; the physician gives advice and treatment. The ruler makes laws; the citizen follows them.

■ Individuals and Institutions

The conception embodied in Figure 11.1 can be applied not only to relationships between individuals but also to relationships between individuals and institutions and even to relationships between institutions. To do this, it is often convenient to treat the institution as if it were an individual. That creates no confusion as long as we remember that institutions are, after all, composed of individuals. A company, church, or government is a group of individuals, all of whom have relationships with some others of the group. You may not be able to say that everyone in a company has a relationship with everyone else, but being part of the institution entails having relationships with, for example, superiors and subordinates.

It makes sense to treat institutions as if they are individuals because institutional functionaries are replaceable. Judges, ministers, doctors, and nurses leave and are replaced by new individuals who serve the same functions. In some institutions, individuals are even interchangeable, at different times switching roles. When you call the IRS or are admitted to the hospital, you usually have no idea which official will answer the telephone or which nurses and doctors will be on duty.

One can talk about relationships to institutions because, regardless of the particular individuals playing the institutional roles, the contingencies involved remain much the same. In a sense this is true by definition—we speak of something as an institution because it has a certain stability. It is not the personnel who are stable, for people come and go. Neither do buildings make an institution what it is; a hospital can move to a new building and still be known as the same hospital. If the hospital is taken over by new owners, however, it may become a different hospital even if it is in the same building. What remains stable is the mode of operating—in our terms, the contingencies of reinforcement and punishment.

As in a relationship between two individuals, in a relationship between an individual and an institution there are two sets of contingencies: those that affect the individual's behavior and those that affect the behavior of the institution. In the terms of Figure 11.1, the individual or the institution could be either the initiator or the responder. If a bank sends you an invitation to apply for a loan, the bank is the initiator. However, if you go to a bank uninvited and apply for a loan, you are the initiator. You make out your application (B_I), which provides the stimulus (S_R^D) for the bank to make its decision (B_R) to offer you a loan, reinforcing your behavior (S_I^R). Now you respond by signing the loan agreement (B_{I2}), which reinforces the bank's granting of the loan. You and the bank will now have an ongoing relationship because you and the bank will have monthly interactions in which the bank will request a payment, you will pay, and the bank will send a receipt.

Some behavior analysts have applied this framework to thinking about international relations, considering interactions between governments analogous to interactions between individuals. Arms races, for example, can be understood this way (Nevin, 1985). When one country presents a threat (S_R^D) to the other. The other responds by threatening, the first responds in kind, and so on. Each action makes sense (is reinforced) in the short run, but the long-term consequences are disastrous. Alternatives to arms races, such as signing treaties and cooperation, pay off better in the long run, but may be difficult to establish because they are risky in the short run.

❖ EXPLOITATION

In our discussion of coercion (Chapters 9 and 10), we saw that social interactions need not serve the interests of both parties, even though both parties' behavior is reinforced. When a robber demands money and gets it, only the robber benefits, because handing over the money is negatively reinforced; the victim "benefits" only by avoiding injury.

Another sort of interaction prompts talk of cheating. Suppose I go into a shop to buy some cloth, and the merchant charges me twice the going rate. Looking at such an interaction in terms of Figure 11.1, we have to agree that the actions of both parties were positively reinforced. I gain the cloth (S_I^R) and the merchant gains the money (S_R^R). We say the merchant cheated me because, in a larger context, we see an inequity between the two reinforcers: the merchant's payoff is too large relative to my payoff. This larger context sets the fair price. I may never learn that I was cheated, but if I look in other shops or talk to people who know prices, I may conclude that I was cheated (these discriminative stimuli change my verbal behavior).

In a subtler form of cheating, the two parties have an ongoing relationship, and the one being cheated fails to come into contact with the larger context that would expose the inequity of reinforcement. This larger context would usually develop over a long time. For example, one person might make promises but fail to keep them, or more likely keep only some of them and then make more promises. We say the promiser "strings along" the other person. Eventually the person being cheated may catch on because the situation goes on long enough and may be compared to alternative courses of action (other jobs, divorce, rebellion). Governments sometimes take steps to protect citizens from long-term cheating, particularly when they might learn only too late that they had been cheated. Child-labor laws, for example, prevent children from entering into relationships with employers that would pay off in the short run but, by depriving them of opportunities to play and learn, would cheat them in the long run. A relationship of this sort, with short-term positive reinforcement but long-term cheating, is called *exploitation*.

■ The "Happy Slave"

The possibility of coercion—out-and-out slavery—may present less of a threat to democracy than the possibility of the happy slave. Coercion is immediately apparent to the person coerced, whereas the happy slave is content in the short run and may discover the exploitation only after a long time. Being content, because their behavior is positively reinforced, happy slaves take no action to correct their situation. Children working in factories in the nineteenth century were paid and often received care; they were mostly content. Only in middle age would they realize how they had been cheated, if they were to realize it at all. Whatever action they could take then would come too late to prevent harm.

Happy slaves can occur in many different kinds of relationships. Parents can exploit children, rewarding them with care and affection for working, begging in the street, or sexual acts. A husband may exploit his wife by reinforcing her service to him and his children with affection and gifts; a wife may exploit her husband by reinforcing long hours of hard work in the same way. An employer may exploit employees by offering them extra pay for working in hazardous or unhealthy conditions. A government may exploit its citizens by reinforcing gambling in a lottery. One nation may exploit another by taking raw materials in exchange for goods manufactured from those same materials. In each of these examples, the one who is exploited may remain content for a long while or even indefinitely.

■ Deferred Consequences

From the standpoint of the exploited party, the trouble with exploitation is that it entails long-term punishment. Figure 11.2 is a modified version of Figure 11.1 showing such punishment. The target behavior B_R results in two sorts of consequences, the more immediate S_R^R and the delayed punisher S^P. S^P is written large to emphasize the key factor that inclines us to call the relationship exploitive—the long-term punishment outweighs the short-term reinforcement.

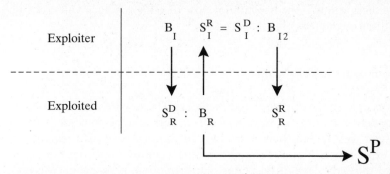

Figure 11.2 An exploitive relationship. The exploited party's behavior (B_R) produces short-term reinforcement for both parties (S_I^R and S_R^R), but leads to major unfavorable consequences (large S^P) in the long run (long arrow). The ultimate punishment is much larger than the immediate reinforcement (S_R^R).

Figure 11.2 omits another common feature of exploitation. The punisher S^P usually grows incrementally as the relationship continues. If a child works for a summer, little loss results, and the experience might even be called beneficial. But if a child works for all the years of childhood, the results are considered disastrous. Each year of work digs the hole deeper, so to speak. That the punishment is both delayed and incremental makes the contingency particularly difficult for the exploited person to detect.

In the terms of Chapter 9, Figure 11.2 illustrates that an exploitive relationship constitutes a contingency trap. (See Figure 9.2.) The target behavior B_R corresponds to acting impulsively in accordance with the short-term reinforcement. Self-control, acting in accordance with the long-term punishment, would mean acting so as to stay out of exploitive relationships or to change a relationship so that it is no longer exploitive. Figure 11.2 represents just the sort of contingency pointed to by rules (Chapter 8) whereby parents and other caretakers warn their charges against impulsive behavior and reinforce behavior that prevents exploitation.

The trouble with happy-slave relationships in behavior management is that they are unstable. The exploited party may wake up to the loss, and the results then resemble those of coercion. The once-happy slave now becomes angry, resentful, and rebellious. The exploited child who has lost in health, education, or ability to enter into normal relationships may now reject the parents. The exploited spouse who has never pursued personal interests may now leave the marriage. Employees who have been exploited eventually punish their employers. Citizens and colonies rebel. As with coercion, in the long run exploitation backfires.

It appears that equity is the only stable policy. Here, however, two age-old questions arise: What is equity? How do we achieve it? Behavior analysis allows us to frame these questions in a way that allows relatively clear answers. The first question can be understood as a question about verbal behavior, and we shall discuss it now. The question of how to achieve equity will come up when we discuss counter-control.

■ Comparative Well-Being

When do people speak of *equity* and *inequity?* These words are notoriously difficult to define. Notions of equity vary from person to person: Shona might say it is right to make convicts work in road gangs; Aaron may regard it as shameful exploitation. Notions of equity within a culture vary from century to century: In the early days of the Industrial Revolution, most people accepted the idea that capitalists should make as much profit as they could and workers should work as hard as they were willing. As time went on, enough people began to call the situation inequitable that reforms occurred; trade unions, welfare legislation, and socialism arose.

Behavior analysts approach variation in verbal behavior, whether from person to person or from time to time, by looking at the consequences and context of the behavior. If Shona says that road gangs are equitable, she is making a discrimination that Aaron does not make. Let us say she regards prisoners as expensive liabilities, draining the taxpayers' money. That is, her verbal behavior about convicts, jails, taxpayers' money, and debts to society has been shaped by a history of reinforcement different from Aaron's; no doubt they travel in different circles, different verbal communities. Perhaps Aaron's parents reinforced talk of equality under the law or in the eyes of God.

The discriminative stimulus for calling a situation exploitive or inequitable is a comparison of consequences. The consequences to one person or group are compared with the consequences to another. For instance, is it equitable for women to be paid less than men for the same work? In the United States and other Western nations, children learn from an early age to make such comparisons between themselves and others. The utterance *She got more than me* is likely to be reinforced with more ice cream, toys, or whatever is being compared. *It's not fair* becomes a refrain in some houses because it is frequently reinforced, with sympathy if not with goods.

As we move into adulthood, our discussions about what is fair become more complicated. The discriminative stimuli controlling verbal behavior about equity become more complex. We learn that sometimes it is fair for one person to receive more than another, especially if one person contributes more effort than the other. Perhaps high-steel construction workers should be paid more than carpenters, if one considers the hazards of high-steel construction.

Equity Theory In discussing equity, organizational psychologists and social psychologists refer to a ratio that compares relatively immediate reinforcement (called *outcome* or *profit*) with longer-term conditions (called *input* or *investment*). In the classic statement of equity theory by George Homans (1961), the ratio is written this way: profit/investments.

Homans argued that decisions about equity depend on this ratio. If two people in a relationship have equal profit/investment ratios, the relationship is equitable. If two people or groups have unequal profit/investment ratios in their relationships with a third party (Acme Lens Company or the United States government), then the disparity between them is inequitable.

The profit/investment ratio can increase in two ways: investment can decrease or profit can increase. If a woman and a man invest equally in a job, then equity demands that the woman's pay (profit) equal the man's. In our supervisor–employee example, however, if Naomi the supervisor invests more than Zack the employee, then their profit/investment ratios can be equal only if she profits more from their relationship than Zack. (She also profits more from her relationship with the company than Zack does.) To determine whether equity exists between two parties, one cannot look at profit or investment alone; one must look at the ratio between the two.

Equity theory conceives of profit to include relatively short-term consequences, such as effort and wages. Profit consists of the party's net gain from the relationship, or gain minus cost (e.g., wages minus effort). When Zack exerts himself to fill orders, the company must reinforce his order-filling adequately with money for his behavior to continue. In other sorts of relationships, the gains are less tangible. If Bill is to wash the dishes regularly, his spouse Liz must make sure that he profits from his efforts enough to keep him at it. According to equity theory, Bill's profit from the marriage would be reckoned by subtracting efforts like dishwashing from gains like affection and opportunities to reproduce.

Homans's concept of investment includes two components: (1) efforts like getting an education, which are investments in the sense that they are supposed to pay off in long-term reinforcement; and (2) personal attributes such as good looks or gender that might be helpful in social interactions but are investments in no ordinary sense of the word. The first type is uncontroversial; it is accepted practice to consider education and experience when setting wages. In terms of equity theory, if the only difference between Jane and Mary is that Jane is a college graduate and Mary only finished high school, Jane's profit/investment ratio equals Mary's only if Jane is paid more. Presumably, Jane and Mary would agree that this was equitable.

The second type of investment raises more controversy. Is it right that, other things being equal, males should be paid more than females for the same work? Regardless of whether it is right, such disparities in pay do occur. Equity theory says nothing about the way people ought to behave; it addresses the way they do behave. Someone who has been brought up to think that males should be paid more than females or that whites should be paid more than blacks sees no inequity in males and whites being paid more. These attributes are investments in that logically they belong in the denominator of the profit/investment ratio: a man who thinks he should be paid more than a woman requires a larger profit before he will say that he is paid equitably relative to the woman. A similar phenomenon occurs in the realm of personal relationships when good-looking people require more profit from relationships than their less good-looking counterparts. Good looks may be called an investment in the same manner of speaking in which people are said to capitalize on their good looks. A beautiful woman may demand expensive jewelry, saying "I'm worth it"; a handsome man may demand to have sex sooner than his partner feels ready for it and see nothing unfair in it.

The mentalistic view of investments appeals to something inside the person, such as an expectation about reinforcement in other settings. The person is said to demand more profit because of the expectation. To the behavior analyst, such an account explains nothing. One might ask what an expectation is and where it comes from.

From the behavior-analytic perspective, the elements of equity theory—gain, cost, and investment—all constitute discriminative stimuli that govern verbal behavior about equity. The usefulness of equity theory is that it points to the various factors that lead to calling a comparison equitable or inequitable. If one party in a relationship receives more pay or other reinforcement than the other party, that is weighed against any difference in immediate costs (e.g., effort expended), differences in experience and education, and differences in personal attributes (e.g., gender, race, and looks). The profit/investment ratio cannot be taken as a mathematical quantity because no one knows how to calculate profit or investment from all the different factors that enter into them, but it does illustrate that various conflicting comparisons all combine to affect the likelihood of words like *equitable* and *inequitable, fair* and *unfair.* Zack may call it fair that his supervisor Naomi is paid more than he is, considering her greater experience, but if Naomi were a man and Zack's training was that men are paid more than women, he might accept a larger disparity in pay and still call it equitable.

Which Comparisons?   This last example illustrates a strength of behavior analysis. Equity theory only points to the various factors that enter into equity-talk, and takes for granted the factors to be weighed. Behavior analysis goes a step beyond to ask what determines which factors will be weighed.

The answer to that question lies in the person's history. Every discrimination depends on past reinforcement and punishment, and calling some disparities equitable and others inequitable should be no exception. There are two ways in which Zack might come to view higher wages to men as equitable. First, it might actually be his experience in jobs he has had that women are paid less than men for the same work. Second, his parents or other authority figures might have taught him this, shaping his verbal behavior about males, females, and fairness. Either way, Zack's history with factors such as gender, race, education, and looks affects which disparities he calls fair and which he calls unfair. When he falls in love with Teresa, who ardently supports women's rights, Zack's judgments about equity change. As Teresa reinforces and punishes his verbal and nonverbal behavior around women, his "consciousness gets raised" and he no longer says that lower pay for women is equitable.

Often, shifts in how factors are weighed translate into shifts in which group is held up for comparison. In the nineteenth century, child labor may have seemed equitable because starving peasant children were held up for comparison. In the twentieth century, when the social costs of child labor became apparent, middle class children who played and attended school were held up for comparison and verbal behavior about child labor switched accordingly. Laborers taught to compare themselves only to other laborers see no inequity if bureaucrats enjoy special privileges; other laborers without such training might compare their plight with that of the bureaucracy and declare inequity. When enough such comparisons are made, we get events like the breakup of the Soviet Union (Lamal, 1991).

❖ CONTROL AND COUNTER-CONTROL

Declarations of inequity occasioned by coercive and exploitive relationships spur revolution as a means to more just arrangements. Overthrowing a government, a marriage, or a business constitutes extreme action. A revolution, a divorce, or a strike seems like the last resort, undertaken only when other means have failed.

The extreme measures change the exploited person's (controllee's) situation by severing the relationship; lesser means, such as threats and promises, make changes within the relationship by changing the behavior of the exploiter (controller). The threat of revolution, divorce, or strike may serve to coerce the offending party into change. Such control exerted back toward the controller adds a new contingency, which can be represented in the general terms of Figure 11.1. Behavior analysts call this *counter-control.*

■ Counter-Control

Counter-control of the coercive sort can be diagrammed as in Figure 9.1. The downtrodden person or group threatens the removal of reinforcement—goods or services—unless the controller complies. Examples need not be so extreme as threats of revolution and divorce; the threats could be of sabotage or disaffection. No matter how asymmetrical the relationship, as long as the controller wants something from the controllee—as long as the controller's behavior can be reinforced by the controllee—the controllee can threaten to withhold. When the threat is effective, the controller's behavior is counter-controlled by negative reinforcement.

Counter-control can also occur by positive reinforcement. Many relationships allow threats to be replaced by promises. Employees can promise higher productivity if their wages are raised. A wife can promise to contribute money to the household if her husband will help her pursue a career. If the controller's behavior changes, it is positively reinforced. The reinforcement may be delayed, but the controller will eventually be better off.

Counter-control implies that the controller has choice, that alternative action is available. The controllee produces a discriminative stimulus that changes the likelihood of one of the alternatives. When their subjects threaten rebellion, the rulers may lower taxes instead of raising them. When employees promise the factory owner an increase in product quality, the owner may switch to the new management scheme the employees suggest.

Figure 11.3 diagrams the two types of counter-control we have discussed. In each diagram, the interactions on the left show counter-control. The controller can act in either of two ways, equitably (B_1; lower taxes and cancel the war) or exploitively (B_2; raise taxes and pursue the war). Each of the two alternatives leads to a different relationship between the parties, symbolized by the boxes on the right. The relationship to which action B_2 leads, in the lower box, may be the present state of affairs; B_2 would keep "business as usual." Action B_1, however, would lead to a new relationship (upper box) that would be more beneficial to both controller and controllee. The controllee promises or threatens (B_C), producing the discriminative stimulus S_C^D ("Increase our wages or we'll strike!"—a rule; see Chapter 8) that points to the upper box (relationship) with its set of contingencies and strengthens the controller's alternative B_1 (e.g., increasing wages). When the controllee counter-controls by threat (top diagram), S_C^D points to the superiority of B_1 on the basis that B_2 leads ultimately to major aversive consequences (S_I^P), to the controller. These result from the behavior of the controllee (B_{R3}) in response to S_R^P, the long-term aversive consequences to the controllee. If rulers overtax their subjects, the subjects will rebel and depose the rulers. When the controllee counter-controls by promise (bottom diagram), S_C^D points to the superiority of B_1 on the basis that it leads ultimately to major reinforcement for both parties (S_R^R and S_I^R). When the subjects enjoy peace and prosperity, they adore and applaud their rulers. Action on the part of the controllee (B_{R3}) may or may not be necessary; a combination of profit-sharing and improved quality control may be directly beneficial to both employer and employees.

Controllees often combine the two types of counter-control, offering both a threat and a promise. Citizens' groups threaten to turn officials out of office if they adopt one policy while simultaneously promising support if they adopt another. This strategy is often called "the carrot and the stick" technique.

The need for counter-control arises because the controller's choice between B_1 and B_2 is a difficult one, for two reasons: (1) of the immediate reinforcers, S_2^R is bigger than S_1^R, and (2) even though the major consequences, S_I^P and S_I^R, outweigh the short-term difference in reinforcement, they are deferred. The controller might have to wait a long time before reaping the advantages of B_1. In the terms of Chapter 9 (Figure 9.2), the choice between B_1 and B_2, without counter-control, constitutes a contingency trap. The controller is likely to behave impulsively, choosing B_2. As we saw in Chapters 8 and 9, when long-term consequences conflict with short-term consequences, rules (threats and promises) can help strengthen the alternative that is better in the long run.

Counter-Control by Threat

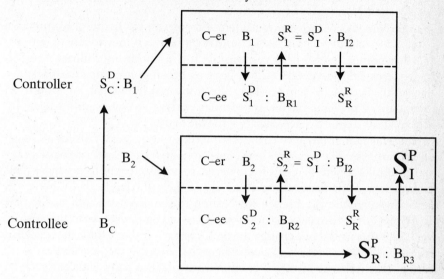

Counter-Control by Promise

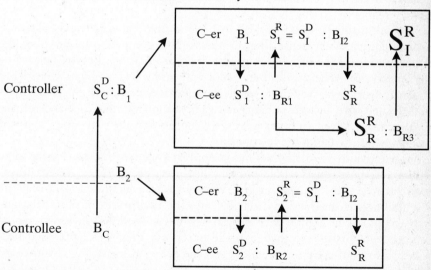

Figure 11.3 Counter-control. In both counter-control by threat (top diagram) and counter-control by promise (bottom diagram), the controller chooses between two relationships with the controllee, shown in the boxes to the right. Action B_1 on the controller's part leads to a better long-term relationship. Action B_2 leads to or continues a less favorable relationship. Counter-control by threat occurs when a discriminative stimulus generated by the controllee, (S_C^D) points to a long-term punisher (S_I^P) for the controller's engaging in behavior B_2. Counter-control by promise occurs when S_C^D points to long-term reinforcement S_I^R for B_1. Counter-control is most necessary when the immediate reinforcer S_2^R is larger than the immediate reinforcer S_1^R.

■ Equity

Counter-control arises from considerations of equity. If the discriminative stimulus for talk of inequity is a comparison between individuals or groups, then that comparison is also responsible for initiation of counter-control. Once successful, however, counter-control becomes a permanent part of a relationship because it helps to keep the compared individuals or groups on par—that is, it prevents the inequity from recurring. It is also a mechanism by which relationships can keep changing for the better.

Since talk about inequity changes from time to time, new calls for counter-control can arise. This occurs when a new comparison is made. As social stratification breaks down, people of a lower class or caste begin to compare their circumstances with those of the strata above them (formerly their "betters"). Historians attribute the French Revolution to the dissatisfaction of the new middle class over their lack of political power in comparison with the aristocracy. Since threats did not change the king's behavior, the middle class rebelled and established a new form of government that afforded the middle class more power—that is, more effective counter-control. In a truly classless society, comparisons would be general in the extreme; any individual or group might be compared with any other. The ideal, "From each according to his ability, to each according to his need,"—was partly responsible for the Russian Revolution.

The ultimate equity is equality. In a relationship between equals, not only is there equity in the sense that no unfavorable comparison exists, but the comparison is made between the parties *in the relationship*. Before the twentieth century, the relationship between a wife and a husband was considered unequal; nowadays, however, equity-comparisons are often made between husband and wife, instead of between this husband and other husbands or this wife and other wives. In other words, we suggest that the two spouses should be equally satisfied with the relationship.

If we stick to our earlier definition of peers as equals who receive the same reinforcers, most equals would not be called peers because they receive different reinforcers in the relationship. We say of a husband and wife that the sources of their satisfaction differ because the reinforcers in their relationship—S_I^R and S_R^R in Figures 11.1 and 11.3—differ in kind, but they may report and otherwise behave so that they and others say they are equally satisfied. When this verbal behavior occurs, it sets the occasion for saying also that the parties are equals.

In terms of equity theory, advocating equality means that the two parties' investments must be viewed as equal, ignoring any differences in gender, race, looks, or education. In practice, people rarely behave this way. The whole point of equity theory is to explain how people are able to call unequal relationships equitable. It admits the possibility, however, that investments could be equal; then equity would require that profits also be equal.

In the special case of relationships between equals, the distinction between control and counter-control disappears, because neither party can be called controller or controllee—neither gains more from the relationship than the other. Each controls the behavior of the other equally.

Shifting from partial equity to equality often leads to profound changes in a relationship. When workers compare themselves only with other workers, they can call a situation equitable even though their employers profit from it more than they do. If the workers begin to compare themselves with their employers, however, to achieve equity they would have to achieve equality. Such movements lead to employee-owned businesses or, on a larger scale, to government-owned businesses and socialism.

■ Power

Discussions about equity usually also involve discussion about power. Definitions of *power* usually appeal to intuition or common sense. Behavior analysis offers a path to a better understanding.

Equity and power refer to different aspects of a relationship. Talk about equity concerns the benefits derived from the relationship. Talk about power concerns the degree of control each party exerts over the behavior of the other. When the parties benefit unequally from the relationship, the one who benefits more also has more power. This greater power, as much as the greater benefit, leads to this party being called the controller.

Strictly speaking, however, contingencies are powerful, not people. A person has power when he or she is the instrument of a powerful contingency. When an employer can deprive an employee of a job for failure to perform, the employee's behavior is under control of a powerful contingency. A person's power depends entirely on the power of the contingencies he or she wields.

Two factors make a contingency powerful: the importance of the reinforcer and the precision of control over the reinforcer. The importance of the reinforcer depends not on its absolute value but on its value relative to other reinforcers in the controllee's life. If we say of Sonya that "her job is her life," we mean that there is little else providing reinforcement in her life. We expect that losing her job would be devastating and that Sonya will do almost anything to retain her job, giving her employer enormous power in their relationship. If, however, Sonya has many other relationships in her life—parents, spouse, children, friends—and particularly if she has other sources of income, the job will have less importance. Then her employer would be less able to control her behavior with the threat of losing her job. In general, since employers are wealthier than their employees, the benefits that employees derive from the relationship have greater importance to the employees even though they are smaller in absolute terms. By pooling the reinforcers that individual workers control, unions allow workers partly to offset the difference in reinforcer importance.

The same difference appears in other relationships between unequals. The grade a teacher gives a student is usually more important to the student than the student's approval is to the teacher. The parent's affection is usually more important to the child than the child's affection is to the parent. The more powerful person controls the more important reinforcer.

The way that reinforcer importance contributes to power is often especially obvious in abnormal relationships. When the child's performance is more important to the parent than the parent's affection is to the child, the child bosses the parent. When students can threaten the teacher with knives and guns, the teacher's behavior is very much swayed by their approval. When an employee has vital skills that are impossible to replace, the employee can order the employer around.

The power of these contingencies also depends on their precision. Even if reinforcers are important, the contingency is less powerful if their delivery is delayed or uncertain. The busy parent who has to tell the child to wait until the weekend for some quality time has less power to control the child's behavior. The employer who has to make wage increases contingent on the business making a larger profit loses power to control employees' behavior. Totalitarian governments increase the precision of aversive control by spying (e.g., wiretapping) on their subjects, thereby making punishment for opposition more certain.

Unequal power may be the basis of unequal benefit. The one who wields the more powerful contingencies also reaps the greater rewards. The controller reinforces controllee behavior that produces the controller's greater reinforcement.

The inequity, however, is limited. If the controllee's reinforcement drops too low or the demands of the reinforced behavior are too high, counter-control becomes likely. When workers in one company are paid less than those in another company, or find they cannot feed their families on what they earn, they begin to leave, protest, or organize. Depending on the comparison serving as the discriminative stimulus, the controllee at some point declares that the controller is abusing his or her power and that the relationship has become exploitive. Even if the controller's behavior continues to push the limit, still the imbalance in power can sustain only a certain imbalance in benefits.

Counter-control acts to redress inequity by decreasing the imbalance of power. Creating contingencies that reinforce or punish the controller's behavior means that the controllee can reinforce (positively or negatively—offering promises or threats) the controller's more giving actions. To avert a rebellion, the dictator lowers taxes. For the sake of a promised gain in quality control, the industrialist institutes employee profit-sharing. Since counter-control increases the relative power of the controllee, it produces more equity by decreasing the imbalance of power, and in the extreme, both benefit and power become equal. When, for example, a husband and wife have an equal relationship, their behavior is not only reinforced equally, but other sources of reinforcement make the reinforcement from the marriage equally important to both.

■ Democracy

Why is democracy so popular as a form of government? Traditional answers refer to citizens' feelings of freedom and happiness. Behavior analysis allows a fuller and clearer understanding of the virtues of democracy.

It is true, as we saw in Chapter 9, that citizens in a democracy feel relatively free and happy. We could, however, imagine a benevolent dictator who controlled the citizens' behavior with positive reinforcement. With such a government, the citizens might feel free, but they would not be able to ensure the dictator's benevolence. The ingredient in democracy that safeguards the people's freedom is counter-control.

Democracy provides citizens with contingencies with which to control the behavior of their rulers. In the United States, the President and congressional representatives periodically come up for evaluation, with the possibilities of being reelected or replaced. If we don't like what they do, we can throw them out.

Counter-control in a democracy can be by threat or by promise. The threat would be that if the ruler's policies (B_2 in Figure 11.3) were to produce punishing consequences (S_R^P) for the constituents, then the citizens will vote (B_{R3}) for someone else and dismiss the ruler (S_I^P). Such threats are made explicit at demonstrations and rallies. The promise would be that if the policies were to produce reinforcement (S_R^R), then the constituents would vote for the ruler (B_{R3}) and return the ruler to office (S_I^R). In everyday terms, we call counter-control by promise *lobbying*.

Democracy is also characterized by a type of equality, symbolized in the French and Russian revolutions by calling everyone "citizen" or "comrade." The relationship between the President and the citizens of the United States cannot be a relationship between equals—while in office, the rulers in a democracy are clearly controllers. Once out of office, however, they again become ordinary citizens—controllees like everyone else. In the long run, they are subject to the same contingencies as everyone else.

Democratic rulers' policies sooner or later affect the rulers themselves. Even while in office, the President and members of Congress must pay taxes. Once out of office, they are even more subject to their own policies. In the long run, democracy tends to take the relationship between controllers and controllees beyond partial equity toward equality.

This description of democracy is, of course, an idealization. Government officials sometimes engage in secret illegal action, and sometimes take bribes. An ex-President only partly returns to the status of ordinary citizen. As a whole, however, democracy is generally considered an improvement over absolute types of government such as monarchy and dictatorship. The imperfection of democratic processes, however, suggests that they could be improved further: perhaps still better means of counter-control can be found. We shall discuss how a society might make such improvements in Chapter 14, when we take up social engineering.

❖ SUMMARY

For an episode between two parties to be called a social interaction, each party must reinforce the other's behavior—the reinforcement must be mutual. Examples discussed in earlier chapters include verbal behavior and coercion. Two individuals are said to have a relationship when social interactions occur between them repeatedly and frequently. This same conception applies to relationships between individuals and institutions.

Although relationships based on coercion are obviously inequitable, a subtler form of inequity marks exploitive relationships, in which both parties' actions are positively reinforced. These are said to be inequitable because one party is cheated in the long run; the exploited party's participation in the relationship is ultimately severely punished. In the short run, the person being cheated might remain content; such a person is called a "happy slave." In the long run, happy slaves often discover or are told about the cheating—that is, they encounter discriminative stimuli that make disaffection and rebellion likely. This long-term instability makes exploitation, like coercion, a poor method of management.

More so than for coercive relationships, the tendency for rebellion against exploitive relationships depends on verbal behavior of people in the society. Talk about exploitation tends to occur in the same contexts as talk about unfairness and inequity. A comparison is made between two individuals or two groups, and the poorly treated person or group is said to be exploited. Since the comparison made depends on the speaker's history of reinforcement, talk of exploitation, equity, and inequity varies from person to person and from time to time.

Coercion and exploitation are redressed by changing the relationship. Relationships can be severed, but often less drastic changes can allow the relationship to continue. The move toward greater equality occurs as a result of added contingencies, or counter-control. The controller is offered a choice of an alternative relationship, a modification of the existing one, and discriminative stimuli from the controllee that point to superior long-term consequences for the controller increase the likelihood that the controller will adopt the new course of action. Counter-control operates by promise and by threat, by stimuli (rules) pointing to future reinforcement and avoidance of future punishment. Introducing a new contingency by which the controllee can affect the controller's behavior changes the relationship toward greater equity.

When new comparisons occur, a relationship may change still further. If the new comparisons are made to a broader reference group, the relationship moves toward greater equity and, ultimately, to equality, in which the parties in the relationship are compared to one another. In a relationship between equals, both parties benefit equally. When reinforcement is equal, the distinctions between control versus counter-control and controller versus controllee disappear, because each party controls the other's behavior equally.

The control that each party in a relationship exerts over the other's behavior is the party's power or, more precisely, the power of the contingencies by which that party controls the other's behavior. The power of a contingency depends on the importance of the reinforcer and the precision of control over the reinforcer. The more important the reinforcer and the greater the precision of control over it, the more powerful the contingency. An imbalance of power in the contingencies of a relationship leads to inequality of benefit derived from the relationship. Since counter-control increases the controllee's power, it tends to reduce inequity by decreasing the imbalance of power.

The great strength of democracy is that it gives the people, the controllees, counter-control. Counter-control occurs by means of elections, demonstrations, and lobbying. Although the relationship remains unequal, even with counter-control, the limited term of office of the rulers ensures long-term equality, because on the rulers' return to being ordinary citizens they are subject to the same contingencies as everyone else. When everyone's behavior is subject to the same contingencies, everyone is equal. That, at least, is the theory; democracy as actually practiced may be open to improvement.

❖ FURTHER READING

Adams, J. S. (1965). Inequity in social exchange. In L. Berkowitz (Ed.), *Advances in experimental social psychology,* Vol. 2 (pp. 267–299). New York: Academic Press. A classic article that extends Homans's equity theory by considering the effects of different standards of comparison.

Homans, G. C. (1961). *Social behavior: Its elementary forms.* New York: Harcourt Brace. A classic text that contains Homans's original equity theory.

Lamal, P. A. (1991). Three metacontingencies in the pre-*perestroika* Soviet Union. *Behavior and Social Issues, 1,* 75–90. This article is a behavioral analysis of some management practices that served poorly in the Soviet Union.

Nevin, J. A. (1985). Behavior analysis, the nuclear arms race, and the peace movement. In S. Oskamp (Ed.), *International conflict and national policy issues. Applied Social Psychology Annual #6* (pp. 27–44). Beverly Hills: Sage Publications. This paper illustrates the way that behavior analysis can be applied to international relations.

Rao, R. K., and Mawhinney, T. C. (1991). Superior-subordinate dyads: Dependence of leader effectiveness on mutual reinforcement contingencies. *Journal of the Experimental Analysis of Behavior, 56,* 105–118. This article describes laboratory studies of superior–subordinate relationships, particularly as they depend on the importance of reinforcers.

Skinner, B. F. (1974). *About behaviorism.* New York: Knopf. Counter-control is discussed explicitly in Chapter 12, "The Question of Control."

Skinner, B. F. (1978). *Reflections on behaviorism and society.* New York: Appleton-Century-Crofts. This contains, among other essays, "Freedom, at Last, from the Burden of Taxation," about the exploitive nature of state lotteries.

**CHAPTER
12**

VALUES: RELIGION AND SCIENCE

Questions about values are questions about good and bad, right and wrong. Growing up in a culture, we learn to call certain things and actions good: we strive after those things and engage in those actions. We learn to call certain things and actions bad, and we avoid those things and shun those actions. The approbation of one's fellows is good, honest labor is good, illness is bad, and meanness is bad. In this chapter we accept that these things and actions are called good and bad, are embraced or avoided. We are interested in how to explain the behavior of calling them good and bad.

In the traditional view, values are ideas or attitudes, mental things somewhere inside. To religious-minded people, these mental values come from God. This assumed divine origin underlies the quote from C. S. Lewis at the end of Chapter 9 that says science can shed no light on questions of value, that it can tell us how we *do* behave but not how we *ought* to behave. Behaviorists today disagree with Lewis; it is possible for science to shed some light on questions about how we ought to behave.

❖ **QUESTIONS ABOUT VALUE**

Behaviorists reject the notion that values are mental entities; if they are any-thing, they are behavior. Lewis is correct that science has nothing to say about what is good or bad in the eyes of God, but it may have plenty to say about what is good or bad in the eyes of people. Even if Lewis is correct that behavior analysis can only address what people do, one of the things people do is to talk about how people ought to behave. Behavior analysis can approach questions about value by focusing on what people do, and particularly what they say (their verbal behavior) concerning good and bad and right and wrong. Science can inquire into why people make the value statements they do.

■ Moral Relativism

There seems to be so much diversity from person to person, place to place, and culture to culture that some thinkers throw up their hands and say there is no universal standard that can explain ideas about right and wrong. Such thinkers talk of *situational ethics*—ethics born of particular situations rather than universal principles—as the only possibility. In other words, these moral relativists hold that each person develops his or her own ideas about good and bad relative to his or her particular situation. The extension of such thinking is the dictum, "Nothing is good or bad but thinking makes it so."

One problem with moral relativism is that it appears to offer no means for resolving conflicts between people whose ideas of good and bad differ. To take an extreme example, suppose a sadist finds it good to inflict pain on other people. If there is no universal standard, how can we conclude that these actions are bad? What could limit the notion, "If it feels good, do it"?

Moral relativism can answer such questions by pointing to social conventions. A group can decide what behavior they will call good or bad, and then that convention becomes part of the individual's situation. The sadist can be taught that the group rejects such behavior. A view like this, however, leaves open some basic questions: (1) How would a group arrive at conventions of good and bad? (2) How would the group persuade individuals to accept the conventions?

■ Ethical Standards

The alternative to strict moral relativism is the idea that there are universal ethical standards, that principles can be discovered by which we can explain people's assertions about good and bad as an outcome of more than their particular situations. Both the religious Lewis and the behaviorist Skinner rejected moral relativism in favor of universal ethical standards. Their ideas about what standard to apply differed, of course, particularly in respect to the origins of such a standard.

The Law of Human Nature   Lewis (1960) begins with the observation that people often quarrel over what is fair:

> I believe we can learn something very important from listening to the kinds of things they say. They say things like this: "How'd you like it if anyone did the same to you?"—"That's my seat, I was there first"—"Leave him alone, he isn't doing you any harm"—"Why should you shove in first?"—"Give me a bit of your orange, I gave you a bit of mine"—"Come on, you promised" (p. 17).

From Lewis's point of view, such statements suggest that when people quarrel they appeal to an ethical standard which they assume everyone shares:

> Now what interests me about all these remarks is that the man who makes them is not merely saying that the other man's behavior does not happen to please him. He is appealing to some kind of standard of behavior which he expects the other man to know about. And the other man very seldom replies: "To hell with your standard." Nearly always he tries to make out that what he has been doing does not really go against the standard, or that if it does there is some special excuse. He pretends there is some special reason in this partic-ular case why the person who took the seat first should not keep it, or that things were quite different when he was given the bit of orange, or that some-thing has turned up which lets him off keeping his promise. It looks, in fact very much as if both parties had in mind some kind of Law or Rule of fair play or decent behavior or morality or whatever you like to call it, about which they really agreed. And they have (p. 17).

This "law or rule" that everyone agrees on Lewis calls the "law of human nature." He carefully explains, as we saw in Chapter 9, that this law is not about what we do, but about what we ought to do. It is a law that can be—and often is—disobeyed.

Reading between the lines, we can see that Lewis's law concerns kindness and fairness. It comes down to the Golden Rule: Do unto others as you would have them do unto you. To Lewis, apparently, we break the rule out of self-interest, and he is interested in why we ever obey it. He implies that our only reason to act selflessly is our God-given inner sense of what is right.

Lewis overlooks the possibility that people might also obey the Golden Rule out of self-interest. In keeping with our discussion of rules in Chapter 8, this rule points to long-term consequences and the likelihood of reciprocation: when we do nice things for others, they often do nice things for us. We resist breaking the rule openly because if we act selfishly toward others they are like-ly to respond by acting selfishly toward us.

In the more technical terms of Chapter 11, the Golden Rule mandates equity. If you fail to reinforce the other person's behavior sufficiently, the desired behavior will disappear. If Naomi gives Shona a piece of orange, and then Shona refuses to give Naomi a piece of orange, it becomes unlikely that Naomi will give Shona anything else. If Zack breaks his promise to Gideon, it becomes unlikely that Gideon's behavior will again be controlled by a promise of Zack's (a rule; Chapter 8). Doing unto others as you would have them do unto you means that you reinforce others' behavior and they reinforce yours.

Evolutionary biologists also recognize altruism (being good to others) and reciprocity (considerations of long-term equity) as human universals. (They recognize other cultural universals, like marriage, property rights, and recognition of relatives.) The biologists' reasoning parallels Lewis's: wherever we look, we find that people share and make sacrifices for others (practice altruism) at least some of the time; that cheating (failure to reciprocate in the long run) occurs too; and that cheating is punished, particularly by those who are cheated. The universality of these phenomena does seem to suggest that kindness and fairness constitute a law of human nature.

In contrast to Lewis, however, evolutionists and behaviorists see the regularities of human behavior as reflecting only various forms of selfishness. Naomi gives Shona a piece of orange only if Shona is likely to reciprocate—reinforce Naomi's act of giving—in the long run. Gideon may donate time and money to his church, but only as long as he gets something back in the long run. Cheating and verbal behavior that may avoid punishment for cheating ("pretending" according to Lewis) differ from the "correct" behavior only in that they are reinforced more immediately. They constitute only a more obvious form of selfishness—acting so as to produce greater short-term reinforcement. Thus, altruism, because it enhances long-term benefit, is still selfish.

The great exception to human selfishness occurs in behavior toward relatives. Parents, in particular, make sacrifices for their children with no expectation of repayment. Brothers and sisters often help one another out even if reciprocity is unlikely, or openly disavow any need for repayment. Uncles and aunts help their nieces and nephews. A well-to-do person may even help a cousin with no ability to reciprocate.

The exceptions, however, prove the rule. The universality of altruism suggests a genetic base. Genes for altruism toward relatives would be selected because relatives share those genes and helping relatives tends to increase the frequency of the shared genes in the gene pool. Genes that promote altruism toward nonrelatives can be selected as long as they go along with genes that make for a sensitivity to long-term reinforcement. This brings us to the question of origins: Where did the law of human nature come from?

The Question of Origins   Lewis rejects the moral relativists' idea that agreed-on values are simply social conventions, as do evolutionists and behaviorists. Here is how he addresses the question, "Isn't what you call the Moral Law just a social convention, something that is put into us by education?"

> I fully agree that we learn the Rule of Decent Behavior from parents and teachers, and friends and books, as we learn everything else. But some of the things we learn are mere conventions which might have been different—we learn to keep to the left of the road, but it might just as well have been the rule to keep to the right—and others of them, like mathematics, are real truths. The question is to which class the Law of Human Nature belongs (p. 24).

Lewis, of course, argues that this law is a "real truth," not one of those conventions that might have been different. He goes to some lengths to reject a related explanation that decent conduct benefits one's society as a whole, stating the argument this way: "Human beings, after all, have some sense; they see that you cannot have real safety or happiness except in a society where every one plays fair, and it is because they see this that they try to behave decently." He dismisses the explanation this way:

> Now, of course, it is perfectly true that safety and happiness can only come from individuals, classes, and nations being honest and fair and kind to each other. It is one of the most important truths in the world. But as an explanation of why we feel as we do about Right and Wrong it just misses the point. If we ask: "Why ought I to be unselfish?" and you reply "Because it is good for society," we may then ask, "Why should I care what's good for society except when it happens to pay *me* personally?" and then you will have to say, "Because you ought to be unselfish"—which simply brings us back to where we started (p. 29).

To Lewis, there has to be some additional factor, some ultimate reason, why we feel as we do about right and wrong and why we ought to behave unselfishly.

Evolutionary biologists make a similar argument against explanations of altruism that appeal to acting "for the good of the species" or group selection. If individuals behaved so as to enhance the fitness of the group at their own expense, then any member of the group that acted selfishly—enjoying benefits of being in the group without making sacrifices (i.e., cheating)—would have higher fitness than the rest. Selfish types would increase in numbers and eventually undo the social arrangement. Any social system based on the good of the group would be vulnerable to disruption by cheaters unless some larger consideration, ultimately selfish, could constrain individuals to remain altruistic.

Although the religious and evolutionary accounts of values agree that some ultimate factor or absolute standard must explain our values, this is as far as their agreement goes. Lewis proposes that the law of human nature comes from God, whereas evolutionists argue that it is the result of natural selection.

❖ A SCIENTIFIC APPROACH TO VALUES

A scientific account of values cannot appeal to supernatural causes like God. Can behaviorists, contrary to Lewis's contention, say anything about what we ought to do, beyond what we, in fact, do?

The answer is "yes and no." Behavior analysts can offer accounts of what people do that is considered good and bad, and particularly people's verbal behavior about good and bad and right and wrong—that is, accounts of what people say about what we ought to do. A religious person like Lewis, however, could remain dissatisfied with such explanations and demand to know why the universe is arranged in such a way that we would come to say things like

Thou shalt not steal to one another. Even if we can explain how that came about, given the way the world is, there remains the question of why the world should be that way. As Lewis (1960) said:

> Science works by experiments. It watches how things behave. Every scientific statement in the long run, however complicated it looks, really means something like, "I pointed the telescope to such and such a part of the sky at 2:20 A.M. on January 15th and saw so-and-so," or, "I put some of this stuff in a pot and heated it to such-and-such a temperature and it did so-and-so." . . . But why anything comes to be there at all, and whether there is anything behind the things science observes—something of a different kind—this is not a scientific question. If there is "Something Behind," then either it will have to remain altogether unknown to men or else make itself known in some different way. The statement that there is any such thing, and the statement that there is no such thing, are neither of them statements that science can make. . . . After all, it is really a matter of common sense. Supposing science ever became complete so that it knew every single thing in the whole universe. Is it not plain that the questions, "Why is there a universe?" "Why does it go on as it does?" "Has it any meaning?" would remain just as they were (p. 32)?

Recognizing the correctness of Lewis's general argument that there are questions that lie outside the scope of science, we can disagree with his assertions about the law of human nature coming from Beyond, as long as we focus on what people do and say that conforms to the law. We can explain why people behave unselfishly and why they speak of selfish behavior as bad and unselfish as good. As before, we will rely on basic behavior-analytic concepts like reinforcement, verbal behavior, and stimulus control.

■ Reinforcers and Punishers

Skinner (1971) offered a simple rule of thumb: Things that are called good are positive reinforcers. Things that are called bad are punishers. Actions that are called good are those that are reinforced. Actions that are called bad are those that are punished.

Some things and actions are good or bad because of the way our bodies are constructed. Health is good; illness is bad. Food and eating are good; pain and falling down are bad. Affection is good; rejection is bad.

Acquired reinforcers and punishers are called good and bad because they have been associated with unconditional reinforcers and punishers. Money is good; the signs of illness are bad. An *A* is a good grade; an *F* is a bad grade. Both their power as consequences and their verbal labels derive from a person's history. They vary from time to time, person to person, and culture to culture. The behavior of many children in the United States may be reinforced with baseball cards, and these children call baseball cards good. This is rarely true for adults, but for some adults the cards remain reinforcers. For a person living in a village in India, baseball cards are unlikely to serve as reinforcers or to be called good; neither are they associated with unconditional reinforcers nor is the verbal behavior of calling them good reinforced.

Most acquired reinforcers and punishers result from our living in society with other people. Grades, medals, reprimands, praise, getting to work on time, catching the bus—the power of all these consequences is social in origin, the outcome of relations arranged by the group. All of them are called good or bad according to whether they reinforce or punish behavior that produces them. Reprimands are bad; they punish lying, cheating, tardiness, sloppiness, and so on. Getting to work is good; it reinforces rising early, eating quickly, catching the bus, and so on.

If most things called good or bad are called so because of social arrangements, so too most actions called good or bad are called so because of social arrangements—that is, because they are reinforced or punished by other people. A child's sharing with siblings and friends is called good and is reinforced by parents and teachers. Donating to charity is called good and is reinforced by friends, newspaper columnists, and the Internal Revenue Service (by reduction of taxes). Lying is called bad and is punished by parents, teachers, and friends. Giving and accepting bribes is called bad and is punished by the judicial system.

Skinner's rule of thumb about reinforcement being good and punishment being bad implies a rule about value judgments—verbal behavior involving *good, bad, right,* and *wrong.* The utterance *Cheating is wrong* occurs because utterances like it have been reinforced by parents and teachers. Thus, someone who never received approval for such utterances will never call cheating wrong, yet this person might never cheat if his or her history has included honesty being reinforced and cheating being punished. Another person might call cheating wrong and yet frequently cheat. Usually, however, people whose cheating has been punished are also people whose verbal behavior of calling cheating wrong has been reinforced. Calling reinforcers good and reinforced behavior right and calling punishers bad and punished behavior wrong is verbal behavior that is usually reinforced.

This account may shed some light on why we call things and actions good and bad, but it leaves at least two fundamental questions unanswered. First, we have strong feelings about right and wrong—about the Rule of Decent Behavior, as Lewis would call it. When we do something good, we feel good; when we do something bad, we feel bad. It is often suggested that we call things good or bad because of the way we feel about them. How are feelings related to things we call good and bad?

Second, even if it is true that good and bad actions are those that are reinforced and punished in our society, we have yet to explain why our society customarily reinforces and punishes those particular actions. What is it about good and bad actions that leads the group to reinforce and punish them? This is the puzzle that Lewis raised and answered by appealing to God. Behavior analysts today generally follow Skinner's (1971, 1981) lead and answer it by appealing to evolutionary theory, as we shall see in this chapter and the next. We shall first take up the question of the role of feelings and then turn to the role of evolution.

■ Feelings

Skinner (1971) discussed the difference between what we can do and what we ought to do as an example of the difference between a fact and the way we feel about the fact. Although people readily embrace this distinction, Skinner pointed out that to a behavior analyst both an act and our feeling about it are facts to be explained: "How people feel about facts, or what it means to feel anything, is a question for which a science of behavior should have an answer. A fact is no doubt different from what a person feels about it, but the latter is a fact also" (p. 103). If Gideon loses his temper, shouts at Shona, and then feels terrible about it afterward, the behavior analyst needs to explain not only Gideon's shouting but also his feeling terrible.

Reports of feeling good or feeling bad are instances of self-knowledge (Chapter 6). To understand such reports, we need to examine a person's history of reinforcement and punishment. Not everyone feels badly after shouting at someone else, so why does Gideon? Most likely, his shouting was frequently punished over the years by parents, teachers, and friends. The result is that when he misbehaves he reports feeling anxiety, shame, and guilt.

Skinner argued that such reports are verbal behavior under the discriminative control of conditions of the body. The conditions can be at least partially public, as when changes in heart rate, breathing, stomach, and sweat glands are recorded in emotionally charged situations. Public or private, they serve as discriminative stimuli, which along with external circumstances (the shouting, the hurt expression on Shona's face) set the occasion for reports of feeling bad, ashamed, and guilty. Reports of feeling good occur in situations like those in which behavior has been reinforced in the past. Naomi's report that she feels good when she gets an *A* in a course results from bodily conditions that are also labeled "joy" and "ecstasy."

The reports, however, do not explain why the situations that occasion them are called good and bad; rather, the reports about feelings and the utterances about good and bad arise from the same source—history. Skinner attributed the bodily conditions to respondent conditioning; they are physiological reactions to situations in which reinforcers and punishers (phylogenically important events; Chapter 4) have occurred in the person's past. They arose as a by-product of the operant contingencies that controlled the reinforcers and punishers—that is, the contingencies that shaped (encouraged or discouraged) the behavior called good or bad. The utterances about good and bad proceed from a parallel set of contingencies in which labels of *good* were reinforced in the presence of reinforcers and reinforced behavior and in which labels of *bad* were reinforced in the presence of punishers and punished behavior. Having yelled at Shona, Gideon says that he did something wrong *and* that he feels bad, but he does not do the one because of the other; the two verbal operants proceed from overlapping, but different, histories of reinforcement.

The difference between the histories explains why people can talk about good and bad without necessarily feeling good and bad. Discussions of right and wrong often engender passion, but they can proceed calmly. I may decide that I ought to carry insurance without having any special feelings about it.

The history of value statements apart from feelings allows us to understand the use of words like *ought* and *should*. Statements involving these words are rules in the sense of Chapter 8 (i.e., verbal discriminative stimuli). If Naomi says to Zack, "To get to the bank, you should turn left at the corner," she could just as well have said "If you turn left, that action will be reinforced by your getting to the bank." The *should* is a cue to Zack that his behavior could be reinforced. Rules are usually called value judgments when they point to social contingencies of reinforcement, contingencies in which reinforcement is delivered by other people. Skinner (1971) argued this point as follows:

> "Should" and "ought" begin to raise more difficult questions when we turn to the contingencies under which a person is induced to behave for the good of others. "You should (you ought to) tell the truth" is a value judgment to the extent that it refers to reinforcing contingencies. We might translate it as follows: "If you are reinforced by the approval of your fellow men, you will be reinforced when you tell the truth." The value is to be found in the social contingencies maintained for purposes of control. It is an ethical or moral judgment in the sense that ethos and mores refer to the customary practices of a group (pp. 112–113).

In the terms of Chapter 8, Skinner is arguing here that a value judgment is a rule that points to an ultimate contingency that is social in nature, the result of the "customary practices" of the group to which speaker and listener belong. We cannot, however, discuss either cultural practices (Chapter 13) or morals (below) without first revisiting evolutionary theory.

■ Evolutionary Theory and Values

Our discussion thus far has left unanswered a basic question, or as Lewis might say, the "real question." If good things and actions are reinforcers and reinforced actions, and bad things and actions are punishers and punished actions, then what makes reinforcers reinforcing and punishers punishing?

A partial answer was sketched in Chapter 4: fitness. Food is a reinforcer to a deprived organism because those types in a population that are organized because of their genotype so that food should be a reinforcer outreproduce other types not so organized. Pain is a punisher because those types that are organized so that the bodily harm inducing pain should be a punisher outreproduce other types not so organized. Occasionally, because of genetic defect, someone is born without the capacity to be punished by painful stimulation. Such people injure themselves frequently and survive childhood only with constant vigilance by their caretakers. Similar problems would arise with people deficient in other personal reinforcers and punishers: shelter, sex, excessive heat and cold, nausea, and so on.

Since our species is social, the fitness of our genes is often tied up with our behavior toward one another. The benefits of group living can be bought only at the expense of mechanisms that make us sensitive to and dependent on one another. Not only the approval of our fellows, but their well-being often weighs heavily with us. Not only a baby's cry, but signs of distress even in a stranger are usually aversive. There is experimental evidence that behaving altruistically toward others functions as a reinforcer even apart from any other personal gain. Our short-term individual interests are often sacrificed on the altar of the greater good of the group, which turns out to be our own greater good in the long run.

More precisely, the greater good in the long run is the greater good of one's genes. The evolutionary biologist Richard Dawkins (1989) puts the position vividly by describing organisms as "survival machines" that make "gambles" depending on the way their genes have organized their bodies:

> Prediction in a complex world is a chancy business. Every decision that a survival machine takes is a gamble, and it is the business of genes to program brains in advance so that on average they take decisions that pay off. The currency used in the casino of evolution is survival, strictly gene survival, but for many purposes individual survival is a reasonable approximation. If you go down to the water-hole to drink, you increase your risk of being eaten by predators who make their living lurking for prey by water-holes. If you do not go down to the water-hole you will eventually die of thirst. There are risks whichever way you turn, and you must take the decision that maximizes the long-term survival chances of your genes. . . . Some form of weighing up the odds has to be done. But of course we do not have to think of the animals as making the calculations consciously. All we have to believe is that those individuals whose genes build brains in such a way that they tend to gamble correctly are as a direct result more likely to survive, and therefore to propagate those same genes (pp. 55–56).

"Gambles" and "decisions" here refer to behavior and usually, in our species, learned behavior. From the point of view of genes, learning implies still more gambling, because the genes can be less assured that the organism will behave correctly. Relinquishing some control to experience with the environment may enhance survival; if so, genes that allow this will flourish. On the other hand, genes that limit what actions are likely to be learned and what aspects of the environment are likely to be learned about will be selected if they generally tend the organism to make good gambles. That is why genes make for learning, but only to a limited extent. One way that genes retain control is to set the things that will be good and bad or reinforcers and punishers. Dawkins (1989) writes of operant learning:

> One way for genes to solve the problem of making predictions in rather unpredictable environments is to build in a capacity for learning. Here the program may take the form of the following instructions to the survival machine: "Here is a list of things defined as rewarding: sweet taste in the mouth, orgasm, mild temperature, smiling child. And here is a list of nasty things: various sorts of pain, nausea, empty stomach, screaming child. If you should happen to do something that is followed by one of the nasty things, don't do it again, but on the other hand repeat anything that is followed by

one of the nice things." The advantage of this sort of programming is that it greatly cuts down the number of detailed rules that have to be built into the original program; and it is also capable of coping with changes in the environment that could not have been predicted in detail (p. 57).

Genes that define reinforcers and punishers and provide the means for operant learning generally will be selected in a species like ours, which lives in an uncertain environment. In turn, the reinforcers and punishers define what is good and bad, even when the gamble has gone awry and behavior fails to advance fitness or even decreases fitness. Dawkins continues:

> In our example the genes are predicting that sweet taste in the mouth, and orgasm, are going to be "good" in the sense that eating sugar and copulating are likely to be beneficial to gene survival. The possibilities of saccharine and masturbation are not anticipated according to this example; nor are the dangers of over-eating sugar in our environment where it exists in unnatural plenty (p. 57).

This last point deserves emphasis: Sugar "exists in unnatural plenty" in our environment because our environment has changed. The environment in which the genes were selected that made sweet taste a reinforcer is no longer with us. Sugar is now plentiful because of cultural change, and cultural change is so rapid in comparison with evolutionary change that shifts in the gene pool can never keep up. But cultural change continues, and now it has become bad to eat too much sugar and good to watch one's diet. These labels, however, have to do with more than the individual because they depend on group practices of reinforcement and punishment. We shall return to culture and cultural change in the next chapter.

Altruism   According to both evolutionary theory and behavior analysis, true altruism in the sense of self-sacrifice with no possibility of long-term gain cannot occur. Evolutionary biologists point out that altruism is most often directed toward kin. Self-sacrifice for the sake of kin can be selected because the kin share the genes making for the altruistic behavior; even if the altruist loses out personally, the genes may increase through the benefit to the kin. Biologists argue further that self-sacrifice extends to strangers only when reciprocation is likely—when, for example, group membership requires self-sacrifice as the price of the benefits of group membership. People are much more likely to help someone who belongs to their club, their neighborhood, or their race than someone who is utterly unrelated.

Behavior analysts take this line a step further by noting that altruistic behavior depends on reinforcement. Skinner (1971), for example, considered acting for the good of others to be an outcome of social reinforcement: "When other people intentionally arrange and maintain contingencies of reinforcement, the person affected by the contingencies may be said to be behaving 'for the good of others'" (pp. 108–109). The recipient of the altruism may benefit more immediately, but the altruist benefits ultimately as well. People behave altruistically toward others under two circumstances: (1) when they are involved in relationships with them, as described in Chapter 11, so that the other party ultimately reciprocates, or (2) when some third party arranges that the action shall be reinforced. A baby-sitter sacrifices time and effort and sometimes risks personal injury for the sake of another person's child, but is rewarded in the end by money and approval from the child's parents. Governments require citizens to sacrifice by paying taxes, but paying taxes is reinforced in the long run by services such as schools and garbage collection. (Of course, paying taxes also prevents fines, jail, and other forms of punishment.)

This long-term reinforcement helps us understand why altruism occurs, and the deferred nature of the reinforcement helps us understand why altruism often fails to occur. In the terms of Chapters 9 and 11 (Figure 9.2), selfish behavior usually constitutes impulsiveness, and altruism usually constitutes self-control. People often behave selfishly because the reinforcement for selfishness is relatively immediate. People lie, cheat, steal, and murder because such behavior pays off in the short run.

A large part of what we call "socialization" consists of bringing behavior into contact with long-term consequences that reinforce kindness and generosity. Verbal behavior about doing good unto others provides rules (in the sense of Chapters 8 and 11) that help people avoid the contingency traps of selfishness. We saw such a contingency trap in Figure 11.3, in which a controller has to choose between an exploitive relationship that pays off in the short run and a more cooperative relationship that pays off in the long run. The controllee provides a rule (e.g., a promise or threat) that strengthens the choice that is better in the long run. As we saw in Chapters 8 and 9, such rules are usually backed up with relatively short-term social reinforcement (e.g., approval). Evil exists because the rules and social reinforcement may be ineffective or altogether absent from a person's environment. To the extent that people behave well, however, the social training works.

Apparently altruistic behavior is never devoid of self-interest, because ultimately it can be traced to genetic influence, a history of reinforcement, or, most often, both. People are usually good to their siblings and cousins both because they share genes with these relatives and because they were taught to do so—the "good" actions were reinforced by parents and other family members.

Because they are reinforced, altruistic acts are called "good." When a church teaches its congregants that it is good to help others in distress, this verbal behavior points to the likelihood that charitable acts will be reinforced by approval and status in the church. A verbal discriminative stimulus that labels an action as *good* or pairs *should* or *ought* with the name of the action constitutes a rule in the sense of Chapter 8. In the long run, since the behavior of both the speaker and the listener is reinforced, the good behavior usually constitutes rule-governed behavior in the context of a relationship.

Although Lewis (1960) was correct that science cannot address ultimate questions like "Why does the universe exist?" he was incorrect when he argued that science could have nothing to say about what is right or wrong or what people ought to do. Even if no scientist can say why the universe is arranged so that societies came to be the way they are, behavior analysts can explain conventions (i.e., verbal behavior) about right, wrong, and ought—the law of human nature—as an outcome of genetic effects and operant learning.

Morals   If quarrelsome statements like "Why should you shove in first?" or "Give me a bit of your orange, I gave you a bit of mine" constitute verbal behavior stemming from past reinforcement, the same applies to moral judgments and injunctions. The commandment *Thou shalt not steal,* which is equivalent to saying that stealing is wrong, is a rule in the sense of Chapter 8. It is a verbal discriminative stimulus that points to a contingency of punishment—stealing is a type of action that is likely to be punished in our society. As a discriminative stimulus, it decreases the likelihood of stealing. The same can be said of the other nine commandments.

Calling such statements commandments or injunctions separates them from other rules, like advice. When a parent advises a child not to lie, the contingencies of punishment pointed to are more personal in nature; not only is lying punished by our society, but the parent also disapproves. The verbal discriminative stimuli called morals, however, point only to the more general contingencies resulting from the practices of the group.

Our discussion of rules in Chapter 8 leads us to take these general social contingencies as proximate and to look further for what ultimate contingencies might explain the existence of the rule. As we saw there (Figure 8.2), we would be looking for an effect on fitness. Does stealing ultimately tend to lower an individual's fitness? This question is best answered in a more general discussion of where cultural practices, including moral commandments, come from. We shall take that up in Chapter 13.

The Good Life   No discussion of values is complete without some attention to the question of what is ultimate good. Toward what ultimate end are group practices and verbal behavior about good and bad directed? Many philosophers, economists, and other social scientists have wondered whether human society could ever attain some ideal state and what that ultimate good life would be like. Is there some goal we could be working toward, some social arrangement which, if not ideal, might at least be the best possible? Plato proposed monarchy with a philosopher-king. The economist Jeremy Bentham proposed an economic arrangement of "the greatest good for the greatest number."

Discussions that presuppose such an end state are often called *utopian,* after the imaginary country Utopia (Greek word meaning "nowhere") that Thomas More wrote about. Would behavior analysts propose some new utopia? Chapter 14 will give a fuller answer to this question, but a brief answer can be given here.

Behavior analysts can no more specify where society is headed than evolutionary biologists can predict where evolution might ultimately end up. Although Skinner's (1948/1976) novel *Walden Two* has often been called

ple, childhood is a relatively recent invention, originating in the sixteenth century. Children's birthdays have been celebrated regularly only since the seventeenth century.

In evolutionary theory, the problem of accounting for diversity of forms coincides with the problem of explaining change because diverse new forms arise as a result of changes in ancestral forms. In theories of biological evolution, for example, one imagines an ancestral population of bears, some of which migrated further and further north and, as a result of selection, became larger and ultimately white, to make different species we see today.

Similarly, the problem of explaining the diversity of cultures coincides with the problem of explaining change of cultures. In a theory of cultural evolution, one might imagine an ancestral culture carried by a group that split in two. From the ancestral customs, new customs might arise by modification, until the cultures of the two groups hardly resembled one another. The possibility of a parallel arises: Might cultural evolution be explained by the same kind of theory as biological evolution—as an outcome of selection acting on variation?

As mentioned in earlier chapters, the details of the account are relatively unimportant. Some may prove wrong, and the explanation of culture will change as new ideas arise. Our goals are only to demonstrate that a behavioral account is possible and to show that the account is sufficiently complex to be plausible.

❖ GENETIC EVOLUTION AND CULTURE

To draw a parallel between biological evolution, which changes a gene pool, and cultural evolution, which changes a group's social behavior, we need to think about selection in very general terms as we did in Chapter 4, where we drew a parallel between natural selection and operant learning. Like those two, cultural evolution can also be seen as the result of variation, transmission, and selection. Cultural evolution, however, cannot be understood independently of the other two, because the behavior involved is operant behavior and depends for its acquisition on a genetic base stemming from natural selection.

■ Replicators and Fitness

What are the units of selection? What are the things that vary and are transmitted and selected? With natural selection and operant learning, we were able to avoid this question simply by talking about genes, alleles, and variation in operant behavior. With cultural evolution, the units of selection are less obvious and more controversial, because talking about culture in terms of behavior and selection goes against traditional accounts. What are the parts that can make up a whole culture and enter into a process of selection?

To answer such questions, evolutionary biologists such as Richard Dawkins (1989) developed the concept of a *replicator*—an entity that, once in existence, makes copies of itself. To qualify as a replicator, the entity must possess three types of stability: longevity, fecundity, and copying fidelity. Reproduction takes time; longevity ensures that the replicator stays around long enough to reproduce. Dawkins imagines a gene, a piece of DNA, in a primordial soup that existed before there were organisms. The molecule or piece of molecule would have to be chemically stable long enough to copy itself, and the longer it lasted, the more copies might be made. After the advent of organisms, genes in a gene pool tended to be chemically stable but could be changed by radiation or broken up during cell division—most importantly during the formation of gametes (meiosis) because gametes carry the copies that are passed on in offspring. Fecundity refers to the tendency toward frequent copying—of two rival replicators (alleles), the one that is copied more often will become more frequent in the gene pool. Copying fidelity refers to accuracy. Inaccurate copies tend to lose their parent's virtues. The copies of a successful replicator resemble it closely—the more closely, the better.

These three requirements favor small units by giving them *stability.* A small piece of DNA is less susceptible to being damaged or falling apart, is quicker to copy, and has fewer possibilities for error. If nothing offset these considerations, replicators would always be the smallest size possible. But there are other considerations that favor larger units.

The factors facilitating larger replicators can be summed up in the word *efficacy.* A large unit can have a large effect on the phenotype (organism) in which it is positioned, and so it can have a large effect on its own future. If a single gene controlled the manufacture of one entire protein molecule—say, an enzyme that would in turn control several chemical reactions—it might ensure that its phenotype possessed traits that would lead it to live long and reproduce often.

Between the advantages of smallness (stability) and largeness (efficacy), replicators tend to be intermediate and variable in size. Sometimes a relatively large piece of DNA might be stable enough to propagate through a population. Sometimes a small piece might be effective enough to be selected, if it controlled a crucial bit of structure in a protein molecule, for instance.

A particularly good way for relatively small units to achieve efficacy might be called "teamwork." Dawkins points out that genes rarely operate on their own. Selection favors genes that cooperate or act in concert with other genes. Say two alleles of a gene, X and X', are matched in fitness on all counts except that X' works together with another gene Y to produce a more successful phenotype. The combination X'Y will flourish and possibly drive out X-allele combinations altogether. This way clusters of genes and traits can be selected—clusters like lungs, breathing, skin, sturdy limbs or feathers, wings, flying, and building nests in trees. Dawkins theorizes that this is how organisms came into existence; genes survived and reproduced better when they were packaged into "survival machines."

■ Societies

If genes generally do better in aggregates, then sometimes they might do even better in aggregates of aggregates. That is, sometimes it might benefit genes to build survival machines that collect together in groups. Much advantage accrues to fish that school or birds that flock. Such aggregates offer, for example, better protection from predators and greater efficiency in finding food than the individuals would enjoy on their own. Groups of predators like lions or hyenas can subdue large prey they could never capture on their own. Other things being equal, if alleles that build social survival machines tend to survive better than alleles that build solitary survival machines, then over time the species will come to be found in groups.

However, it takes more than aggregation to make a society. An aggregation may be a sort of limited partnership, with each individual's behavior confined to keeping close to the rest while feeding. In a society, however, the individuals do not behave only for their own benefit. When a group of wolves tracks and kills a moose, they all behave together in ways that benefit them all. The behavior of each is necessary to the attainment of the goal, and without the efforts of all none would benefit. This is cooperation.

For the wolves, a moose is a shared goal in a literal sense: once killed, it is shared among the members of the group. If each individual's participation depends on benefiting from the group's activities, then each individual must get a share. Any tendency to cheat must be curbed because each individual's benefits would cease if the group fell apart. Genes will be selected that help to subordinate the individual's short-term interests (cheating) to the individual's long-term interest in maintaining the association. Such a tendency to act for the good of others in the short run, but for the sake of greater benefit in the long run, is what we have called altruism.

Altruism is the hallmark of a society. When a group lives together in a stable association and behaves altruistically toward one another, that is a society. In a society like an ant colony, in which everyone is closely related, altruism can be selected by the benefit to the shared altruistic genes; between close kin there need be no reciprocity. Between unrelated individuals, however, mutual benefit depends on reciprocity. Along with genes for altruism, genes for remembering the other members of the group and for accounting of debts and dues must be selected, all as a cluster. Knowing who is who and who did what for whom makes it possible for even a group of unrelated lions to band together, capture large prey, protect one another, and feed one another's offspring. (Of course, some relatedness does help.)

Not only altruism but much other social behavior is selected when societies are beneficial to fitness. In his studies of marmots, David Barash (1982) found dramatic differences between woodchucks, which are solitary, and Olympic marmots, which are social. Woodchucks live in low-lying fertile areas with relatively long growing seasons, whereas Olympic marmots live high in the mountains where the growing season is short and the weather severe. Woodchucks apparently manage well in the milder climate on their own. They maintain territories from which they exclude others of their kind. Males and females come together only to mate, and females keep their young with them only until they are weaned, when the offspring disperse. For them, the costs of a social existence would outweigh the benefits. In Olympic marmots, selected along with warm coats are the necessities of living in groups: greeting calls, recognition of members, alarm calls, group maintenance of burrows, food sharing, and cooperative defense. Along with this, offspring typically stay with the group through two or three growing seasons; presumably they cannot be brought to maturity quickly with this harsh climate's limited resources. Barash theorizes that the slow maturation may be the key factor that makes the benefits of society outweigh the costs.

For all their living in societies, would we say that ants, or even Olympic marmots, have culture? Ants show an amazing range of adaptations. They may be the only creatures besides humans that have wars—group fighting to the death. Some species farm—grow edible fungus on pieces of leaves brought into the colony for the purpose. Still, we do not see, nor do we expect to find, culture in an ant colony. What is missing?

■ Definition of Culture

What is missing is learning, for culture is the learned behavior of a group. It consists of operant behavior, both verbal and nonverbal, acquired as a result of group membership. It might be said that ants and Olympic marmots learn as a result of group membership because they recognize other members of their societies. Ants kill strangers that enter their colonies because they give off the wrong odor; a stranger painted with the chemicals of the colony is accepted. Olympic marmots greet group members and drive off strangers. These discriminations must be learned, because each ant colony's odor and each marmot society's membership is unique. Although such learning might suggest the rudiments of culture, it still seems too little to qualify. For one thing, the behavior involved is probably not operant behavior. The discriminations consist of the occurrence or nonoccurrence of greeting displays and aggressive attacks, which are fixed-action patterns. The learning involved appears to be more like classical conditioning than like operant learning; it depends entirely on context and hardly at all on consequences. For another thing, no actions are transmitted from one individual to another and nothing like instruction is involved. Operant learning as a result of group membership implies that the behavior of the group arranges consequences for its members. Human parents arrange reinforcement for their children's behavior. We shall return to this shortly, but first we need to see how evolutionary theory explains why culture exists at all.

Culture and Society   For culture to come into existence, there first had to be societies, for a culture is the possession of a society. Robert Boyd and Peter Richerson (1985) explain that culture is a "population-level phenomenon."

Like a gene pool, a culture can only be seen when one looks at a whole population. They compare the "pool of cultural traits" with the gene pool: every population has a gene pool, but only some—possibly only human populations—have pools of cultural traits.

Just as a gene pool is transmitted from generation to generation, so a culture pool is transmitted. A child growing up in Japan or the United States carries part of the gene pool and eventually, as he or she learns the customs of the culture, part of the culture pool. The child grows into an adult, passes the culture on to other children, and then dies. Thus, the individuals die but the gene and culture pools go on. Most people in Japan eat with chopsticks, whereas most people in the United States eat with forks, knives, and spoons, but exactly who eats in these different ways changes from century to century. The individuals carry the genes and they carry the cultural traits, but the gene pool and the culture pool transcend the individual. At the population level, there is a real sense in which the individuals, as survival machines and behaving organisms, are only the means by which the gene pool and the culture pool are transmitted.

When two societies with different cultures come into contact, rarely does one culture so dominate that all traces of the subordinate culture are lost; usually the two cultures merge to form one comprising elements from both. When this happens, traits from each culture compete for acceptance with traits from the other. Some win out from one and some win out from the other. The reason that the traits of one culture would displace the traits of another must be linked to the reason that cultures exist at all—directly or indirectly there must be an effect on fitness.

Culture and Fitness   Learning like that involved in culture, from the point of view of genes, is a risky business, for the survival machine with preprogrammed behavior is less likely to behave inappropriately. However, if on the average survival machines that learn are more likely to survive and reproduce than survival machines that do not, then genes for learning will tend to survive and increase. Even if learning goes wrong some of the time, if it is beneficial across many individuals and over many generations, its genes will be selected.

Imagine a variable environment or, to be more accurate, several potentially habitable environments, where resources and dangers are too numerous and diverse to catalog easily. Consider the possibilities of dispersion, if members of a species could survive in the tropics, in the desert, in temperate climates, and in the arctic regions. To open all these possibilities, the ability to learn which resources and dangers are present and how to obtain or avoid them would be essential. Humans and other species learn because genes that make for learning open up possibilities that outweigh their riskiness.

A similar line of reasoning explains the existence of culture. If it is useful to learn, it might be useful to learn from others of your kind—the members of your society. That is to say, if an average benefit to fitness can select genes that make for learning, then an average benefit to fitness can select genes for culture. If there is much to learn or if there are many possibilities to be eliminated, then learning from others would be a valuable shortcut. How can you know whether it is better to wear shoes or what sort of shoes would be best to wear? How better to find out quickly than from those around you? A person living in isolation might never arrive at an adequate solution to the problem. Cultural transmission prevents us from having to "reinvent the wheel."

If culturally transmitted traits like wearing shoes or speaking English can enhance the fitness of the genes in a survival machine, then the genes that make for the traits that ensure cultural transmission will be selected. What sort of traits make the shortcut possible?

■ Traits for Culture

There are at least three requirements for learned behavior to be transmitted from the group to the individual by means that we recognize as teaching or instruction. The first two, constraints on stimuli and imitation, allow an individual to learn from the group but serve as the basis of only a rudimentary sort of culture, which we shall call *imitation-only culture*. The third requirement is social reinforcement, the addition of which distinguishes imitation-only culture from *full-blown culture*. Social reinforcers allow the key element of human culture, instruction.

Constraints on Stimuli   If learning is risky, then it is likely to be constrained—that is, guided or directed by the structure of the organism, particularly the structure of the nervous system and sense organs. This means that certain stimuli are much more likely to affect behavior than others. If illness follows ingestion, a rat is likely to avoid the taste of the food that preceded the illness. Quail and pigeons, birds that find food by sight, avoid food that looks like what they ate before getting sick. Humans seem to be prone to both biases; someone who became sick after eating lobster Newburg later becomes queasy at both the smell and sight of lobster Newburg.

When the stimuli toward which we are biased are those produced by other members of our species, then we learn quickly from those others. Evolutionary biologists point out that many creatures besides humans display this sort of sensitivity. For example, the white-crowned sparrow shows a special sensitivity to the songs of other white-crowned sparrows, and a young white-crown must hear the song of an adult male before it can sing that song when it grows to adulthood. If the bird is reared in a laboratory and hears no song at all or only that of a related species, the marsh sparrow, it grows up to sing only a rudimentary song with little resemblance to the typical song of its species. It must hear a white-crowned sparrow song—a tape recording will do—and no other, if its singing is to develop correctly, and its song will resemble the one that the little bird heard. Such transmission from adult to young allows for local dialects in the song; white-crowned sparrows from different areas sing different variations of the song. So far no one knows why this is advantageous.

Human language learning appears to be constrained (guided) in ways similar to white-crowned sparrow song-learning. The human auditory system appears to be specially sensitive to speech sounds— there is evidence that the ability to make important phonemic discriminations is present shortly after birth. There is evidence too that infants can discriminate faces from other patterns, an ability that may serve in language learning as well as many other social outcomes.

Far from being "blank slates" on which experience writes, human babies apparently come into the world constructed so as to be affected by crucial stimuli from other humans. These social stimuli are essential enough to normal development that genes have been selected to take much of the chance out of their occurrence in caretakers and their reception by infants. Parents take great interest in babies, and babies take a great interest in parents.

Just as all normal male white-crowned sparrows begin their first attempts at song around a certain age, so do all human infants begin to babble when they are several months old. For the sparrow's song to develop, the bird must be able to hear itself sing. The same appears to be true of human speech; children with chronic ear infections develop abnormal speech (usually correctable by speech therapy).

Special sensitivities to stimuli go hand in hand with special behavioral tendencies (like babbling). In particular, there may be great adaptive value to coupling a sensitivity to the behavior of others with a tendency to behave as they do. Special sensitivities, in other words, frequently go together with a tendency toward imitation.

Imitation Culture would probably be impossible without imitation. If there is any fitness advantage to learning about variable environments, then there would be an advantage to imitation because it would help ensure the acquisition of appropriate behavior. To make this argument more concrete, Boyd and Richerson (1985) consider a hypothetical population of acultural organisms living in an environment that varies from time to time (goes through cycles of drought and rain). Imagine that in each generation individuals had to learn on their own the behavior that succeeds in the current environment: some would manage and some would fail. They continue:

> Now, consider the evolution of a hypothetical mutant "imitator" gene that causes its bearers to eschew individual learning and copy the behavior of individuals from the previous generation. As long as the environment does not change too much between generations, the average behavior of these models will be close to the currently adaptive behavior. By copying behavior of individuals from the previous generation, imitators avoid costly learning trials, and, if they average over a number of models, have a better chance of acquiring the currently adaptive behavior than non-imitators (p. 15).

In other words, individuals that imitate have a better chance of behaving in ways that will result in survival and reproduction in the current environment, so the imitator genes will tend to increase in frequency in the gene pool.

Imitation occurs in a variety of species, many of which we would consider acultural. Epstein (1984) found that when a pigeon with no training is placed in an apparatus in which it can observe another pigeon pecking at a Ping-Pong ball and receiving food reinforcement, it soon begins to peck at a Ping-Pong ball on its side of the apparatus, and will still peck at the ball after the trained pigeon is removed. The pigeon would doubtless cease to peck after a while, but if the apparatus were arranged so that the pecks produced food, the pigeon's pecking would be reinforced and would move from being induced behavior to being operant behavior. However, even if an entire flock of pigeons learned to peck at Ping-Pong balls through imitation, we might still hesitate to say that pigeons have real culture, although we might grant them an extremely rudimentary culture.

The same would apply to the group of monkeys that all learned to wash sweet potatoes put out on a sandy beach. Researchers providing the potatoes observed that one monkey individually began washing her potatoes. A few others, and then the rest, followed suit. The spread of this trait, presumably by imitation and reinforcement, could qualify it as part of a rudimentary culture, confined to food-washing and a few other traits unique to the group. (See Goodenough, McGuire, and Wallace [1993; pp. 138–140] for a summary of social learning in nonhuman animals.)

We can call such a pool of traits transmitted by imitation alone an *imitation-only* culture; although it shares much with human culture, the element of instruction, teaching, or training is still missing. In an imitation-only culture, the behavior of other group members serves only as an inducing stimulus or context. The consequences of the imitated behavior (potato-washing) arise from nonsocial aspects of the individual's environment (sand sticking to the potato). With instruction, the two individuals have a relationship (Chapter 11); the reinforcement for the learner is delivered by the instructor. Such social contingencies push human culture far beyond the possibilities of imitation-only culture.

We shall discuss the effects of instruction on culture later. First we turn to the way that evolution may have provided a genetic basis for instruction by selecting powerful social reinforcers.

Social Reinforcers   For children growing up in a human culture, learning all the things they need to learn would probably be impossible without continual shaping by adults. If there was an advantage to learning more skills and subtler discriminations, then genes that aided such acquisitions would be selected.

In Chapters 4 and 12 we discussed the likelihood that genes making certain important events reinforcers—food, potential mate, shelter—and genes making certain events punishers—pain, illness, predators—would be selected in any species for which operant learning might enhance fitness. The extension of this reasoning explains how subtle social cues could come to be potent reinforcers and serve as a base for culture. In Chapter 12, for example, we saw that Dawkins included in his list of reinforcers *smiling child* and in his list of punishers *screaming child*. Most parents would testify that the sight of a smiling child is both a potent reinforcer and an inducing stimulus (unconditional stimulus or releaser; Chapter 4). The sound of a crying baby, though quieter than many sounds we accept, is one of the most aversive sounds we experience, and parents rush to feed or change diapers or do whatever might be needed to stop the crying. No consideration of the parents' individual health or survival can explain why a child's smile or cry should affect them so powerfully. Taking care of the child, however, has everything to do with the survival of genes, and a gene package that included the tendency for such effects might well prosper. The child's smile and cry are the means by which genes induce and reinforce caretaking by the parents.

If the child shapes the parents' behavior, how much more is it true that the parents shape the child's behavior! Adults exhibit a variety of behavior shifts around children. They smile, gaze affectionately, and raise the pitch of their voices, all fixed-action patterns (Chapter 4). For the child, the parent's smile, regard, voice, and touch offer powerful reinforcers, but were it not for the advantages of culture there is no obvious reason why this would be so. If the child had nothing to learn from its parents, genes making such subtle cues into reinforcers would never be selected. Given these potent social reinforcers, however, the possibilities of cultural transmission far exceed those of an imitation-only culture.

Social reinforcers are especially effective because they are so handy. Imagine a parent trying to shape a child's behavior with nonsocial reinforcers like food and money. Each time the child makes the desired response, the parent has to hand over a cookie, which the child eats, or a coin, which the child later spends. How ungainly and inefficient, in comparison with the ease and immediacy of a smile, praise, and a hug. Unlike money, these social reinforcers are ever-available to the parent, no matter the situation. Unlike cookies, affection can be given again and again and the child won't get full. Ready delivery and slow satiation mean that these reinforcers allow the child's instruction to go on during all waking hours.

❖ VARIATION, TRANSMISSION, AND SELECTION

The types of traits that we have been discussing—stimulus constraints, imitation, and social reinforcers—not only produce culture but also allow cultural change. Cultural evolution can occur in a manner analogous to genetic evolution—that is, by the combination of variation, transmission, and selection (the selective transmission of variation). To understand how this might be, we need to answer some basic questions. What varies and how? How are variants transmitted? What are the mechanisms of selection?

■ Variation

Evolution is impossible without variation. In genetic evolution, gene locations on chromosomes must be habitable by various alleles—various gene packages must be possible. Similarly, cultural evolution requires that various cultural "alleles" must compete and various trait packages must be possible. But what are the analogs to genes, alleles, and packages, and what are the mechanisms of their variation?

Cultural Replicators   The question "What varies?" is a question about units. In Dawkins's terms, it becomes, "What are the replicators of culture that possess longevity, fecundity, and copying fidelity?"

The problem here is exactly analogous to the problem of identifying units of operant behavior (Chapter 4), and the solution is much the same. Here, as there, the units are identified by their function. A cultural replicator is an action, engaged in and transmitted by the group, that serves a certain function, results in a certain effect, or accomplishes a certain result. In other words, a cultural replicator gets a certain job done. Wearing warm clothes in the winter keeps us healthy. Computer programming allows a person to earn a living and gain status.

Like gene packages, cultural replicators can be thought of as varying in size. Anthropologists, for example, distinguish among cultures on a variety of grounds, some specific and some general. Producing a specific artifact can be thought of as a relatively small replicator; in a technological culture, an example could be making television sets of a certain brand. Larger replicators, or packages of replicators, are defined by interdependent clusters of customs. Customs about marriage and family, for example, tend to go together. In cultures with extended families, arranged marriages are the rule, presumably because too many people are involved for the association of two families to be left up to the vagaries of romance. Love matches become more common as fewer people are involved beyond the married couple themselves. In the last 300 years in the West, we have seen a shift from extended families to nuclear families and the predominance of love matches.

Speaking English could be thought of as a replicator, though it is so broad that it is of little help in understanding cultural customs. More specific verbal-behavior replicators would be greeting and bargaining over prices or goods. "Hello, glad to see you" and "My donkey is worth at least three of your sheep" can be said in a variety of languages, and the language is usually less important than the result—that is, the job done. Most cultures include different greetings for different relationships, and the different greetings are replicators. In some cultures, it is common practice to lie about the quality and origin of goods, as Westerners who have bargained with shopkeepers in countries like Turkey or India can testify. Different bargaining practices in different cultures constitute replicators.

Meme, Culturgen, Practice   Different names have been proposed for cultural replicators. Lumsden and Wilson (1981) suggested culturgen and Dawkins (1989) suggested meme (rhymes with cream); Skinner (1971) used practice. The history of science includes examples of new terms being invented (oxygen and acceleration) and of terms being appropriated from everyday talk (force and response). For our purposes, we will stick to words like practice and custom, which remind us that cultural replicators are actions.

Among evolutionary biologists, discussion of cultural evolution has been handicapped by a failure to recognize that cultural replicators are actions. Lumsden and Wilson and Dawkins write of the evolution of beliefs, ideas, and values. The belief, idea, or value that stealing is wrong, if thought of as a thing, could never evolve by physical mechanisms because it is nonnatural. The problems with mentalism that we discussed in Chapter 3 apply to cultural practices as much as to any other type of operant behavior. No understanding is gained by imagining that the units of cultural evolution are mental entities (Boyd and Richerson, 1985) or unknown neural structures (Dawkins, 1989). Such explanatory fictions remain superfluous as ever and cannot explain how cultural practices originate and change, a question that demands attention to history and behavior over time for its answer (Chapter 4).

Just as the frequency of a gene in a gene pool can be assessed only across all the individuals in a population, so the frequency of a practice can be assessed only across all the individuals in the group. For example, more American women wear lipstick today than in the 1970s or in colonial days; this cultural change could be measured only by studying many women. The thing that changes in frequency, across women and over time, is the practice (wearing lipstick) itself; that is the replicator. Clusters of practices that function as replicators are categories of actions (Chapter 3). For example, "disapproving of stealing" is a category label. Since it denotes something natural, a set of interdependent actions, it denotes something that could evolve by the natural process of selection: Group members may punish stealing, may reinforce behavior incompatible with stealing, and may talk about how wrong stealing is ("Thou shalt not steal").

That talk is part of culture deserves emphasis. Among the practices of a culture are traditional utterances: sayings, stories, and myths. In New Hampshire, the saying "If it ain't broke, don't fix it" is part of the local culture. Part of ancient Greek culture was its myths. Particularly important to culture are utterances that in Chapter 8 we identified as *rules*. These include moral injunctions (Thou shalt not steal), instructions (Always say "Please" and "Thank you"), and knowledge of the environment (You need a warm coat around here in the winter). Even the stories and myths of a culture have some characteristics of rules because they usually convey lessons or morals—that is, they usually point to contingencies of reinforcement and punishment. The story of the boy who cried "wolf," for example, contains a lesson about verbal discriminative stimuli, reliability, and reinforcement. C. J. Sommerville (1982), in his book about childhood, argues that even children's fairy stories about brave young men, fair maidens, dragons, and wicked stepmothers serve socially useful functions, indirectly teaching lessons about life and encouraging confident interaction with the world. He writes, "They offer something that must precede moral development by encouraging the child to choose sides. By sympathizing with one character and against another, the child acquires the habit of identifying with those he wishes to emulate" (p. 139). In other words, like moral injunctions, the fairy stories of a culture help engender behavior that will be reinforced by the practices of the group. When biologists and anthropologists talk about the beliefs, ideas, and values of a culture, they are probably referring particularly to the culture's traditions of verbal behavior.

We may distinguish rule-making from rule-giving as we would distinguish invention from repetition. People make up rules from time to time, in the sense that they emit novel utterances in the form of injunctions, advice, or instructions. Only some of these become part of the culture's characteristic rule-giving, which spreads from person to person and generation to generation by imitation coupled with reinforcement. Rule-making and rule-giving are both parts of human culture.

The particular rule-giving that goes on in a group helps distinguish one culture from another and changes in a culture from one period to another. A young man of marriageable age in India today may be told by his parents, "When you meet the woman we have picked for your wife, if you don't like her, you may refuse." In the United States he may be told, "When we meet the woman you have picked for your wife, if we don't like her, we may refuse." Three centuries ago, he might have been told something more like the young man in India. Rules vary from place to place and time to time.

Social Contingencies   It is characteristic of every culture that certain actions are reinforced or punished by members of the group. A child's obedience to parents results in approval and affection. Lying, cheating, and stealing result in disapproval and rejection. These social contingencies constitute the most important practices of the culture because they form the base for cultures that go beyond imitation-only culture. The operant behavior we call teaching, correcting, or instructing consists of reinforcing behavior that is normal for the culture and punishing behavior that is deviant. As operant behavior, the teaching itself also must be reinforced, often by the students' correct behavior, but also by other practices within the culture, such as paying a salary.

Skinner (1971, 1974) regarded social contingencies as so important to human culture that he suggested the word *practice* be used only to refer to such contingencies. In his view, social contingencies shape the behavior that is normal for the culture. Since the behavior results from the contingencies, the contingencies are more basic than the behavior. Thus, to know a culture would be to know its contingencies. The making of bowls of a certain shape would be secondary; the reinforcing of making bowls of that shape would be a primary part of the culture. Whether cousins marry or not would be secondary; whether proposals of marriages between cousins were reinforced or punished would be primary.

Skinner's position has two main implications. First, it rules out imitation-only cultures, and limits the possibility of culture in nonhuman species. (The nonhuman species would have to engage in operant behavior that had the effect of reinforcing or punishing the behavior of other group members. It would not be enough that potato-washing spread from parent to offspring; the parent would have to reinforce the offspring's potato-washing.) Second, Skinner's view shifts focus away from a difficult and possibly unanswerable question: How many group members must behave in a certain way before that type of behavior is "characteristic" or "normal" for the culture? Skinner answers, in effect, that the number is irrelevant, as long as some members of the group reinforce that type of behavior in others. If some group members, whether few or many, reinforce the behavior, it will persist as part of the behavior of the group.

Evolutionary biologists differ with Skinner on both points. First, even those who acknowledge the importance of instruction define culture as consisting of behavior learned as a result of group membership. This definition draws no line between imitation-only cultures and those including instruction; nor does it draw a line within a culture between behavior acquired by imitation combined with nonsocial reinforcement (e.g., potato-washing) and behavior acquired as a result of interactions with another group member—that is, as a result of a relationship in the sense of Chapter 11. For this more inclusive view, it would be enough that group members serve as models; they need not also be the source of reinforcement. Second, they get around the question of what is normal for the culture by likening the culture to a gene pool. In a culture pool, certain practices may be common and others may be rare. What matters is whether they remain in the pool or disappear.

Mutation, Recombination, and Immigration   If a culture pool is like a gene pool, then it must contain within it the means for novelty. In the gene pool, three processes make for novelty: (1) mutation constitutes a source of new alleles; (2) recombination, or "crossing-over"—the breaking and rejoining that occurs during meiosis—arranges new combinations of alleles; and (3) immigration of individuals from one population to another allows whole new combinations to appear in the gene pool. Analogs to these three processes occur in the culture pool.

The cultural analog to mutation is accident or error. We have already discussed the impossibility of repeating the same action exactly. Variation is inherent in behavior, and some variants may be more successful than others. Another type of accident may be imposed by some uncontrollable environmental event. When I injured my right hand, I was forced to brush my teeth with my left hand and discovered I could do a better job on the teeth on the right that way. Now I switch hands when I brush. When you are prevented from doing things in the usual way you may discover better ways of doing them. Finally, as with genetic replication, copying errors can occur. An athlete may imitate a tennis coach incorrectly and discover a better way to serve the ball. A child may imitate a parent imperfectly and discover a better way to tie shoes. As with mutations, however, most mistakes are for the worse; happy accidents that turn out for the best are rare.

A possible behavioral analog to recombination is failure of stimulus control. You might make a wrong turn driving home, or put on the wrong item of clothing, or say something inappropriate to a relative, even though you have behaved correctly hundreds of times in the same situation. Patterns of behavior that would ordinarily remain separate get mixed this way. Although such mixing is usually disastrous, occasionally it may lead you to discover a better route, a better mode of dress, or a better way of interacting with your relatives.

As there can be immigration into a gene pool, so there can be immigration into a culture pool. This can occur when individuals from one society enter another society. For instance, westerners living in Japan during the nineteenth and twentieth centuries transferred many practices into Japanese culture. Immigration into the United States has introduced new methods of cooking, new verbal expressions, new ways of doing business, and new forms of religion.

Novel practices may also enter the culture by immigration from a subculture—that is, from a set of practices characteristic of a subgroup within the society. The effects of immigration into the United States have often been delayed because an ethnic group has remained partially segregated from the rest of the population, moving into the main culture only over several generations. Almost all Americans know the meaning of expressions like *jive*, *pasta*, and *chutzpah* even if they don't know their origins.

◼ Transmission

The second essential ingredient for evolution by selection is transmission from one generation to the next. In genetic evolution, transmission occurs by transfer of genetic material (DNA) from parent to offspring. In cultural evolution, it occurs by more direct means: transfer of behavior from one group member to another.

Inheritance of Acquired Characteristics   Before the twentieth century, it was sometimes suggested that traits might be passed from parent to offspring by direct transfer, so that characteristics acquired by the parent might appear in the offspring. If a blacksmith's arms grew muscular as a result of his work, then the muscular arms might be passed on to his children. Although the notion never found any evidence to support its operation in genetic evolution, it is exactly the means of transmission in cultural evolution.

In a culture-possessing species like ours, children tend to learn whatever their parents learn. Everything from modes of dress to table manners to dialect to social mannerisms may be passed directly from parent to child. For some cultural traits, transfer of genetic material from parent to child may play no direct role, but genetic inheritance from parent to child may also guide or bias cultural transmission; children may be disposed to learning certain things as a result of genes they inherited. For example, child and parent might share a disposition toward acquiring a fear of heights, learning music, or learning manual skills.

Since, however, transfer of genetic material can be irrelevant to cultural transmission, one's *genetic parents* may differ from one's *cultural parents*. A child may acquire cultural traits from a variety of adults—uncles, aunts, teachers, ministers, coaches. People may also acquire practices from peers; children typically learn the "code of the playground" from other children, and adults are "taught the ropes" of a situation by other adults. Such transmission, impossible for genes, is called *horizontal*. Since horizontal transmission occurs within generations, cultural traits can spread through the group even within the span of a single genetic generation.

This means that cultural evolution is much faster than genetic evolution. Whereas genetic transmission is limited to only one point in an individual's life, cultural transmission occurs throughout the life span. Cultural transmission allows new traits to displace old ones throughout even a large population in the space of just a few years. Sometimes the speed of cultural evolution relative to genetic evolution creates problems; examples are our present problems with our "sweet tooth" and nuclear weapons. The practices of making sugar and weapons have evolved too fast for the genes underlying our attraction to sweet taste and our aggressive tendencies to decrease at all in the gene pool. Instead, other cultural practices have evolved to offset the bad effects of the earlier ones. We diet and brush our teeth; we engage in peace talks and disarmament.

Imitation One way that acquired cultural traits are transmitted is by direct copying—imitation. In genetic evolution, copying of DNA occurs during the formation of germ cells, and the DNA then affects the development of the individual into which it is transferred. This is relatively uncertain and indirect compared with the direct copying of phenotype comprised by imitation.

Children imitate adults and other children. Adults usually imitate other adults, but sometimes they imitate children. Slang expressions used by children, such as *far out* and *totally awesome,* tend to slip into the speech of adults who hear them.

Imitation provides a base for operant learning. Once an action has been induced by imitation, it can be reinforced and shaped into more evolved forms. Once a child utters *abbuh,* listeners' responses (approval and giving apples) reinforce and eventually shape it into *apple.* If no reinforcement occurs or the action is punished, it remains at a low frequency or disappears. One child may hit another, imitating aggressive behavior shown on TV, but whether the aggression continues depends on whether the behavior is reinforced or punished.

We can distinguish learned imitation from unlearned imitation. Imitation in pigeons and monkeys is probably unlearned, and much imitation in children (and perhaps adults) is unlearned in the sense that it requires no special experience. It is as if some of our genes instructed our bodies, "Watch and listen to people around you, and do as they do." Without instruction, a small child watching a parent hammer nails will pick up a hammer and pound a board.

Unlearned imitation combined with shaping explains why children learn to speak and behave socially as those around them do. Even adults away from their home regions or countries may pick up new dialects and social mannerisms without noticing.

Learned imitation is another matter. It is a type of rule-governed behavior, in the sense of Chapter 8. When one person tells another to "do like this," the ability of the one being instructed to behave appropriately depends on a history of reinforcement for imitating in such situations. The transition from unlearned to learned imitation may occur in many different contexts: in the home, when parents say "Look at me"; on the playground, when a peer says "Look what I can do"; in the classroom, when the teacher plays games like Simon Says.

Although unlearned imitation allows speedy cultural transmission, learned imitation speeds it even faster. With learned imitation, a single social episode may suffice to pass on a trait. One person says to another "Comb your hair like this," and the other immediately does so. Assuming that the environment provides reinforcement—social or nonsocial—for the behavior, it will persist.

Rule-Governed Behavior   Learned imitation is an example of a more general type of cultural transmission: transmission by rules. One of the earliest lessons that children learn is to obey their parents and other authorities. Rather than merely to imitate, they are taught to do as they are told. When there is a conflict, they are told, "Do as I say, not as I do." No doubt children are predisposed to learn rule-following because of their sensitivity to stimuli from their parents, particularly their speech sounds, and because of their susceptibility to the social reinforcers delivered by their parents.

Woe to the child that fails to learn to follow rules, for that child will fail to acquire all sorts of socially acceptable behavior. Many of the utterances that a parent directs at a child are equivalent to statements of the form "In our culture, we do X, and X is reinforced by members of our group," or "In our culture, we avoid doing X, and X is punished by members of our group." Such rules point to relations we usually call *conventions.* A parent tells a child "Say bye-bye," "Hold your fork in your left hand," or "Shake hands when you meet someone," and all these actions are reinforced by members of the group. The parent tells the child "Don't hit Uncle John," "Don't pick your nose in public," or "Don't laugh too loudly," and all these actions are punished by members of the group.

Such conventions derive their power ultimately from the benefits of group membership to fitness. In the terms of Chapter 8, the ultimate contingency takes the form "If you behave so, then you will be eligible for the protection and sharing of resources that go on in this group." To deviate too far from acceptable behavior is to risk ostracism. In the public TV series *The American Experience,* one episode describes the plight of a woman who lived during the early nineteenth century in a remote New England town, had given an illegitimate baby up for adoption when she was a teenager living away from the town, and then unknowingly married her own son many years later. When the mistake was discovered, the son was removed and the woman was ostracized. Although a few people took pity on her, she was eventually left to starve to death in a shack on the edge of town. Nowadays, people who are cast off like this wind up "on the streets."

Social conventions differ from rules pointing to contingencies involving personal health and welfare. A rule such as "Dress warmly in winter" is good advice in a temperate climate regardless of whether any other group members approve. Social conventions are value statements that point to reinforcement and punishment that is predominantly social. They often include words like *should* and *ought*. An American parent might say to a child, "You should never steal from your friends, but a little cheating on your income tax is okay." As we saw in Chapter 12, *should* and *ought* point to ultimate contingencies of reinforcement and punishment. In social conventions, including moral statements like "Honor thy father and thy mother," the reinforcement and punishment is delivered by other group members.

■ Selection

Besides variation and transmission, evolution of the practices in a culture pool requires some mechanism of selection. In genetic evolution, selection occurs because of differential survival and reproduction. Something analogous must be true in cultural evolution. As with genes, some variants among the cultural replicators are longer-lived, more fecund, or more faithfully copied.

Selective Transmission   Individuals (survival machines) that indiscriminately copied whatever practices occurred around them might fare poorer than individuals that copied selectively. Ones that imitated selectively might be more likely to acquire the most adaptive behavior, provided that there is some handy criterion—some manifest character—on which to base the selection.

The best rule for selective imitation would be *imitate success.* In a variable environment, in which the best clues to adaptive behavior are the actions of those around, a gene or set of genes that contained this directive would fare better than others. However, genes could never code any directive so abstract; instead, they would need to guide imitation toward concrete criteria that generally correlate with success. Boyd and Richerson (1985), for example, point out that circumstances might often make it more useful to imitate individuals other than one's parents. "For example, offspring frequently must emigrate. Individuals native to the new habitat are likely to be much better models than the immigrant's biological parents" (p. 15). In such a situation, how could one know who or what to imitate?

One concrete criterion that Boyd and Richerson suggest is frequency. The commonest actions—the norms—of a social group are likely to be the ones that have proven most successful. It would be relatively simple to arrange for the most frequently encountered actions to be imitated; it might be necessary, for instance, only to slow imitation down, so that several exposures were required for an action to be copied. Such a rule could go wrong if some better practice were less frequent, but it need only make for higher fitness on the average and in the long run for the genes to be selected.

A second possible concrete criterion might be imitate those individuals encountered most frequently. In our species, these would usually be the biological parents, but they could be adoptive parents, uncles, aunts, or teachers. Genes for recognizing family members and significant others could be selected for a variety of reasons besides guiding imitation—for example, guiding altruism toward kin or toward those who are likely to reciprocate. The rule "charity begins at home" might be coupled with the rule "imitation begins at home."

Imitating frequently encountered individuals, like imitating frequently encountered actions, entails some risk. Human beings seem to imitate the adults who rear them, often with good results but sometimes regretfully. People who were abused as children may swear never to strike their own children, but may find it difficult to refrain when they actually have children. From the genes' perspective, such copying of maladaptive behavior would be offset as long as copying one's parents was advantageous most of the time—on the average and in the long run.

To imitate less frequent actions or individuals other than parents, yet another criterion of success is needed. In his poem "The Road Not Taken," Robert Frost wrote, "Two roads diverged in a wood, and I—/I took the one less traveled by,/and that has made all the difference." What was that difference?

A successful action is an action that is reinforced, and a successful person is a person whose actions are reinforced. People tend to imitate actions that are reinforced and to imitate other people who possess reinforcers. Motorists in a traffic jam usually stay in their lanes, which is the socially correct (reinforced) thing to do, but if one car goes whizzing past in the breakdown lane with no apparent punishment, several more are sure to follow suit. Typical role models for children and adults are people with wealth and status—movie actors, professional athletes, politicians, corporate executives—people whose behavior is highly reinforced.

Genes could code for the tendency to imitate successful actions and people by causing an increase in the tendency to imitate whenever reinforcers are present. This would be equivalent to an instruction such as, "Whenever you see events in your list of reinforcers, imitate the people around them." Alternatively, the tendency could be largely or entirely shaped by the culture. Children could be instructed to imitate success: "Look at Aunt Martha. Wouldn't you like to be rich like her when you grow up?"

Whether provided mostly by genes or mostly by culture, the tendency to imitate actions and people associated with reinforcement constitutes a powerful selective force. It explains why even relatively rare practices can spread in a social group. In the early twentieth century, automobiles were rare, and many horse owners scoffed at them. As the advantages (more reinforcement and less punishment) of cars over horses became more apparent, however, the practice of automobile ownership spread and, within a generation, all but eclipsed horse ownership. This change probably never could have occurred so rapidly if it were not for selective imitation.

Rule-Following and Rule-Making The same considerations that tend to make imitation selective also tend to make rule-following selective. People often follow commands and advice, for example, but not just any commands and advice. Just as we are more likely to imitate practices that occur frequently in the culture pool, so we are more likely to follow rules that occur frequently in the culture pool. In this way, dominant practices tend to be carried on. While growing up, a child may hear so much on all sides about the wrongness of stealing that he or she may become extremely careful to avoid even the appearance of stealing. The high frequency of exhortations against violence may explain why so few children imitate the violence they see on TV.

As we are inclined to imitate successful people, so too are we inclined to follow rules given by successful people. If you were lost in a city, who would you ask for directions—a person sitting on the sidewalk dressed in rags or a person striding along dressed in expensive clothes? We are disinclined to follow advice given by people who show few signs that their behavior is reinforced, but we are sometimes even willing to pay money for advice from people who show signs of success (buying books about how to succeed in business, gardening, or weight control).

Along with the tendency to imitate success, the tendency to follow rules given by manifestly successful people explains how a rare practice can spread rapidly through a culture pool. When videocassette recorders became available at reasonable prices, the majority of households in the United States bought them within just a few years. This rapid spread in the use of VCRs was largely due to advertising and word of mouth—that is, successful people (i.e., people whose behavior is reinforced) telling other people that their purchase and use of a VCR will be reinforced. Testimonials in advertisements capitalize on our tendency to follow rules given by successful people. The people urging you to buy the product are usually famous and always good-looking, expensively dressed, and well-spoken.

In their book *Programmed to Learn*, Ronald Pulliam and Peter Dunford tell a story called "The Legend of Eslok" that illustrates how culture is shaped by variation combined with selective transmission. In it, we see some people succeeding and others failing and the growth of a rule in response to short-term reinforcement in conflict with long-term effects on fitness. Here is a brief retelling.

The Legend of Eslok

Once upon a time, long ago and far away, there existed an agricultural community, a village, in a remote fertile valley. The people were neither poor nor rich—they managed to get along. One day, Mephistopheles came to the village in the form of an old man. He befriended some of the farmers, and offered them gifts such as seeds and tools. At first, they hesitated to accept the gifts, but after a while a few accepted. Almost at once, those farmers began to prosper. Their harvests were bigger than all the others. Seeing their success, the other villagers began accepting the old man's gifts also. Soon everyone was prospering, and Mephistopheles left.

The villagers had no way of knowing that a few years after a family accepted the gifts, all their children would die. Since every family in the village had accepted the gifts, all the children died. Finally, when all the adults were growing old and dying, a man named Eslok left the community and the valley to travel.

Eslok journeyed many days until he came to another community. He settled there and told the people the story of the old man and the gifts. After
Eslok died, the story was still told, and a moral was added: "Beware of
strangers bearing gifts."

Several generations passed, and Eslok's story came to be regarded as a
myth. Eventually, the community became overpopulated, and some adventur-
ous young people set out to found a new community. They traveled far in
search of a good place, and came upon the fertile valley, now uninhabited, that
had been Eslok's home. They settled, became established, and grew into a village.

Once again, Mephistopheles came offering gifts. As before, some people
accepted the gifts. But this time, some people remembered the saying,
"Beware of strangers bearing gifts," and refused the gifts. After a few years,
the children of those who accepted began dying; on seeing this, the villagers
drove Mephistopheles from their midst. Since some people had refused the
gifts, the community survived the disaster and returned to their modest
lifestyle. Afterward, the myth became a firm rule in the village: "Never accept
gifts from strangers."

As shown by this story, both rule-following and rule-making depend ultimately on their enhancing fitness.

Self-Interest   In *The Selfish Gene,* Dawkins emphasizes that replicators—
whether genes or practices—act out of self-interest. Yet many genetically
coded traits and many cultural practices seem to promote the survival of the
group or the culture, often at the expense of the individual survival machine.
We saw in our discussion of the benefits of sociality how it is possible for
genes to be selected that make for subordination of the individual's welfare in
favor of the group—those genes need only do better on the average and in the
long run than genes that put the individual's short-term benefit first. This is
the explanation of altruism and cooperative behavior in general.

Something similar might be true of cultural replicators, which could also
increase at the expense of the individual survival machines. As a result of imitation and rule-following, soldiers go off to war and are often killed. When
weapons were primitive, the genes that make for affiliation with the group and
obedience to authority were probably benefited by war. As a result, the cultural practices of war could survive and flourish, because they were reinforced on
the average and in the long run (perhaps by increased goods and territory).

The analogy to genes suggests further that certain practices can be selected
because they help maintain other practices. Such practices would tend to be
conservative—that is, would tend to resist cultural change. For example, xenophobia could be explained this way, as killing or driving off strangers would
help protect the culture from invasion by foreign practices, helping all the
other practices of the culture to survive. During the seventeenth and eigh-
teenth centuries, Japanese culture successfully resisted influence from Western
visitors by extreme xenophobia. Not until modern warships came to their
shores and further resistance became dangerous did this resistance crumble.
The short-term benefits of xenophobia might explain the resistance, whereas

the long-term welfare of the people might explain the eventual opening up to Western culture.

The logic of evolutionary theory dictates that cultural evolution must operate within limits set by genetic evolution (Boyd and Richerson, 1985). Before culture existed, genes were selected that set those limits on what can be learned and what can be reinforcing. In the short run people may engage in practices that are reinforcing but deleterious to health or reproduction; but in the long run they tend to act to preserve health and foster reproduction. This is the reason that the ultimate contingencies of rule-governed behavior concern fitness (Chapter 8). When a conflict occurs between cultural practices and the fitness of genes, the conflict is eventually resolved by a change in the culture. One of the points implied by the legend of Eslok is that when short-term success (accepting the stranger's gifts) conflicts with long-term reproductive success (dying children), then new practices ("Never accept gifts from strangers") evolve to compensate. For example, when practices evolved that made sugar readily available and the manufacture of candy profitable, people began to consume more and more sugar and candy. In the United States, the long-term cost to health slowly became apparent, and practices such as tooth-brushing and using sugar substitutes have evolved. Similarly, the hazardous effects of building nuclear weapons is being offset by the move toward disarmament. In the final analysis, cultural change is guided by the welfare of our genes. This point will be especially important to us in Chapter 14, which concerns purposeful cultural change.

❖ SUMMARY

A group's culture consists of learned behavior shared by the members of the group, acquired as a result of membership in the group, and transmitted from one group member to another. Evolution of culture occurs in a manner parallel to shaping of operant behavior and genetic evolution—variation coupled with selective transmission. The units of selection—the things that vary and are selectively transmitted—are replicators. A replicator is any entity capable of producing copies of itself. A good replicator possesses longevity, fecundity, copying fidelity, and efficacy.

One requirement for culture is society. A true society includes cooperation—altruistic behavior that benefits others in the short run and benefits the altruist in the long run. A second requirement for culture is the ability of group members to learn from one another, for this is how cultural traits are transmitted through time.

In genetic evolution, the pool of replicators possessed by all the organisms in a population is known as the gene pool; in cultural evolution, the pool of cultural traits possessed by a society is called the culture pool. These traits constitute the replicators of culture, and as they are passed along in the culture pool, their frequencies may wax or wane depending on how often they are learned.

When learning from others benefits the learner's genes in the long run, as in our species, traits that make learning from others likely are selected. Three such traits are constraints on stimuli, imitation, and social reinforcers. Our bodies are so constructed that we are tuned to stimuli produced by other people, such as faces and language sounds. If one organism imitates another and the result is reinforcing, then rapid operant learning takes place. Social reinforcers such as smiles, pats, and hugs allow still more and faster learning from others because they introduce the practices of teaching and instruction.

The replicators of culture are the actions of group members passed along by imitation and instruction. These units are defined functionally, like operants, because they are operants. They include not only nonverbal practices such as dietary selection and manufacturing, but also verbal behavior such as stories, sayings, and moral injunctions. These verbal practices are useful either because they are rules or because they offer instruction analogous to rules—that is, they provide discriminative stimuli inducing behavior that is socially reinforced. Human culture includes practices of following rules, giving rules, and making rules. All of these depend on contingencies of reinforcement arranged by other people—social contingencies. These social contingencies, apart from the behavior they produce, may be the most fundamental replicators of human culture.

The first ingredient of evolutionary theory is variation. Just as genes vary, so cultural replicators vary. Like genetic accidents, behavioral accidents occasionally are beneficial. Like a gene pool, a culture pool can profit from immigration.

The second ingredient is transmission. Unlike genetic transmission, cultural transmission means inheritance of acquired characteristics. The possibilities for cultural transmission far exceed those of genetic transmission because those transmitting a practice—cultural parents—may be genetically unrelated to those receiving it—cultural offspring. Cultural transmission also differs from genetic transmission in that genetic transmission occurs only at conception, whereas cultural transmission can occur any time during life. Many sources and many opportunities for cultural transmission mean that cultural evolution occurs much faster than genetic evolution. Social problems arise when cultural evolution changes the environment in such a way that a mechanism enhancing fitness in the old environment makes for a practice detrimental to fitness in the new environment. When such problems arise, new practices tend to evolve to offset them.

Cultural transmission occurs by imitation and by rules. Learned imitation is a form of rule-governed behavior. Children are taught to follow rules because transmission of practices by rule-following is especially fast.

The third ingredient in cultural evolution, selection, occurs because transmission is selective. If the organism is likely to fall into a variety of environments, mechanisms might evolve by which transmission would be biased toward receiving practices that are successful in a particular environment. One likely criterion of success is frequency. People might imitate frequently encountered practices and frequently encountered individuals. Rule-following might be selective in a way even more directly related to success if people tended to follow rules coming from people whose behavior is frequently reinforced.

The idea that cultural practices are replicators analogous to genes helps explain why people often act to their personal detriment for the good of their community or country. "Selfless" practices (donating money, time, effort, and risking one's life) will remain part of the culture as long as the consequences are reinforcing on the average and in the long run. The social reinforcers that maintain such practices derive ultimately from their effects on fitness of genes.

❖ FURTHER READING

Barash, D. P. (1982). *Sociobiology and behavior* (2nd ed.). New York: Elsevier. This textbook lays out many of the theories underlying an evolutionary account of behavior. It contains discussion of sociality, including the comparison among marmots.

Barash, D. P. (1986). *The hare and the tortoise: Culture, biology, and human nature.* New York: Viking Penguin. This is a comparison of cultural evolution and genetic evolution.

Boyd, R. and Richerson, P. J. (1985). *Culture and the evolutionary process.* Chicago: University of Chicago Press. This book presents a scholarly treatment of cultural evolution that clarifies many of its similarities to, differences from, and interactions with genetic evolution.

Dawkins, R. (1989). *The selfish gene* (new ed.). Oxford: Oxford University Press. See especially Chapter 11, "Memes: The New Replicators."

Epstein, R. (1984). Spontaneous and deferred imitation in the pigeon. *Behavioural Processes, 9,* 347–354. This article reports experiments showing that pigeons imitate each other.

Glenn, S. S. (1988). Contingencies and metacontingencies: Toward a synthesis of behavior analysis and cultural materialism. *The Behavior Analyst, 11,* 161–179. This paper represents one of the first attempts to apply behavior analysis directly to the study of culture.

Goodenough J., McGuire, B., and Wallace, R. (1993). *Perspectives on animal behavior.* New York: Wiley. This textbook offers up-to-date information on mechanisms and theories of animal behavior.

Harris, M. (1980). *Cultural materialism.* New York: Random House. The title of this book names the behavioral approach to the study of culture within anthropology.

Lamal, P. A., ed. (1991). *Behavioral analysis of societies and cultural practices.* Bristol, PA: Hemisphere Publishing. This book is a collection of papers by behavior analysts.

Lumsden, C. J., and Wilson, E. O. (1981). *Genes, mind, and culture: The coevolutionary process.* Cambridge, MA: Harvard University Press. One of the first books to discuss the interaction between cultural and genetic evolution.

Pulliam, H. R. and Dunford, C. (1980). *Programmed to learn: An essay on the evolution of culture.* New York: Columbia University Press. This is an entertaining book exploring the way that genes guide learning and the way that such guidance contributes to culture. See Chapter 8 for the original telling of the legend of Eslok.

Skinner, B. F. (1971). *Beyond freedom and dignity.* New York: Knopf. See especially Chapter 7 on evolution of culture.

Skinner, B. F. (1974). *About behaviorism.* New York: Knopf. This book, in which Skinner answered his critics, contains a discussion of rule-governed behavior in Chapter 8, "Causes and Reasons."

Sommerville, C. J. (1982). *The rise and fall of childhood.* Beverly Hills, CA: Sage Publications. This book discusses practices about children throughout the history of western civilization.

CHAPTER
14

DESIGN OF CULTURE: EXPERIMENTING FOR SURVIVAL

Perhaps nothing Skinner had to say stirred up more controversy than his ideas about design of culture. Critics saw in this the specter of totalitarian government, regimentation, and stagnation. It seemed to them a dangerous idea, a formula for disaster. How could anyone be wise enough to design a culture? What would happen to people who disagreed with the design? Fueling the fire of such objections, Skinner wrote also of behavioral engineering, which sounded even more ominous.

Although some behaviorist ideas—about free will, mind, and language, for example—are truly controversial, design of culture and behavioral engineering seem like controversial ideas only when they are interpreted in the light of common prejudices about the words *design* and *engineering*. To critics, these words suggest something like a master plan, a fixed idea about how a culture should run, that is put into action whether anyone objects to it or not. However, the logical extension of a behavioral analysis of freedom (Chapter 9), government (Chapter 11), and values (Chapter 12) leads to no such idea. The view advanced in Skinner's *Beyond Freedom and Dignity* and *Walden Two*, for example, resembles more the process of trial and error that engineers and designers go through when they are trying to create a product that works. An architect designing a house makes a sketch, perhaps builds a model, examines this prototype for flaws, and tests it by showing it to the client. At any point in the process, and particularly if the client rejects the design, it's"back to the drawing board." Few people object to government-funded experimental projects like job training or tax incentives; they seem to be legitimate attempts to get people to behave in socially desirable ways. As we shall see, behavior analysts suggest only that we should engage in such experimentation more systematically and more generally.

❖ DESIGN FROM EVOLUTION

Once we recognize that culture changes by an evolutionary process as a result of variation, transmission, and selection, then we should be able to act to enhance that evolution by improving on all three aspects. We could increase and guide variation by purposefully trying out new practices. We could guarantee transmission by teaching practices we consider good (in the sense of Chapters 12 and 13) in schools. We could sharpen selection by training experts to evaluate experimental programs.

▧ Selective Breeding

Darwin's ideas about natural selection came partly from studying selective breeding. He had no definite theory about how traits passed from one generation to the next, but there was no doubt that animal breeders were able to improve their stock by breeding parents that possessed the sorts of traits they wanted in the offspring. Horses could be bred for speed; cows for size and milk production. Darwin reasoned that if the environment arranged for some members of a population to be more likely to become parents, even if in a relatively haphazard manner, then over time the population would tend to comprise more and more individuals possessing the traits that make for greater reproductive success.

Selective breeding differs from natural selection in one important way: purposefully choosing which members of the population get to reproduce results in more powerful selection. As selective breeding is to natural selection, so is design of culture to evolution of culture. Just as agricultural experts can experiment, selectively breed, and produce improved strains that farmers can use, so it should be possible for cultural experts to experiment, evaluate, and produce improved practices that society can use.

Such experimentation exists to some extent already. In the 1930s, many people viewed Social Security and unemployment benefits as an experiment, as many view affirmative action today. Occasionally individual states try out new practices—for example, negative income taxes to help the poor and lotteries to fund education. Most experimental practices occur on a smaller scale—in cities, school districts, or even a city block—trash recycling, parental choice of schools, crime watch. Some experiments prove ineffective or disastrous, as with negative income taxes and the deregulation of savings and loan institutions.

■ Evaluation

Design of culture means only that we do more experimenting and do it more carefully—that is, with planning and evaluation. When experiments are undertaken with no plan for evaluation, then decisions on whether they have succeeded or failed require that their results be spectacular. The results of cultural experiments, however, are likely to be subtle—changes, for example, in the frequency of certain events (teenage pregnancy or drug-related deaths) or individual performances within a group (scores on standardized tests). Even if some people change a lot, some may change less and some not at all; thus, evaluation demands more than casual observation, and data must be gathered and analyzed. Just as laboratory scientists must use statistical tests and graphs to decide about the results of experiments, so cultural experimenters must use similar methods. This is why agencies that fund new experiments often require a plan for evaluation before a project is approved.

Large-scale funding usually depends also on small-scale demonstrations, or pilot experiments. Should a cultural pilot experiment go wrong, its small scale allows relatively quick detection and easier remedy of any ill effects. Trying deregulation initally on a small scale might have averted the U.S. savings and loan catastrophe. Even if deregulation seemed to have worked well in other contexts (and in the absence of careful evaluation, this remains debatable), the savings and loan industry represented a new context in which deregulation should first have been evaluated in a pilot experiment.

Evaluation, however, raises a question. In agricultural experiments, breeders assess new strains according to definite goals or standards, such as resistance to disease and productivity. Everyone can agree about the success or failure of some cultural experiments, but many experiments leave room for disagreement because our conclusions depend on the standards we apply. Someone viewing state lotteries in the light of the revenue they produce might consider them highly successful, but someone looking at the way they draw the revenue primarily from lower socioeconomic groups might regard them as a dismal failure. By what sort of standards should cultural experiments be evaluated?

■ Survival as a Standard

In addressing this question of standards, Skinner often wrote of survival. Sometimes, when looking at global problems, he seems to have meant survival of the human race. At other times, however, he wrote about the survival not of peoples but of their cultures.

To survive, a culture must be able to change, for only in a world without new environmental challenges and competition from other cultures could a particular culture remain stable. In today's world, since the environment is deteriorating and global communication allows constant contact between cultures, survival depends on coping with environmental changes and absorbing practices from other cultures. Practices compete, not only within a culture, but between cultures. If a foreign practice proves reinforcing, it moves into the indigenous culture and may even replace traditional practices. The Japanese adopted mass production and quality control from the West; Americans today enjoy sushi and karate. Since practices tend to occur in clusters and depend on one another, adopting one practice often leads to adopting others. A person interested in karate may become interested in Zen; the Japanese adoption of mass production led to their adoption of quality control. Interdependence of practices leads to competition between large cultural patterns and even whole cultures. When a group drops its traditional culture and adopts another wholesale, the traditional culture can be said to have died.

In a changing environment, if one culture changes to meet new challenges and another does not, only the first is likely to survive. Such challenges are particularly crucial when they are produced by the culture's practices themselves. For example, the practices of manufacturing nuclear weapons and dumping toxic wastes threaten the welfare of generations to come. A great deal depends on how a culture responds to these self-created challenges.

Survival as a standard implies not only change, but change in response to long-term relations. Responding only to short-term relations usually spells disaster, because short-term and long-term relations usually conflict. In the short run, plastic bags have proven popular with Americans because they are convenient and cheap; in the long run, they wind up in landfills and pollute the environment. Their real cost is high, in the long run, because it includes satisfactory disposal. In the short run, fossil fuels seem a convenient and cheap source of energy, but in the long run, their use promotes destruction of an irreplaceable resource, traffic jams, and air pollution.

Most of the problems we face constitute contingency traps in the sense of Chapter 9. Acting in accordance with short-term consequences is reinforced relatively immediately; the reinforcement is obvious. Long-term relations, however, present difficulty because their consequences are usually delayed and incremental. The discharge of a little toxic waste into a stream may have no major lasting consequences, but discharging a little every day for years may eventually produce a disaster because of the cumulative effect.

If individual companies cannot be relied upon to respond in accordance with long-term contingencies, then regulatory contingencies need to be imposed. Electric companies cannot be expected to encourage conservation as long as greater consumption of electricity raises their profits. In Maine, the public utilities commission has experimented with a way to remove this disincentive to conservation. If consumption increases, rates go down, and if consumption decreases, rates go up, so the electric company's profits remain roughly constant. The result has been that consumption has declined. When promotion of consumption was no longer reinforced and the company began to encourage conservation (or at least ceased to encourage consumption) individual consumers became more likely to conserve. The regulatory contingency brought the company's behavior into line with the long-term contingencies that favor conservation.

Responding to such long-term contingencies requires prediction, often guesswork. Sometimes action should be taken even if the prediction is uncertain. For example, it appears that our practices of consuming wood and fossil fuels, which release large quantities of carbon dioxide into the atmosphere, may result in a warming of the entire earth—the "greenhouse effect." The connection, however, is far from certain because temperature rises and falls for other reasons. A general upward trend might take many years to confirm. If we wait until we are sure there is a problem before taking action, it may already be too late to avert a disaster.

Only small numbers of experts can be trained to make guesses about long-term environmental, economic, and social consequences. A society is forced to rely on these specialists to reveal long-term relations and to recommend new practices to deal with them. These recommendations, however, can produce change only if the society includes groups who respond to the experts' verbal behavior and work for the survival of the culture. Groups who encourage people to recycle waste, for example, play this role.

Whether they help people to eat a better diet or to conserve electricity, new practices that solve problems generated by the old practices they replace have two effects: they ensure the survival of the culture and they promote long-term reproductive success of the society's members. In Chapter 13, we saw that the likeliest explanation of why societies and cultures exist at all is their enhancement of fitness. Practices change so as to increase the fitness of the practitioners, or, with problems produced by our own practices, to prevent significant decrease in fitness. In discussions of the need for change, people often talk about the health and survival of their children and grandchildren.

■ **Guided Variation**

In their book *Culture and the Evolutionary Process,* Boyd and Richerson (1985) took what Skinner called design of culture so much for granted that they gave it a technical name—*guided variation*—and listed it as one of the forces of cultural evolution. They equate guided variation with individually learned behavior that is then transmitted by imitation or teaching. This is broader than Skinner's notion because it includes instances involving no verbal behavior—say, one creature learning by trial and error and then others imitating it. Boyd and Richerson concentrate, however, on what they call rational calculation, which corresponds to Skinner's precurrent behavior (Chapter 8). Precurrent behavior, such as experimenting with diets or trying out biodegradable plastics, results in solutions that set the occasion for verbal behavior, rules such as "Eat more leafy vegetables for better health" or "Use biodegradable plastic bags to prevent pollution." These rules induce rule-governed behavior in those who listen, and this rule-governed behavior must ultimately be reinforced.

Boyd and Richerson introduce reinforcement in the form of an "adaptive standard":

> The effect of the guided variation force on evolution depends on the existence of some adaptive standard such as taste or a sensation of pleasure or pain. For example, adaptation through rational calculation proceeds by the collection of information about the environment, the estimation of the results of various alternative patterns of behavior, and the evaluation of the desirability of the alternative outcomes according to some criteria. It is these guiding criteria that translate variation in the environment into a directional, often adaptive, change in phenotype, which then is culturally transmitted to subsequent generations. The source of these criteria clearly must ultimately be external to the guided variation process itself. In the final analysis, we will be driven to explain the guiding criteria as the product of some other process (p. 9).

Interpreting the mentalistic phrasing here, we see that "taste or a sensation of pleasure or pain" corresponds to the reinforcing and aversive properties of various consequences (children, wealth, nausea, and so on), and "criteria" means reinforcers and punishers. The phrases "collection of information" and "estimation of the results" correspond to precurrent behavior, some verbal and some perhaps manipulative, that produces various discriminative stimuli (outcomes) that control further verbal behavior. A "change in phenotype" here means a change in some practices of the culture. The "source" or "process" responsible for the "criteria," of course, is natural selection. As we saw already in Chapters 4 and 13, events gain reinforcing and punishing power if such power generally enhances fitness.

If Boyd and Richerson's guided variation means much the same as Skinner's design of culture, why does only Skinner's idea seem controversial? The main reason is probably that whereas Boyd and Richerson's discussion is strictly descriptive, Skinner's discussion often becomes prescriptive. Although both point to a process that already occurs in our society, only Skinner goes on to insist that we should do more such guided variation and do it more systematically. This raises the fear that experts will gain too much influence and threaten our democracy.

In answering this and other objections, Skinner (1971) usually accepted the fear as legitimate, but urged a broader view. A well-designed culture would include contingencies (counter-control; Chapter 11) that would prevent the experts from gaining undue influence. His vision, which he called the *experimental society*, included experimentation on many fronts, not just in a few limited areas.

❖ THE EXPERIMENTAL SOCIETY

Fearful for the survival of humanity and civilization, Skinner worried that we adapt our cultural practices to deal with environmental challenges too slowly to avert destruction. Practices that have worked in the past may become maladaptive and may need to be replaced. Skinner proposed that, instead of clinging to old practices, we should constantly be trying new ones to see if they might work better, making experimenting with new practices one of the practices of our culture. Instead of an experiment*al* society, he might better have written about an experiment*ing* society.

▨ Experimenting

Skinner (1971) compared experimenting with cultural practices to experimenting in the laboratory:

> A culture is very much like the experimental space used in the analysis of behavior. Both are sets of contingencies of reinforcement. A child is born into a culture as an organism is placed in an experimental space. Designing a culture is like designing an experiment; contingencies are arranged and effects noted. In an experiment we are interested in what happens, in designing a culture with whether it will work. This is the difference between science and technology (p. 153).

Skinner points here to the difference between the science of behavior analysis and behavioral technology. Whereas the science aims only to understand, the technology aims at practical results. The technology and the science are partially interdependent: the science explains why practices might work, and the technology draws on the science to discover practices that actually do work.

▨ Happiness

How do we know when a practice works? This brings us back to Boyd and Richerson's adaptive standard and guiding criteria. The commonest answer is couched in terms of happiness. What works is what makes people happy.

This, however, results only in a restatement of the problem: Under what conditions are people said to be happy? We have already seen (Chapters 9, 11, and 12) how behavior analysts approach this question. First of all, it seems apparent that people report greater happiness when they are free from threats of aversive consequences (or removal of accustomed reinforcement). In Chapter 9, we noted that people report happiness when their environment provides choices (alternative possible actions) and those choices have reinforcing consequences rather than aversive consequences. People tend to be happy in the same conditions in which they report feeling free, especially from coercion, but also, as our analysis of spiritual freedom suggested, from some types of positive reinforcement.

One qualification has to be made about happiness as a criterion of what works in a culture: We are speaking here of happiness in the long run. Long-term happiness derived from one's culture often conflicts with short-term personal reinforcement. In the short run, no one enjoys paying taxes, but everyone benefits from schools and trash collection in the long run.

In Chapter 11, we introduced a long-term perspective by examining exploitation and equity. The contingencies of a culture are manifested concretely in relationships, which consist of the repeated exchange of discriminative stimuli and consequences by which people control one another's behavior and institutions control people's behavior. People report greater long-term happiness when they are free from exploitive relationships and receive equitable reinforcement—that is, reinforcement equivalent to that received by a comparison group. Historically, the tendency in the United States has been toward making broader and broader comparisons. Wives are compared not just with other wives, but with husbands. Minorities are compared not just with other minorities, but with the majority. Ultimately, if the population at large became the comparison group, everyone's standard for equity would be the same.

In Chapters 12 and 13, we reminded ourselves that, ultimately, because we are products of natural selection, our happiness tends to coincide with the fitness of our genes. For most people, happiness (reinforcement) derives from conditions in themselves and others (reinforcers) ultimately tied to fitness: personal survival and comfort, the welfare of children, the welfare of family members and other relatives, and the welfare of nonrelatives with whom we have mutually beneficial relationships (Chapter 11)—spouse, close friends, members of a community.

■ *Walden Two:* Skinner's Vision

One way Skinner tried to convey his idea of the experimental, or experimenting, society was by describing one in his novel *Walden Two*. As a novel, the book offers concrete illustrations of what an experimenting society might be like. As an essay advocating the virtues of the experimenting society it is indirect because Skinner makes his points through dialogue between characters. To appreciate the book fully, you have to interpret it in light of Skinner's viewpoint.

Interpreting *Walden Two*   The book begins with two middle-aged college professors, Burris and Castle, deciding to visit an experimental community located in Midwestern farm country. They find an attractive layout of buildings and land with about 1000 inhabitants. The days they spend there are dominated by conversations with Frazier, the originator of the community, who lives there but has become peripheral to its operation.

One way to read the book is as a battle between Frazier and Castle for the loyalty of Burris. Castle, described as comfortable in his role as an academic, is an overweight and verbally pugnacious philosopher—the personification of mentalism. Frazier, the man of action, is described as vigorous and argumentative, confident to a fault. He represents the hope of a new world based on behavioral technology. Burris, uncomfortable as an academic, dissatisfied with his life, is open to persuasion. None of the three can be said to represent Skinner, although we can imagine that the discussions that occur among them, especially between Frazier and Burris, might resemble arguments Skinner had with himself.

As Frazier shows them around Walden Two, Burris and Castle learn about the various aspects of the culture, the practices concerning economics, government, education, marriage, and leisure. Frazier explains that the practices are founded on behavioral principles. Castle finds fault and urges mentalistic arguments, which Frazier rebuts. Burris vacillates. One after another, objections to the idea of the experimenting society are raised—most by Castle, some by Burris—and answered.

Every aspect of Walden Two is portrayed as working better than in the United States at large. No money is needed; people earn labor credits for doing useful work—more credits per hour of onerous work (washing windows), less for enjoyable work (teaching). The government is so sensitive to feedback from the citizens that elections have become obsolete. Children are taught how to educate themselves and require only loose guidance from teachers. The people enjoy enormous amounts of leisure time and use it productively. Dress is varied. Social interactions are direct and kind. Most of all, everyone is happy. Burris eventually goes through a sort of conversion experience, leaves Castle on their way back to the university, and returns to Walden Two to stay.

Is *Walden Two* Utopian?   Of course, Walden Two seems too good to be true. The book has often been classified as a utopian novel. There have been many such novels, usually about some small isolated community where life is far better than in the world we know. On the surface, *Walden Two* conforms to this mold.

Skinner, however, denied that the book was utopian, maintaining that it aimed to portray the basic idea of an experimental (experimenting) society. The concrete particulars of economics, government, social life, and so on were included only by way of illustration. Unlike typical utopian novels, in which the particulars are the point of the book, *Walden Two* points past the particulars to a method—the experimental method. To take the particulars as Skinner's recommendations is to misread the book. Indeed, the logic of Skinner's position would preclude his having any definite idea of the particulars of Walden Two, because those would have to evolve over time as a result of experimentation and selection. Who knows whether the labor credit system, government by constant feedback, or self-education would work? In an experimenting society they could be tried, modified, and retained or dropped.

Over the years, *utopian* has gained the additional meanings of "impractical" or "unworkable," and *Walden Two* might be called utopian in this sense. You might say that experimentation could be fruitful in a community of 1000, but could never be implemented in a country of 250 million or even a state or city of any large size. So, even if a community like Walden Two succeeded, it would remain a little island unto itself. In the book, Skinner imagined other communities similar to Walden Two springing up around the country. Eventually, he implied, enough people would live in such communities that they would begin to influence the nation at large.

It is hard to know whether Skinner's guess will prove correct, for attempts to start such communities have had little success. One such American community started during the 1960s, Twin Oaks, survives in the 1990s; recent accounts, however, indicate that it has abandoned the practice of experimenting. A Mexican community, Los Horcones, has retained the practice of experimenting, but remains too small to have much influence.

Perhaps the growth of cultural experimentation need not rely on small communities. We could argue that all levels of government have shown increased tendency to experiment since the Great Depression. Newspapers often describe pilot projects testing new ways to deal with trash collection, drug use, teenage pregnancy, unemployment. Practices in other societies come up for discussion and possible adoption. A pessimist might point to the power of entrenched interest groups to oppose innovation, whereas an optimist might say we are moving, slowly and haltingly toward the experimenting society after all. Skinner would probably insist that we should move faster and more systematically to deal with our (behavioral) problems, before it is too late.

❖ OBJECTIONS

In *Walden Two* and *Beyond Freedom and Dignity*, Skinner attempted to answer the objections to his vision of the experimenting society. He started with the point that, whether anyone likes it or not, a behavioral technology—rudimentary perhaps, but growing—already exists. There is no longer any question that people's actions can be controlled by designed contingencies of reinforcement. The question is how this understanding will be used.

The first objection runs like this: The vision is false, because even if it is possible to control the actions of people in the laboratory, these are artificial and simplified conditions having nothing in common with the complexities of the real world. Skinner answered by pointing out that the experiments of physics and chemistry are equally artificial and simplified, yet no one doubts that their results can be applied in the real world. Control need not be perfect to be useful—the advertising industry demonstrates daily that history can be exploited. Happily, more constructive uses occur also—behavioral management in classrooms and mental institutions, for example. In *Walden Two*, Frazier suggests that there have been failures, but there is no question the technology works. Skinner (1971) urged those who would reject behavioral technology because it is too simple to examine the alternative:

> . . . the really great oversimplification is the traditional appeal to states of mind, feelings, and other aspects of the autonomous man which a behavioral analysis is replacing. The ease with which mentalistic explanations can be invented on the spot is perhaps the best gauge of how little attention we should pay to them. And the same may be said for traditional practices. The technology which has emerged from an experimental analysis should be evaluated only in comparison with what is done in other ways. What, after all, have we to show for nonscientific or prescientific good judgment, or common

utopian, Skinner always disavowed any such label, because for him the imaginary community in that book represented a method rather than a goal.

Although behavior analysts cannot specify some ideal end state, they can offer methods for change and for deciding whether changes are sending society in the right direction. For instance, democracy has proven to be a good practice because it has increased many people's satisfaction over what went before and in comparison with existing dictatorships. Democracy as we know it, however, may not be the final word in governmental systems. Shockingly low percentages of people vote in American elections. Too many people are uneducated, unemployed, homeless. Can we make changes to increase participation? Can we move away from coercive and exploitive contingencies to more equitable ones? As we seek ways to eliminate the flaws in our system of government, behavior analysts can suggest deliberate changes of contingencies, to be made on an experimental basis and to be assessed for their ability to increase societal satisfaction. These ideas of social experimentation and assessment we shall take up in Chapter 14.

❖ SUMMARY

Behavior analysts approach questions about value by focusing on what people do and say about things and actions that are called good and bad or right and wrong. Moral relativism, the idea that labels of good and bad vary arbitrarily from culture to culture and arise strictly as social conventions, is rejected by religious thinkers and behavior analysts, both groups instead favoring a universal standard, some principle that all humans share in common. The religious C. S. Lewis argued that everyone seems to have a grasp of the rules about how we ought to behave, even if we often break those rules. Behavior analysts also recognize such universals of decent behavior, in the form of altruism and reciprocity. Lewis parts company with behavior analysts, however, over the question of origins. Whereas religious thinkers see the standards of right and wrong as coming from God, behavior analysts like Skinner see the standards as arising from evolutionary history.

Skinner's rule of thumb about good and bad is things called good are positive reinforcers, things called bad are punishers, actions called good are reinforced, and actions called bad are punished. Although unconditional reinforcers and punishers, and actions associated with them, come to be called good and bad because of the construction of the world and our bodies, many things and actions also come to be called good and bad because of our social environment, because much of the reinforcement and punishment for our behavior comes from other people. From early childhood, other people not only train conditional reinforcers and punishers, but teach us to call bad those things that punish and those actions that are punished and to call good those things that reinforce and those actions that are reinforced.

A person's history of reinforcement and punishment explains not only why the person labels things good and bad but also why the individual feels good and bad about those things. People say they feel bad in situations in which their behavior has been punished; the physiological events called "feelings" serve, along with the public context, as discriminative stimuli inducing such reports. People say they feel good, for analogous reasons, in situations in which their behavior has been reinforced. The feelings do not explain the talk about good and bad; rather, the physiological events and reports of feeling good and bad arise from a history of reinforcement and punishment that parallels and partly overlaps the history that engenders talk about good and bad things and actions (i.e., value judgments). Value judgments, most clearly when they involve *should* or *ought,* are rules (verbal discriminative stimuli) that point to ultimate contingencies that are social—that arise from the practices of a group to which the listener belongs.

When behavior analysts address the question of where reinforcers and punishers, particularly social ones, come from, the answer is natural selection. Genes that made certain events reinforcing or punishing, thereby promoting the reproductive success of the individuals carrying them, would be selected. This explains not only why sweet tastes and orgasms are reinforcers, but also why helping others of our own kind, even at our own expense, is a reinforcer. Altruism toward children and other relatives is selected because it promotes the shared altruism-inducing genes. Altruism toward nonrelatives depends on long-term benefit to the altruist. Either the nonrelative ultimately reciprocates because he or she is in a relationship with the altruist, or practices of the group arrange for other members of the group to provide ultimate reinforcement. Either way, the altruism ultimately benefits the altruist (is reinforced).

In the context of such social contingencies, moral and ethical injunctions constitute verbal discriminative stimuli (rules) that point to ultimate social reinforcement or punishment. Behavior analysis may help our society work toward "the good life" by offering ways to identify and implement better social contingencies.

❖ FURTHER READING

Dawkins, R. (1989). *The selfish gene* (new edition). Oxford: Oxford University Press. This excellent book presents modern evolutionary theory in a readable form.

Lewis, C. S. (1960). *Mere Christianity.* New York: Macmillan. This book is a collection of essays on Christianity and Christian values. The title essay takes up science and religion.

Midgley, M. (1978). *Beast and man: The roots of human nature.* New York: New American Library. A moral philosophical discussion of values in the perspective of evolutionary theory.

Skinner, B. F. (1971). *Beyond freedom and dignity.* New York: Knopf. Chapter 6, in particular, takes up values.

Skinner, B. F. (1948/1976). *Walden two.* New York: Macmillan. Skinner's novel about an experimental society contains discussions about values and social contingencies.

Skinner, B. F. (1981). Selection by consequences. *Science, 213,* 501–504. Reprinted in *Upon Further Reflection* (pp. 51–63). New York: Prentice Hall. A classic article in which Skinner compares operant learning, natural selection, and cultural evolution.

Weiss, R. F., Buchanan, W., Altstatt, L., & Lombardo, J. P. (1971). Altruism is rewarding. *Science, 171,* 1262–1263. This article reports a study in which human subjects demonstrated, without instruction, reinforcing effects of reducing another person's level of discomfort.

CHAPTER
13

THE EVOLUTION OF CULTURE

I f there is one thing that distinguishes human beings from other species, it is culture—not in the sense of better-educated or high-brow, but everyday customs shared and passed on by a group of people. The world contains such a diversity of cultures that for a time anthropologists who studied culture concentrated simply on classifying and cataloging human cultures according to their main characteristics because there seemed to be no scientific way to account for the diversity. That situation changed in the 1970s as psychologists and evolutionary biologists extended their explanations of behavior to include culture.

Since these explanations focused on behavior, one result of the biologists' and psychologists' influence was to redefine culture in terms of behavior. Before the 1970s, most anthropologists defined culture in terms of abstractions (mentalistic concepts), such as a set of shared values and beliefs. One notable exception was Marvin Harris, who defined culture more concretely in terms of shared customs (behavior). Skinner (1971), like Harris, defined culture concretely by pointing to the practices, both verbal and nonverbal, that a group of people might share.

Not only are customs diverse the world over, but customs within any group can change drastically over time. If an American of today were transported back to colonial days, the modern would have difficulty talking with the colonists because spoken English has changed so much in the past 300 years. There would also be misunderstandings about dress, social behavior, marriage, sex, and property. According to C. J. Sommerville (1982), for exam-

sense, or the insights gained through personal experience? It is science or nothing, and the only solution to simplification is to learn how to deal with complexities (p. 160).

He went on to acknowledge that behavior analysis, like any other science, cannot answer every question. As it progresses, however, it produces answers to more and more of the puzzling problems we face:

> A science of behavior is not yet ready to solve all our problems, but it is a science in progress, and its ultimate adequacy cannot now be judged. When critics assert that it cannot account for this or that aspect of human behavior, they usually imply that it will never be able to do so, but the analysis continues to develop and is in fact much further advanced than its critics usually realize (p. 160).

A second objection equates design with meddling. Unwise innovations could lead to catastrophe: we will try some experiment, fail to foresee its consequences, and do damage instead of good. Rather than risk unforeseen consequences, we would do better to let events take whatever course they will. Skinner answered this by pointing out, "The unplanned also goes wrong." If we refrain from intervening, we leave our fate to accident. That may have worked well enough in the past, but in a world where our actions threaten our very existence, it seems irresponsible to sit by and hope for the best.

Skinner's Walden Two community includes a group of Planners, each of whom serves for a certain term. They assess practices on the basis of feedback they receive from the Managers, each of whom is attached to a certain job-defined group—health, dairy, food preparation, child care, and so on. The Managers gather the data; the Planners analyze it. Using the data, the Planners decide which practices work, which could be improved, and which new practices to try.

The Planners are experts; they must have the training to evaluate and to design innovations. Responsible government relies on experts to suggest solutions to complex problems. As with problems like setting standards for bridge construction or evaluating new drugs, so with behavioral problems like pollution and crime—solutions require experts. Behavior analysts are increasingly being called in to design practices for schools, prisons, and hospitals. As they make themselves useful, their role may grow.

A third objection takes design to mean stagnation. Planning would produce a stultifying environment with no room for innovation. As we discussed earlier, this view misinterprets "design." A strength of the experimental approach is that it encourages innovation. Any happy accident can be exploited, and any promising new proposal can be tried. But should we rely solely on happy accidents?

A related objection sees design leading to regimentation and uniformity. If certain styles of dress or food preparation were judged best, then everyone would be obliged to conform to those. Only the products judged best might be available in stores. This fear overlooks its own basis, the value of diversity.

The history of western civilization teaches us that people are happier when they have choices. The kind of diversity that we enjoy today not only can be preserved by plan, but could be increased. If diversity has value, we can design for it.

A fourth, and more well-aimed, objection is that such a society would be no fun. As Skinner (1971) put it, "'I wouldn't like it,' or in translation, 'The culture would be aversive and would not reinforce me in the manner to which I am accustomed'" (p. 163). Life in a community like Walden Two, where there is no privation, little danger, and lots of leisure, where everyone is healthy, pleasant, and unstressed, might be dull. In a world without suffering, would there be a Dostoevsky or a Mozart? Skinner acknowledged that this criticism had some merit, and he doubted whether he himself would wish to live in Walden Two. In answer, however, he pointed out that this society would be good, not for us who live in today's world, but for the people who would live in it. In *Walden Two*, Frazier makes this point to Castle and Burris. Frazier himself is described as a Walden Two misfit. He loves the community, but as a product of the ordinary culture he finds himself ill at ease in the new culture he helped to create.

This "I wouldn't like it" criticism has less to do with the idea of an experimenting society than with the idea of a welfare state. If the experimenting society set as its criteria for choosing good practices that they produce comfort, health, order, and safety, then we would move toward a welfare state in which everyone's behavior would be positively reinforced as much as possible and away from coercive relationships and most aversive control. For many people this would entail a large change in the reinforcers and reinforcement relations that control their actions. Productive and creative activity might be explicitly reinforced. Presumably there would be little need to "prove oneself," to compete with the next person, to cheat, to steal, or to lie.

Whether or not such a world sounds dull to someone living in our world, if we moved to make the changes, the move would be gradual. Even the imaginary Walden Two evolved over a period of time. It seems likely that most of us would welcome what changes could occur in our lifetimes, and each generation would grow up in a culture substantially different from the one before. It is unlikely they would find it dull.

The fifth and biggest objection to design of culture is that it threatens democracy and will lead to dictatorship. Alongside of the utopian novel are what might be called nightmare novels, such as George Orwell's *Nineteen Eighty-Four* and Aldous Huxley's *Brave New World.* Orwell imagined a totalitarian state in which behavioral principles were used to frighten people into compliance. Practically all the methods used by the state are coercive, and even though the people are miserable and constantly in fear, the state is powerful enough to maintain itself. In Huxley's book, the populace is kept in line with positive reinforcement. There is no privation, but everyone becomes addicted early in life to a pleasure-giving drug, something like cocaine, which is made abundantly available. People are taught to spend their time enjoying promiscuous sex, games, and light entertainment, and they are kept ignorant of literature, philosophy, science, or any part of what we regard as the heritage of an educated person.

Two responses can be made to the concern raised by these novels. First, how realistic are these nightmares? Orwell's society reminds us of Nazi Germany and the Soviet Union, neither of which lasted. As we noted in Chapters 9 and 11, coercive relationships are inherently unstable; people eventually escape or rebel. Huxley's nightmare seems more worrisome, only because the use of positive reinforcement he depicts seems unlikely to breed rebellion. The management methods he describes are exploitive. As we saw in Chapter 11, people rebel against or act to change exploitive relationships only when they perceive inequity—that is, only when a comparison is made to a better-off group. In Huxley's novel, although no such comparison is made, there is a ruling class that leads a much better life than those they exploit. One can only wonder how this ruling class would prevent people from making comparisons. In hierarchical societies of the past, like ancient Greece and Rome, even members of the ruling class often spoke out against inequity. In the long run, exploitive management, too, is unstable.

Second, stable management includes effective counter-control (Chapter 11). The relationship between the governors and the governed cannot be a relationship between peers or even equals. Such a relationship can be stable, however, if the means of counter-control go beyond the simple threat of disruption. In a democracy, the threat of rebellion hardly arises, because the people have alternative forms of counter-control—elections, lobbying, and demonstrations.

A second essential feature of democracy that we noted in Chapter 11 is that, in the long run, rulers and ruled share the same contingencies. When the ruler's term of office expires, the ruler again becomes an ordinary citizen. The same laws apply to the ex-ruler as the rest of the citizenry. Shared contingencies constitute an additional, long-term form of control over the ruler's behavior; actions taken while the governor is in office ultimately have the same effects on the governor as on the rest of the community. Such long-term contingencies need to be supplemented, however, by the relatively immediate contingencies of counter-control, which affect the governor's actions more because they are shorter-term.

Yet, after all is said in its favor, democracy as practiced in the United States is far from perfect. As a method of counter-control, elections are unsatisfactory: to provide immediate consequences for the governors' behavior, elections should be frequent, but frequent elections would be too disruptive. When an election occurs, often as few as half of the eligible voters actually vote. Those who do vote cannot be assumed to have considered the issues, because campaign propaganda often fails to cover the issues. Since conducting an election campaign is expensive, wealthy people exert more than their fair share of influence. Delegation of power (over reinforcers) also presents problems, because appointees may be less susceptible to counter-control than those who appoint them. Most Americans can tell stories of frustrating encounters with bureaucrats. The person who takes your application for a driver's license may be rude to you with impunity because you have no idea what to do about it, and you need this person's cooperation to get the license. The degree of variation from one office to another can be astonishing. Whether it is a government office, a bank, or a grocery store, in the well-run organization the service people are courteous and helpful. What makes the difference? What makes an institution well-run?

In *Walden Two*, Skinner guessed at answers and solutions to the questions of what is good about democracy and how it could be improved. The Planners have fixed terms of office, of course, so that they share contingencies with everyone else in the long run. There are no elections, however. Instead, Skinner proposed reliance on frequent opinion polls and solicitations of suggestions, mostly by the Managers. He may have anticipated today's concern with "communication." When we examine what people mean when they speak of communication, particularly in discussions about management, it appears that they are talking about counter-control. Bureaucrats and service people are responsive and courteous when listening and courtesy are reinforced. Since customers have relatively little means to reinforce it, the reinforcement has to come from higher-ups. This depends, however, on the higher-ups' acting to be aware of the behavior of the supervisees and instructing them how to behave. (This "acting to be aware"—observing—and instructing must themselves be reinforced, too.) When the higher-ups thus "communicate" with their supervisees, not only is appropriate behavior toward customers increased, but customers gain more counter-control. The favorable and unfavorable responses of customers make more of a difference because they are observed. Skinner suggested that a government could be similarly well-run. In his vision, the Managers (service people) took polls of their constituents (customers) so that the Planners could be aware of the effects of their practices. In other words, the polls provided discriminative stimuli that, besides reinforcing and punishing the Planners' behavior, also served to induce action (maintenance or change). Polling the U.S. public has increased to the point where it is almost continual; such a practice might be put to good use.

The problems we face today are formidable. There is reason to be pessimistic about our ability to solve them. We hear still about the need to change people's minds without a recognition that we need to change people's behavior and that changing their minds usually doesn't work. We hear still about the need for more punishment to prevent unwanted behavior. As long as mentalistic talk about feelings and inner self dominate the discussion, as long as moralistic talk induces the use of aversive control instead of positive reinforcement, we will fail to approach our problems as behavioral and to use behavioral techniques to solve them. We need to plan, experiment, and evaluate. Will we make the needed changes of contingencies soon enough? As long as long-term contingencies fail to control our policies and short-term contingencies continue to control our behavior, disaster seems inevitable.

Still, there may be cause for optimism. Although short-term considerations may dominate in our culture, it appears that we are tending toward more control by long-term contingencies. In the past, each generation has bequeathed ever greater problems to the next—pollution, weapons, debt—by acting only on the basis of short-term considerations. As we move from one crisis to the next, practices evolve that may finally help us avert the crises. Such practices inevitably depend on experts who can assess and predict likely long-term relations. They depend also on enough informed and outspoken citizens acting to provide discriminative stimuli and consequences for those who govern. Judging from news reports, experts and concerned citizens seem to be succeeding little by little in instigating new practices for protecting the environment, reducing poverty, and improving health in many countries of the world, including the United States. These practices are increasingly being evaluated and compared with alternatives. Whether we wanted it or not, whether we thought it possible or not, we may be moving toward Skinner's experimenting society anyway. Let us hope so.

❖ SUMMARY

Although behavior analysts' recommendations about design of culture have sometimes generated opposition, understood properly they are hardly controversial. The concept of design, far from suggesting some fixed plan to be imposed on people whether they like it or not, implies a process of experiment and assessment in which practices are selected according to the long-term happiness of the people. Design in this sense relates to cultural evolution analogously to the way that selective breeding relates to natural selection. Just as selective breeding takes advantage of genetic variation and transmission by purposefully selecting traits, so cultural design takes advantage of cultural variation and transmission by purposefully selecting practices. Systematic experimenting and selection will make for faster cultural change in response to social and environmental problems.

Experimental practices aim for survival—survival of the society, but more often survival of the culture (the way of life). To survive in the long run, a culture must change in response to shifts in the environment and must adopt practices on the basis of their long-term consequences. Predicting the likely outcomes of various practices requires that data needed to detect long-term effects be gathered and analyzed by trained experts. Adoption of new practices depends on the conclusions of such experts. Change often depends also on groups within the society responding to the experts' predictions by "working for change"—that is, by engaging in verbal behavior that generates discriminative stimuli strengthening new practices.

The selecting standard for survival and change of a culture is reinforcement. A successful practice is one that provides more long-term reinforcement (or less long-term punishment) than the variants with which it competes. Experimenting and selecting the more reinforcing alternative correspond to precurrent behavior, which strengthens various possible solutions to a problem and then may lead to verbal behavior about solutions and nonsolutions—that is, behavior that is and is not reinforced.

Ultimately, change and survival of a culture depend on fitness. Unconditional reinforcers and punishers, social and nonsocial, result from natural selection. Since they are the proximate means by which the genes responsible for them have been selected, practices selected by their consequences enhance fitness in the long run.

An experimental society, according to Skinner, is one that experiments with and selects new practices on a regular basis. A better name might have been experimenting society. Skinner's novel *Walden Two* depicts such a society. It has been called utopian, in the sense that it describes a relatively isolated, idyllic community. This is a misreading of the book, because the concrete particulars of the community served only to give substance to the main point, the experimental method of cultural design. A better reading treats the novel as an essay in which the characters raise and answer the common objections to design of culture.

These objections include that behavioral techniques cannot work in the real world, that design will result in catastrophe or regimentation, and that an experimenting society would be no fun. These are readily answered: behavioral techniques have been shown to work in the real world; experimentation aims to avoid catastrophe and to encourage diversity; cultural change is gradual, and the culture of the experimenting society will be suited to the histories of those who live in it.

The biggest objection is that cultural design will lead to dictatorship. Dictatorship, however, depends on coercion or exploitation, relationships that are inherently unstable. An experimenting society that aims at people's happiness can hardly be dictatorial because people are happy when their behavior is positively reinforced and they are free from coercive and exploitive relationships. Stability and happiness depend on equity and counter-control, the two hallmarks of democracy. Elections as a means of counter-control might be replaced by some more efficient means of communication, but that would enhance democracy, not curtail it.

Although humanity today faces unprecedented problems, there may be reason for hope. The more we experiment and gather data, the more we listen to trained experts, the more informed citizens call for better practices, the more likely it is that we shall succeed.

❖ FURTHER READING

Boyd, R. and Richerson, P. J. (1985). *Culture and the evolutionary process.* Chicago: University of Chicago Press. Material on guided variation appears in Chapters 1 and 4.

Huxley, A. (1989). *Brave new world.* New York: HarperCollins. This is a nightmare novel, originally published in 1946, in which the ruling elite keeps the populace in line with drugs and light entertainment.

Orwell, G. (1983). *Nineteen eighty-four.* New York: New American Library. This is another nightmare novel, originally published in 1949, about a society dominated by coercion—aversive control.

Skinner, B. F. (1961). Freedom and the control of men. In *Cumulative record* (enlarged ed.), 3–18. New York: Appleton-Century-Crofts. Originally published in 1955, this essay discusses many of the objections to design of culture.

Skinner, B. F. (1971). *Beyond freedom and dignity.* New York: Knopf. Chapter 8 treats design of culture and its objections.

Skinner, B. F. (1976). *Walden two.* New York: Macmillan. This is Skinner's novel, originally published in 1948, describing an experimental society and responding to objections to design of culture. This edition includes an essay called "Walden Two Revisited."

INDEX